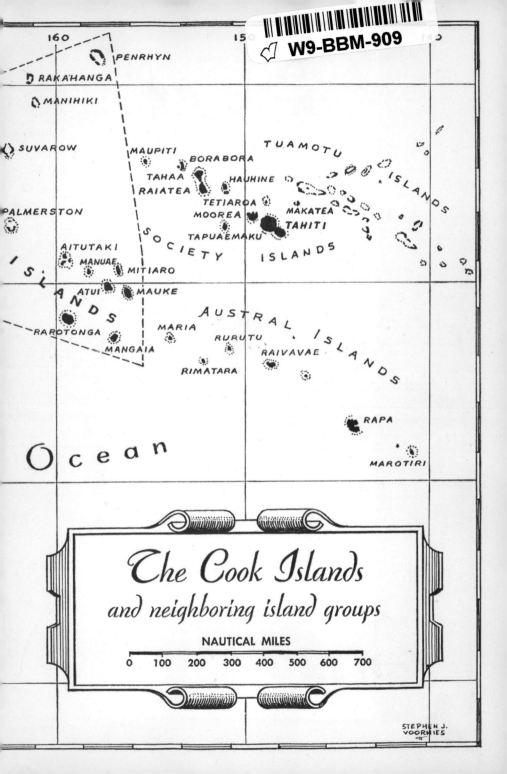

160

150

PENRHYN

RAKA'HANGA

MANIHIKI

SUVAROW

MAUPITI

BORABORA

TAHAA

HAUHINE

RAIATEA

TUAMOTU

ISLANDS

PALMERSTON

TETIAROA

MOOREA

MAKATEA

TAPUAEMAKU

TAHITI

AITUTAKI

SOCIETY

ISLANDS

MANUAE

MITIARO

ISLANDS

ATUI

MAUKE

AUSTRAL

ISLANDS

RAROTONGA

MARIA

RURUTU

MANGAIA

RAIVAVAE

RIMATARA

RAPA

Ocean

MAROTIRI

The Cook Islands

and neighboring island groups

NAUTICAL MILES

0   100   200   300   400   500   600   700

STEPHEN J.
VOORHIES

DOCTOR TO THE ISLANDS

Tom and Lydia Davis

This is the true story of a young doctor,
Tom Davis, part Polynesian and part Welsh,
who left his home island of Rarotonga at
the age of eleven to be educated in New
Zealand and who returned sixteen years
later as a full-fledged doctor to help his own
people in their struggle for health and well-
being. It is the story of Lydia Davis, his
wife, a New Zealand girl, who came to
Rarotonga knowing nothing of its ways and
language; who stood by "Dr. Tom" and was
his stanchest ally; who raised their two
sons, John and Timmy, and somehow found
time to organize the desperately needed
children's clinics, making the Islands so
proud of their infants that they were soon
conducting annual baby shows.

Lydia traveled with her husband to the
furthermost atolls in the Cook group —
Palmerston, Manahiki, Puka Puka — assist-
ing him in his clinics; she took an intense
interest in the lepers of Makogai; she helped
her husband write his unsparing reports;
with her candid grin she got on easily with
the Islanders — though she ran into more
than the usual difficulties with her mother-
in-law.

During his six years as a medical officer
on Rarotonga, Dr. Tom Davis rose from the
bottom to the top. He overcame the superstitions of the Rarotongans, and the opposition of the European and New Zealand
administrators. He insisted that the hospital be supplied with the new drugs, and
when they arrived he personally destroyed

the fear of inoculation. He instituted a program for mosquito control which he knew would reduce the death rate from the dreaded filariasis. He fought the scourge of whooping cough when his own son, young Tim, was desperately ill. He helped to train the Islanders as assistant medical practitioners. He gained the help and confidence of the witch doctors, and he worked hand in glove with the Island leaders in a desperate effort to revive the economy of their plantations, which had been disrupted by the depression and lost sight of during the war years.

Anything could happen in Rarotonga and usually did. There were hurricanes and tennis matches; the dock workers went on strike and police were flown in; there was a whooping cough epidemic in which three hundred infants died, and Dr. Tom literally had to steal the drugs when his superior wasn't looking; when a patient went to the hospital or sanatorium, he took his whole family and his aunts and cousins and there they stayed cooking and chatting for days. The people seemed to live with a happy-go-lucky spirit; but the place was also permeated with a loyalty and integrity which Dr. Tom knew how to tap and which came forth in overflowing affection in the last months of his administration.

In the end, the Davises sailed away on their dream schooner, the *Miru*, a 45-footer bound for Boston, Massachusetts. With their sons and two deckhands, they made the most hazardous crossing of the Pacific imaginable — 12,000 miles in 155 days, and this, an epic in the annals of small craft, forms the conclusion of a unique book.

D O C T O R
to the Islands

by TOM and LYDIA DAVIS

With illustrations by Tom Davis

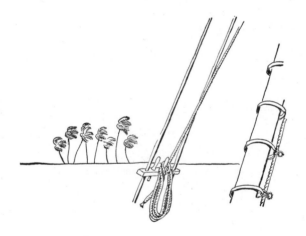

An Atlantic Monthly Press Book
Boston · Little, Brown and Company · *Toronto*

Endicott College Library

BEVERLY, MASSACHUSETTS

920

D264t

11417

FOR THE CHILDREN

Foreword

IT MAY BE hardly respectable to publish one's memoirs before the required three score years and ten have passed. But our lives, now only half spent, seem to have been unusually full. Neither of us relishes the prospect of spending our declining years writing of the past, and our "papers" have been lost during our numerous changes of address.

And so, at our halfway mark, we have joined to recall our ups and downs together, to remember our difficulties and our small successes, and in some measure to tell of the problems of the people of the Pacific Islands and pay tribute to those who we believe have found the secret of living. We wish here to salute the Government of New Zealand in that it has never lost sight of the fact that it has the care of a Polynesian population as well as a European one, and the Otago Medical School and its Dean, Sir Charles Hercus, which continues to provide medical graduates with a qualification they can be proud of anywhere in the world.

Our thanks go to Mr. Edward Weeks of the Atlantic Monthly Press for so tactfully keeping the peace between us during the writing of this book and so patiently sorting out our contradictions and eliminating our nostalgia-born ramblings. We would also like to thank Mr. Harold Coolidge, who, in his position as Executive Secretary of the Pacific Science Board, has done so much for the people of Polynesia, and for us too . . . and we do not forget our brave little ship the *Miru*, who led us so surely into this new chapter in our lives.

THE AUTHORS

Contents

	Foreword	*vii*
I	In the Registrar's Office	3
II	The Giddy Days	15
III	First Year	32
IV	Return to Rarotonga	43
V	The Hospital and the Home	58
VI	The Island Way	74
VII	Hurricane	93
VIII	Paradise	99
IX	Emergency at Atiu	123
X	The Lonely Islands	136
XI	Showdown	163
XII	The Spark	167
XIII	The Cricket	185
XIV	. . . And Cure My Own	197
XV	Visitors	203
XVI	On Leave	221

Contents

XVII   Samoa and Fiji   232

XVIII   In Charge   248

XIX   Trouble in the Laundry   269

XX   Below Deck   289

XXI   At the Helm   311

    Postscript   326

DOCTOR
to the Islands

CHAPTER I

In the Registrar's Office

I WAS married in Dunedin in the South Island of New Zealand on the 4th of September, 1940, and for my wedding I wore a black fur coat. It was a birthday present from my mother for this was also my twenty-first birthday. Actually I had warned my family that I intended to be married on this date but they simply would not believe me. "Don't talk nonsense," they said. "This is a birthday party we're planning, not a wedding breakfast. Now, how many people do you want to ask?" Yet here we were in the Registrar's Office.

The bridegroom also wore black; his only suit, very tight about the shoulders and concealing a badly split shirt.

My parents would have been quite prepared to provide the customary orange blossoms and champagne for my wedding had they believed that I was really going ahead with the event. They had assured me that they approved my choice of a husband, yet they still seemed vaguely disturbed. My father, good businessman that he is, raised the usual objection that Tom, being only in his second year at medical school, could hardly support a wife — it might be years before he could hope to achieve that financial status. I think Mother's uncertainty increased as she heard Tom describe his ambition to return to some remote Pacific Islands associated with a history of cannibalism and fire-walking — certainly no fit place for a respectable New Zealand girl to make her future life.

After discussing my problem between themselves my parents announced that if I would wait until I had attained my majority, then I could do just what I liked; no blame would attach to them if things worked out to be a disappointment for me.

Yet my determination to be married the very minute I turned twenty-one they continued to dismiss as "just talk." Clearly it was up to Tom and me: in place of the lofty cathedral where I had attended my confirmation classes, we chose the rather furtive little office of the Registrar of Births, Deaths and Marriages. Mother, who will rise to an occasion with complete efficiency, agreed at the last minute to see me through the ceremony. But Dad, whose offices happened to be right across the road from the Registrar's, refused to be convinced that the wedding was actually happening. While on one side of the street I was taking the most important step of my life, he, on the other, went stubbornly on with his usual routine.

The Registrar was small and cross-looking. The veiled glances he shot from beneath his dark eyebrows gave us the impression that he had had more to do with deaths than with births or weddings. He matched his surroundings rather well: he and the damp-stained walls and the scuffed carpets had all seen better days. His desk, grimy, ancient and ink-stained, served as an altar to the Bible.

Tom and I grinned at each other. Behind us on a row of painfully hard chairs sat Tom's friends from the medical school. Having been sworn to secrecy, each looked owlishly solemn as if repeating to himself, "Tom and Lyd are really getting married and I've promised not to tell." At the end of the row my precious mother sat straight and dignified, her disapproval of the surroundings quite open and disconcerting. Perhaps she was thinking of how I might have looked in her long-treasured wedding dress and that handmade veil brought all the way from Belgium. But I was quite happy in my new fur coat and not to be subdued by my older sister, Sybil, who, overpowered by her sense of the ridiculous, was having difficulty keeping a straight face.

None of Tom's family was present. Tom's widowed mother lived in the Cook Islands over a thousand miles distant across the Pacific, and his only sister, Mary, was far out of reach at the other end of New Zealand. He had not yet informed them of the significance of this 4th of September.

"Do you, Myra Lydia Henderson of Dunedin in New Zealand, take this man, Thomas Robert Alexander Harries-Davis of Rarotonga in the Cook Islands, to be your lawfully wedded husband, to love and to cherish, for richer for poorer, in sickness and in health, until death do you part?"

Secretly pleased that he had omitted the "obey" I mumbled that I did.

Tom mumbled that he did too. With no more than the usual amount of fishing, he produced the solid gold ring.

Then the Registrar beckoned Tom into a corner and out of earshot. I saw my new husband's jaw drop.

"For Pete's sake, Lyd," he muttered, "lend me a pound. I must have misread that marriage license. I thought it said twenty-five shillings, but it's not, it's two pounds five shillings."

I turned to the row of supporters along the wall. Even though each was wearing his best suit I knew quite well that they were not much better off than Tom. Medical students in New Zealand do not have large allowances and the sheepish looks they gave me were no help.

"Good heavens, child, what's the matter now?" said my mother in what she is pleased to call her stage whisper.

"That man wants another pound before he'll let us go and we just haven't got it," I confessed. Overcome with embarrassment Mother passed over the pound note that launched me on a most adventurous married life.

As we drove away I looked at Tom. He is a nonesuch. He doesn't look, talk, or behave like any of the other young men

who attend medical schools. What does he look like? Well, because his grandmother was a Polynesian, he has black wavy hair and high cheekbones, but because all the rest of him is Welsh, he has green eyes and a straight nose. As a boy he was brought up with the Island people; he spoke their dialects before he spoke English so that now, although his English is perfect and without accent, there is still a hybrid quality to his manner of expression that makes one listen. Tom throws his hands about when he talks, describes forms and directions with a violence almost frightening and is everlastingly resorting to pen and paper when stuck for a word. He draws with a facility which has not been impaired by a few hours' instruction in night school. Because his mind is full of a great variety of subjects, he can ignore a conversation for hours on end; his long silences are not attacks of sulkiness, he is merely hatching a new plot. Fortunately for me he is tall, and fortunately for him he is hefty; men don't interfere with him lightly, he was one of the best heavyweight boxers in the University.

Tom's grandfather, a hearty and much-beloved Welshman who is responsible for the Harries part of Tom's rights and titles, was a powerfully built schoolboy when he climbed out of a downstairs window at school and ran away to sea. He shipped aboard a coastal coaling vessel and learned the ways of the sea he had always loved. Being an able young man he earned his mate's, then his master's tickets in record time, and this helped to allay his parents' wrath. More important, it enabled him to buy a schooner and sail to the South Sea Islands, there to try for his fortune in the pearl and pearl-shell trade flourishing in that area. Papeete, port of Tahiti in the Society Islands, was a congenial headquarters for the young sea captain, and it was here that his roving eye lit on a Rarotongan princess who was visiting her illustrious Tahitian cousins. From all accounts she was a striking beauty. Captain Harries lost little time in marrying his six-foot ladylove and immediately sailed with her to her home seven hundred miles south to Rarotonga. They must have been an imposing couple.

Delightfully archaic tintypes which still adorn the walls of Rarotongan houses show Tom's grandmother, Te Paeru, as the essence of regality. The royal families throughout Polynesia were careful whom their offspring married; they insisted on size and breeding, the result being an exclusive circle of six-foot women and veritable giants of men. Te Paeru was no exception for in her maturity she must have weighed well over

two hundred pounds while her husband could top and out-
span her by several inches.

Captain Harries prospered. Disdaining the dangers of the
hurricane seasons he left his schooners in the water; while his
competitors cowered up on the slipways for three full months,
he kept right on trading. The fact that he lost three vessels
one after the other did not dismay him — no one was
drowned, and he was making so much money from his extra
trading that he could afford to replace lost ships.

Tom inherited his love of the sea and ships, and perhaps a
certain audacity, from Grandpa Harries and it is my one regret
that he did not also inherit a little of his business acumen.
Maybe that will come with age.

When Captain Harries died, he left only one daughter,
Tom's mother, christened Mary Ann. Mary Ann had been
spoiled and overcherished by her father, and when very young
had followed her mother's example and married a young
Welshman, then cruising in the Pacific. Tom's father proved
to be a rover while Mary Ann, despite her many voyages with
old Captain Harries, was so much a martyr to seasickness that,
to her, marriage meant a return to Rarotonga and a chance to
settle down on dry land for once and for all. This was more
than the seafarer could stand. Shortly before Tom's birth,
Davis deserted Rarotonga, preferring the freedom of the seas
and the call of strange lands to the more conventional island
life that Mary Ann had dreamed of.

With her father's legacy and the rents from her mother's
lands, Tom's mother could have lived very comfortably, but
she seemed possessed by the fear that her son too would grow
up to be a wanderer. The conviction grew with the years that
the only way she could make a success of Tom was to keep
him well away from his island home and its attendant pitfalls

of scented *leis* and hula girls and to allow him so little money that his mind would be completely occupied thinking up ways of keeping body and soul together.

This was the picture of my mother-in-law that I had put together from what Tom had told me. He had left no doubt in my mind that he *would* return to the Islands as soon as his medical education was completed, and what kind of welcome I would find awaiting me I could only imagine. Tom's reasons for wanting to return he can explain far better than I.

Our marriage had not been hastily considered. Lydia and I had known each other for more than two years. We were both studying at Otago University, she in the law school and I in medicine, and I first saw her at a dance where, as I remember, she was having such a rush that she couldn't — or wouldn't — dance with me. It provoked me, and I remember that I made a pastel sketch of her when I got back to my shack. But the next time we met — and again it was at a party — the shoe was on the other foot. One of her boy friends had been making himself obnoxious and she turned to me to ask if I would take care of her for the evening and eventually see her home. I said candidly that I didn't have money enough for a taxi, and if I was to see her home she would have to pay the fare. Which she did.

Then we played opposite each other in an undergraduate comedy in which I had been cast as the hero and she as the heroine. I agreed to the role on one condition, that my dog Tiger be given a walk-on part. Tiger was a big tawny half-breed — half Labrador, half German shepherd. He weighed over one hundred pounds, was smarter than most humans, and beyond doubt the best dog I have known or ever shall. He did all right in the play which in itself was rather ham. Lydia did better than all right. She is a very competent actress, good enough for the professional stage, and would have made it except for parental disapproval. She was the star of the show. The rehearsals threw us together; it was natural for me to see her home (in her car), and so I was introduced to her parents. I wasn't quite sure if they approved of me or not.

It was about this time that Lydia changed her course from law to nursing. She became a student nurse in the very hospital where I was getting ready to be an interne. She denies that I had anything to do with this decision, yet her training was of value to us later. Our paths almost never crossed while we were on duty, but I would look for her as I came off and sometimes she would invite me home for cocktails or a meal. I began to see in Lydia more and more of those qualities which I wanted in a woman, more indeed than I had encountered in any other.

Lydia is a complex personality, high-strung, vivacious, temperamental, willing to take a chance, and one had to see through all this to know the real person. I had a premonition of the kind of life my wife would have to live when we went back to the Islands, and I wanted a woman who would stand up to this challenge and even enjoy it. I had looked for this quality in all the women I had known up to this point and had not found it in any of them; all they seemed to be after was an insular kind of security. But Lydia was different. When I began to talk to her seriously about my plans to return to Rarotonga, I felt the sympathy of her response. There was nothing superficial in her attitude, she really believed, and I had to know this.

Lydia is adaptable, but she can also be very inflexible once the course has been set and she has made up her mind to take

it. As we fell in love and our courtship began in earnest, I realized that she was something of a worrier, despite the fact
that she had led a sheltered, well-ordered life. On the other
hand, I have never been a worrier and family life was something I had scarcely known.

The part of me that is Polynesian, no doubt, accounts for
my phlegmatic nature. If a rooster escapes from the chicken
run on one of our Islands, you can hear the resulting uproar
for miles around, though no one really takes it seriously; but
if a tidal wave threatens to engulf us, you will find it is the
Europeans who are rushing around in a panic of misdirected
organization. The natives cope with disaster quietly — quietly
and efficiently.

As Lydia has said, my mother and my grandmother were
Polynesians of royal blood; my grandfather was a Welshman,
my father part Welsh, part English. I was the second of two
children and shortly after my birth my father broke away
from the Islands never to return. He was a born rover and all
I ever knew of him was hearsay. He was a soldier of fortune;
he had served with the Anzacs in the First World War; a traveler reaching for new horizons, until tuberculosis to which he
had been exposed in the war pulled him down. I was told he
was a dreamer, impractical, a lover of music, above all a wanderer. My mother was naturally embittered when he deserted
her; she left strict instructions at our boarding schools in
New Zealand that neither Mary nor I was ever to see or com-
municate with our father. I know he tried to reach us, but the
wall had been built and I never did see him.

It is not unusual for the boys from the Cook Islands to have
their schooling in New Zealand, but however absorbed we
may get in our books we never cease to hear the call of the sea.
My great-grandfather on my mother's side was the last prac-

ticing Polynesian navigator. My Welsh grandfather made a
tidy fortune as sea captain and trader. Although my mother
would have opposed it had she known, by the time I was ten
I had paddled and sailed out of sight of land in my own outrigger canoe. Actually the older men kept a weather eye on
me. They taught me a knowledge of small boats that became
almost instinctive. I soon learned to do things on my own, to
discover things, to depend on my own resources in getting out
of trouble and keeping out of trouble. If other boys came
along, I sometimes got a scolding from their parents. So I began to prefer my independence and learned to use my own
resources either to get out of trouble or, more important, to
anticipate the trouble that might arise at sea.

The first small, deep-sea vessel I ever saw was the *Svaap*
which William A. Robinson of Winchester, Massachusetts,
had sailed around the world. Later he was to write his adventures in a popular book, *10,000 Leagues Over the Sea*, but
this was in the year 1926, and his voyage was only half completed. I shall never forget how kind he was to me, a mere
eight-year-old. He allowed me the run of his ship and gave
me a free hand with his dugout Indian canoe which he used
as a tender and which by an odd freak of circumstance I was
again to see in Marblehead in 1953. My hours aboard the
Svaap were happy ones, and I resolved some day to make a
trip that other small-boat sailors like Bill Robinson would
remember.

In my mother's eyes I spent my boyhood trying to kill myself, but my narrowest escape she never knew of. It happened when I was just eleven and about to be packed off to
school in New Zealand. I had gone out for one last sail and on
this occasion took with me in the outrigger two New Zealand
boys of my own age. The weather was deceptive for with al-

most no warning a squall came up that threatened to drive us straight onto the breakers hardly a hundred yards away on the reef. Young though I was, I had already seen what happened to the Islanders who had been thrown onto that reef. The only way to escape was to put out to sea.

I attempted to head the canoe away from the shore; one of the boys was bailing with his sand shoe, the other paddling sturdily with me as we struggled to keep the bow onto the open sea. Then I made the mistake of shouting, "Keep paddling and don't look behind you!"

More fool I. Of course they immediately looked behind and the sight of the great breakers pounding in on the coral started them screaming with fear. They were quite paralyzed, the bailing stopped, the paddling forgotten. To revive them I had to hit them with my paddle. This was my first knowledge of what hysteria can do. Our only chance was to inch along to the point where at last we could angle in and head for the only opening in the reef. We just did make it.

Fear is no help in an emergency and from that day I learned to keep danger signals to myself; it was the sea that taught me my lesson.

As we left the Registry office that afternoon I began to have qualms about the coming showdown with Father. Evidently Mother was thinking of the same thing.

"Lydia, before we break the news to Father," she said, "I think it would be fun to stop at the nearest cocktail lounge, and I'll treat everyone to some Dutch courage."

So by the time we reached home and faced Father life had taken on a rosier tint. Dad looked at the marriage license and was struck dumb. But as the guests to my birthday party were starting to come in the front door, the time was not right for the lecture he knew he could deliver so well. He set his jaw and began to mix and dispense drinks. In this way he ignored us. Tom and I kept making little rushes out of the room to admire the wedding ring and each other. Mother also made little sorties, digging through her linen cupboards to produce something with which to lay a foundation for the "glory box" I had forgotten about.

That night when we drove away from home in a borrowed car, only a few friends knew that we were off on our honeymoon. It would have to be one of the shortest honeymoons on record, for of the twenty-four hours' leave granted every nurse on her twenty-first birthday there remained only a few short hours.

In my innocence I believed that this rather ragged start was merely an unfortunate prologue to a life of medical routine, permanent surroundings bounded by solid walls and a neat paling fence, pleasant neighbors, a steady income, and a sizable reserve for a rainy day.

Tom knew where he was going; I only thought I did.

CHAPTER II

The Giddy Days

TOM had rented for us two sparsely furnished rooms at the back of a small shabby house. The rent came to thirty shillings a week, which will give you some idea of their elegance. The third member of the household, our dog Tiger, was happy at the prospect. The landlady, whom we called Ma, kept a pieshop on the ground floor, and Tiger had always had an eye for a good pieshop.

Ma was large, bosomy and scarlet-faced with a temper to match. She wore hand-knitted cardigans pinned over her chest with a real diamond brooch, and in this odd costume she would flap up and downstairs between her rooms and her pieshop, her flat feet tucked into red felt slippers with pompons on the toes. Pa, her husband, was a stevedore although he was so quiet and self-effacing that he didn't look like one. He always wore his coat collar turned up all round, and his hatbrim right down over his nose; it saved him from looking his fellow men in the eye and, besides, Ma couldn't always find out what he was thinking. With Pa's earnings and Ma's pie money they had bought their house and were now acquiring (on the installment plan) a Chevrolet, a radio, a vacuum cleaner, washing machine, electric stove, and a bedroom suite.

In the front room on our floor lived a sinister couple called Steve and Lil. We never did find out how they made a living, they stayed home all day and came forth only at nights; I

think Steve had something to do with betting. Tom and I
were installed in the two remaining rooms at the back of the
house, our windows commanding an uninterrupted view of
the brick walls of an adjoining factory. The view was rather
depressing, but the rooms were sunny — and what more could
we expect at that price?

In my ignorance I had assumed that we could keep our marriage a secret, at least until I had completed my course of
nursing. I was in my second year of training and at this time
doing a three months' stint at the Talboy's Benevolent Insti-
tution, a hospital founded in 1850 and unchanged thereafter,
always referred to by the nurses as "the Benny." It was in
reality an old people's home, a hospital full of chronic patients, many of them suffering from mental complaints and
most of them to remain there for the rest of their days. The
female patients wore Mother Hubbard gowns and poke bonnets; they kept their old shoulders warm with little fur tip-
pets; the men, those who were dressed, sported black cloaks
and red woolen bonnets with pompons on top while at night
they wore gray flannel nightshirts, sleeping caps, and, if I
didn't watch them closely, went to bed with their boots on.
It was a little as if one were living in an illustration for a
book by Dickens.

The day after our marriage I returned to cope with these
old dears, and it was my bad luck to be assigned to night
duty. Needless to say by 10 P.M., when I signed on, I was
yawning my head off and wondering how I could keep awake
until seven the next morning.

The Dickens characters seemed bent on mischief. No sooner
would I have everyone neatly tucked in with their boots off
and their nightshirts on than — crash! One of the old men
would topple out of bed taking with him his bed table and

everything on it. Then would follow a short struggle while 112-pound me wrestled 200-pound grandpa back into his sheets where he belonged. After "shushing" the rest of the ancients who would by this time be complaining loudly of the disturbance and demanding cups of hot tea to help them back to sleep, I would return to the kitchen premises (the warmest in the hospital), to find a dear old lady pottering about in her nightgown and bare feet cooking up brews on my stove and before I could escort her back to bed her voluble protests would have again waked everyone in the building, of course producing further requests for cups of tea.

Next evening I had an inspiration: when I went on duty I gave each patient a nice big cup of warm milk, heavily spiked with chloral bromide, a potion guaranteed to put the strongest to sleep and make them stay that way. I placed the cups on the lockers beside each bed with careful instructions that, should any of the patients feel restless during the night, they had only to put out their hands and there would be a good nourishing drink. It worked. Never have the patients at the "Benny" enjoyed better rest and I was at last free to catch up on a little sleep myself.

I stoked up the kitchen stove, removed all the cushions from the matron's sitting room, dragged over the blankets from my unused bed in the nurses' home and curled up on the floor to sleep till morning. Outside the door fifty oldsters were peacefully snoring.

Unfortunately I had overlooked one small matter. The kitchen door admitted a freezing draft which blew steadily all night, right onto the small of my back, and next day I was reduced to a creaking and complaining bundle of woe. I don't know yet if it was the rheumatics, the lumbago, or just plain aching back. Whatever it was, I had it.

Nurses were required to report to the matron when they fell ill: if I were questioned as to how I had contracted my complaint, what could I say? I called in Tom's friends and held a council of war; they decided that I had better go to the matron, tell her my name was now officially Davis and risk the consequences. By this time I was feeling so wretched that to walk the one block to Matron's office seemed like a trek to Africa. To buck me up the boys emptied their pockets and with the pooled proceeds bought me a bottle of port wine. Matron's reactions to my announcement regarding the change in my status remain very blurred in my memory, but in the morning I was again and firmly reminded that despite the fact that the war had created a shortage of nurses, those with the title of "Mrs." were unwelcome.

Now that I was unemployed I could be Mrs. Davis publicly and share what we were pleased to call our home. But the budget was in too precarious a state for me to remain unemployed. Tom had been working his way through Medical School and he knew better than I how narrow was our margin.

⟨෴⟩

Since my first year in medical school, I had been living from hand to mouth. Mother paid my tuition fees which came to about fifty pounds each year, but I had to find my own lodgings, food, clothing and everything incidental. I did. During the winter while the school was in session, I served as an usher in a movie theater, which paid about five shillings a night, plus a free view of the show, while in vacations I did a variety of chores, shoveling phosphate, hauling sacks of coal, working in a wool store, or on a farm as a teamster, shearer or harvest hand. These vacation jobs were supposed to roll up a surplus for the months I would be in class; there was never very much leeway.

I had found a little wooden shack on the bank of the River Leith within the city limits for which I paid a rent of eight shil'ings a week. Here I lived with my dog Tiger, a black ki en which I had taken in, and a half-tame gray mouse v ich holed up under my wardrobe. When I was in funds I bought my food from my landlady; when I was hard up I ate polished rice and milk. I used to fry that rice, boil it, steam it, do everything I could with it, but no matter how often I rang the changes it was mighty monotonous.

It was a one-room shack measuring at the outside twelve by fifteen feet, and furnished with the barest necessities: a bed, one chair, a small chest of drawers, a small table and a wardrobe. On the walls I had tacked my unframed etchings, pastels, and a few oils. (Actually my total time in art school had been one night a week over a half year.) I had an easel in one corner and the usual bachelor clutter in every available space. There wasn't room enough to swing a cat much less to park a dog of Tiger's size.

Tiger joined me during my first year in the shack; a gangling pup of six months, he was given to me because his previous owners found it impossible to discipline him. They had tried the normal methods in vain, he would have none of it;

they did not realize that, even though a pup, Tiger was very much an individual. The first thing I taught him was to carry. We began with a foot rule and before he got tired of having it in his mouth I had a pat for him and perhaps a piece of meat by way of encouragement. Then he learned to shake hands with either paw, to sit up on his haunches, to stack his already oversized self onto a chair and keep his balance with his paws on the back — all the usual tricks and disciplines helping to condition the loyalty between us. I could talk to him as if he were another human being, could say "Tiger, please bring me the matches," and he would fetch the box in his mouth. If I left a towel behind me on the beach I could tell him to run back and get it. In fact, in those days Tiger was my picker-upper. But with Tiger everything had to be purposeful, there could be no fooling. Of course he had the run of the place and while I was in class attached himself to the boys of the neighborhood hunting rabbits with them. At nightfall when I returned he would always be there first, waiting.

That big brown dog with his smooth coat, dark on top and buff on the underside, was one of the best-known figures in the town. When he wrestled with the kids, even though it was all in mockery, you could hear his growls two blocks away. He wouldn't have touched a hair of their heads but strangers wouldn't know this and sometimes in the newspapers there would start up a vigorous correspondence in the Letters to the Editor column about the ferocious Tiger.

It was Tiger who made my bachelor quarters endurable. He was his own breadwinner and sometimes mine too. When I was in funds we followed a regular routine. I had trained him to carry an empty sugar sack with a threepenny bit in it. I would give him the bag, open the door and watch him as, with the bag in his teeth, he would trot away; I knew his routine, he would head for a friendly butcher, rear himself up on his hind legs and, disregarding the large sign which read NO DOGS ALLOWED, drop the sack on the counter. The butcher (I said he was a friend) would open the bag, take out the threepence and then, dominated by Tiger, let generosity do the rest. If others were in the shop they too would fall under Tiger's spell, for there were few people who could resist the look in that dog's eye. They would donate bits from their own parcels and soon his sack would be as full as he could carry — and he could carry a heavy load. He would bring his meat and bones back to the shack, and the four of us, the kitten, the mouse, Tiger and I, would share.

Tiger and the kitten got along well but the only time that the cat and the mouse would come out together was for food. I had taught Tiger to sit up and beg at mealtimes and the little ones had learned to copy him, knowing that food was the reward. It sounds unbelievable, there would be the three of them sitting up on their haunches waiting for me to divide the supper.

When I lived in that shack I was a poor tenant, often weeks behind in my rent, yet when the pinch came it was Tiger who, by endearing himself to the landlady, would ensure that I was not thrown out.

I was never really ahead of the game, and I knew there would be no additional help from my mother. I realized that she disapproved of my studying medicine — I wasn't sure why — and from her letters, as well as from the Islanders who came to New Zealand for work, I learned that Rarotonga was suffering from a severe depression. The prosperity which they had enjoyed when I was there as a boy seemed to be slipping away. It had been a prosperity built wholly on shipping, mostly the shipping of fruit which had declined in tonnage year after year until from 6000 tons a month it had now dropped to only 600. Mother's letters told how the natives had abandoned their old cars, the chassis had been stripped and the axles and rubber-tired wheels were now being used on their horse-drawn carts. Some of the people could no longer afford to repair their European-type houses, so that if a hurricane lifted the iron roof it stayed off. It seemed that families were reverting to living in the old-fashioned thatched houses; but the pandanus trees which in the old days had supplied all the building materials had, through parasite destruction, disappeared, and the Islanders were now stripping the leaves from the live coconut trees — of course injuring the valuable coconut crop. Things seemed to be in a very low state, it saddened me to hear of it.

I knew that if Lydia and I were to eat I had to have a steady job, and soon after we were married I signed on as a taxi driver for a sixty-hour week. It wasn't too tough and on good nights I could salt away as much as £3. From the hospital I would go straight to the garage, check the cab and be out on the streets by 5:15. Over week ends I drove as late as three A.M., but on week nights managed to get off shortly after one. Even so it was quite a long day.

Sleep began to seem more important to me than food: I took cat naps whenever the opportunity arose and I spent the whole blessed lunch hour sleeping. My only big meal of the day came at nine in the evening when I used to park my cab at the curb and dine at the Pie Cart run by my friend, Dick Orr. Dick's wife did the cooking and I looked forward all day to her dinners of steak, fried eggs, onions, peas and mashed potatoes. I think Mrs. Orr took pity on me, at all events she gave me the choice cuts and extra helpings and it was thanks to her that my weight — I weighed about 190 — never fell off. Her meals were a gift from the gods at this time when Lydia was just learning to cook.

⟨⟩

My mother and father refused to pay us any formal calls in our slum, but Dad would drop by quietly to deliver large boxes of Mother's home cooking. We would have welcomed raw steaks and a dozen or so of fresh eggs, but Mother's idea of food for the young did not extend beyond chocolate éclairs, cream puffs, and meringue cakes. However, we soon worked out an exchange system with other students who were only too willing to swap a couple of pounds of sausages for one of Mother's mince tarts, and our meals were almost regular.

Tom wrote the news of our marriage to his mother, but her letter by return post was not exactly one of congratulation; in it she gently reminded him that at his birth she had followed the Polynesian custom of betrothing her first son to the offspring of a suitable Rarotongan family. Tom (who had never seen his bride-to-be) had, of course, forgotten all about this small matter. He apologized to his mother and we shelved the whole problem until that distant day when Dr. Davis would return to Rarotonga and face the embarrassment of being introduced to his deserted bride.

As if to soften this rebuke, my mother-in-law enclosed a five-pound note in her envelope, and I thought, "Hooray, I won't have to find work for a week or two yet."

But I had not counted on Tom's ingenuity. The next afternoon I heard a rattling and banging at the front door, and when I went out I found him pushing an antique motor bike right into the house.

"Tom," I said, "where in heaven did you get that? And don't bring it in on Ma's carpets, she'll go mad."

"Lyd, isn't it a beauty?" he said affectionately. "I got it with Mum's five pounds." He was much too busy fondling his new treasure to notice my rising wrath.

"All right, keep your old motor bike. Let's both starve," I exploded, hoping that the tragic catch in my voice might impress him.

It was no good. Although we had only been married a few weeks Tom decided that he loved the bike more than me. He took it into the kitchen, of all places, and completely dismantled it, lining up all the nuts, bolts and screws on the sinktop, numbering each one and jotting down notes as to where each came from. Two days later he had put the bike together again. Lubricating oil on the kitchen linoleum testified to his thoroughness. The bike, now christened Hurry Up, went — with persuasion. It did not, however, go for long at a stretch, and we became a familiar sight taking turns pushing the darned thing home.

I know by now that I owe my life several times over to that accursed motor bike. From disemboweling it times innumerable Tom learned what makes an engine work. What he learns he does not forget, so that when the hospital power plant breaks down, or when the anesthetic machine goes on the blink, or when our car develops odd squeaks, Tom applies the lessons he learned from Hurry Up.

Thanks to our families, we now owned a bed, sheets, blankets — and a motor bike — but our bank account was low, we were down to our last pound, really bust this time, and it was up to me to find a job with a steady income. Like most of my sex, I had long wanted to go on the stage, preferably into musical comedy; in college I had qualified for a scholar-

ship to a distinguished dramatic school in London, and I had
once received a definite offer from a musical comedy company. But my family were adamant in their disapproval, in-
sisting that I study to become a lawyer rather than spend
my life in the back row of the chorus. Now that I was married and a free agent, this would be my chance.

I arranged for an audition with the National Broadcasting
Company and to my delight was offered a position as an an-
nouncer at the munificent salary of nearly eight pounds a
week. I rushed home to tell the great news.

"Did you say you're going to work at a radio station?"
Tom asked, not showing the least enthusiasm.

"Yes, isn't it wonderful? Think of it, Tom, eight pounds
a week — steak every day and roast pork on Sundays!"

Tom stuck his jaw out and looked aggrieved. "Lyd, I don't
want you to do it. No good your working with a bunch of
actors. See what you can get in a law office — plenty of positions there with all the law clerks off to the war. You'd like
it better — more respectable too."

I explained that radio announcers were not actors, that
they did not marcel their hair or call each other "dahling."

"Eight pounds a week, Tom! Think what a difference that
will make. I'll be lucky if I get two pounds as a law clerk.
Please, please let me do it."

"I'd rather have you get two pounds and be respectable
than eight pounds with a bunch of hams."

So I was committed to the mustiness of a law office, where
each week I collected a miserable two pounds ten shillings
from an equally musty accountant. Still the job was fun. As
Tom said, the war had stripped the legal profession of men so
that there was an opportunity for me to see the more interesting side of common law. I was sworn a bailiff's warrant and,

armed with a handful of summonses, rushed around cornering my victims with a "pay up or else." Sometimes the debtors turned out to be my own friends, and they were easy. I would chat about the weather and the latest party, then throw the summons at them and run. I once chased a debtor in and out of a string of railway carriages shouting "Stop thief," but my quarry escaped by crawling under the guard's van. If I had to go out at night and obtain statements of evidence for my employer's court cases, I would take Tiger with me. He was large enough to discourage angry witnesses from beating me up in alleyways and besides, with Tiger along, Tom could rest assured that I was remaining "respectable."

I had not gained Tiger's loyalty without a struggle. At first that big tawny-colored hound regarded me with suspicion. He had no intention of sharing his master with me and, as soon as I moved my belongings in with Tom's, Tiger decided to be difficult. When I called him to come out for a walk, he hung his head and sulked; when he knocked over glasses with his tail and I marched him out of the room, he snapped at me; when he hopped up on the bed and I promptly threw him off, he turned out his upper lip and sneered. (I think that Tom was privately relieved that he no longer had to share his bed with his dog. Tom told me that they used to start the night with Tiger on the outside and himself against the wall. But once Tom was sound asleep Tiger would step carefully across and snuggle down on the wall side. Next he would place all four paws against the wall — and push. Tom would wake up wondering why he was on the floor.)

I did not intend to let my life be ruled by a dog, even such a paragon as Tiger, so we declared open war. I bought a collar and a heavy chain and when he refused to walk along the street with me clipped on the harness and dragged him. Tiger and I were exactly the same weight, so we must have looked very silly as I tugged and pulled on one end of the chain while that large dog sat firmly on his bottom at the other end, his paws dug into the ground and a look in his golden eyes that can best be described as insulting. When he became tired of pulling in the opposite direction, he would get up and walk — on three legs, with an expression of agony in his eyes and the once-broken paw held well out in front for all to see.

"Look at this fiend of a woman," he would say to passers-by, "she has taken my master away from me, she is sleeping on my bed and eating up all my food, and me only a poor dumb animal, and lame to boot. Just look at this poor paw of mine, all broken and sore. How I suffer!"

Tiger knew he wasn't lame. He was fat, healthy, and active, but by pulling down his mouth at the corners and fluttering his very human set of eyelashes he could fool anyone.

Well, I'd show him. With a carefree disregard for the future, I spent part of my first week's salary buying another dog, a coal-black Labrador, as big as Tiger and nearly as heavy. I had introduced Tom to the delights of Kipling's

Jungle Books, and as we already had Shere Khan, the lame Tiger, in the family, we felt that to call the Labrador Bagheera, the black panther, would be very suitable.

Tiger sniffed at Bagheera, then stared me straight in the eye. I stared back.

"All right, Lyd, you win. I didn't mean any of it really. I'll be friends now," said this condescending animal and rushed off for a game of tag with his new playmate.

From then on Tiger was his usual self. It was Bagheera who became defiant, and I am afraid that in their long chats together Tiger encouraged this. Soon no one would dare shake hands with me for fear of having a hundred pounds of black fury at his throat. Tradesmen refused to deliver our food and friends telephoned, "We're coming to see you, but only if you chain that black dog." When the police began to call, I decided that rather than have him destroyed I should send him to the country to be used as a hunting dog. For a short time Tiger was lonely but when he realized that Bagheera was never coming back he turned to me with disarming affection.

With my two pounds ten a week and Tom's earnings from the taxi, it seemed that we would be able to scrape by. Then Ma dropped a bombshell.

One morning she marched up the passage past our rooms holding in front of her a well-filled bedroom receptacle which it was her wont to empty "out the back." The next thing we heard was a resounding crash. The bomb had slipped out of her hand and completely smashed the major toilet installations.

Surveying the damage, Ma went berserk. She rushed into the front bedroom, threw some furniture at poor Pa who was cowering behind the bedrail, then flung open the door to

Steve and Lil's love nest and gave them twenty-four hours' notice because they had been sinning in her house without benefit of clergy. She then headed in our direction. Never let it be said that the Davises were asked to leave. We beat her to it and with dignity announced that we could not tolerate such living conditions — we were leaving within the hour!

Our belongings were parked for the rest of that day on the footpath, but by nightfall I had found new lodgings. Luck was with us this time. We had the chance to share a house out in a quiet suburb for only twenty-five shillings a week. Our landlord and his lady, whom we still affectionately remember as Win and Ned, were childless, and they admonished us to stay the same way. They were uncertain as to their attitude towards Tiger, but after his courtly reception of their very elderly Pomeranian they felt assured that he was truly a gentleman.

Tom's student friends were eager to inspect our new lodgings, and almost before he had dragged our suitcases and boxes inside the door they arrived. As usual in emergencies they brought with them bottles of beer and Tom, blissfully ignoring the havoc around him, invited them to sit on the various packages and started to take the tops off the bottles. At first I was reasonably pleasant about the situation. I politely asked the boys to sit somewhere else so that I could open a case. I said "Thank you" when they picked up a hammer I had dropped. But when, struggling into the bedroom with a mirror that was far too heavy for me, I fell off the stepladder and broke the glass for seven years' bad luck, my temper exploded.

"All right, Tom, you idiot. Sit there and drink beer while I kill myself. You and your friends can drink till you burst, I'm going home to Mother and I won't be back."

It was all most convenient, my bags were still packed, and before the boys had quite realized what I was doing I was out the door and into a taxi. On my way to peace again!

"Why how nice to see you this afternoon," said Mother, welcoming me in. "I thought you were going to be too busy moving . . ." At this point she caught sight of my suitcases. "Lydia, what on earth have you got in those bags?"

"Everything I possess. I've left Tom. I'm home for good."

Mother never batted an eyelid. "Oh, really. Well, in that case leave those bags right where they are and I'll ring for a taxi to take you straight back. Don't bother to come in. You can wait on the veranda. I never heard of such nonsense."

In twenty-five minutes I was back where I had started. I will say that in that interval Tom and the boys had been quite busy, everything was unpacked and in the wrong place, but at least it was unpacked. The bits of mirror were swept up and the beer bottles sitting tidily on a table. Luckily I did not deign to give an explanation for my hasty return — and the lesson was one we both remembered.

Win and Ned must have appreciated that something was up for they brought in a hot steak and kidney pie for our supper. It was delectable and Tom and I stowed it away grinning.

There are turning points in every marriage and it was at this time that my family began to reconcile themselves to ours; maybe after our bad start we might be able to make a success of life together. When an unexpectedly fat check arrived from Tom's mother, we bought a motor car, a 1929 Austin, old but reliable. Mother and Dad had given us a piano as a delayed wedding present and this, with a few other pieces of furniture from my old home, turned our two rooms into a kind of cosy clubhouse for the other students.

At week ends we all ate together, pooling our week-end food and taking turns at the cooking. There were still cynics who told Tom that he could not possibly support a dog, bike, car, home and wife at the same time, but somehow we were doing it and the future would take care of itself.

Win and Ned had never had young people living with them and they treated us more as their own children than as tenants. Win carefully taught me how to cook and, when I returned late from the office, would share her meals with us. She seemed to take as much interest in our friends as we did. She entered into a conspiracy with my mother to ensure that we were behaving ourselves and getting enough to eat.

And then . . .

To my great consternation, Mother's delight, and Tom's smug assertion that "he knew it all the time," I realized that to the list of dog, bike, car and wife, we should soon have to add "child."

CHAPTER III

First Year

NOW I would have to stop being a law clerk and learn to be a mother; our income would be halved and perhaps we would have to find new lodgings. Win, our landlady, was not happy at the prospect of having a baby in her house. Her own childlessness had been an overwhelming sadness in her life; she loved children but was afraid that someone else's baby so close to her would serve only to remind her of her sorrow. We persuaded her to give us a trial and hoped for the best.

This was 1942 during the worst days of the Second World War. Japan was threatening New Zealand's shores and most of our young men were overseas fighting in North Africa or in Nazi prison camps where they had been taken from Greece or Crete. Those were gloomy times and very fretful to men in Tom's position, for medical students were not allowed to enlist until after graduation — our country was now suffering a severe shortage of doctors, in part the result of the heavy medical casualties in the First World War. Tom had tried to volunteer for the Air Force in 1940 only to be told that he must finish his medical studies. Thereafter his military efforts were confined to brief and perfunctory training periods in local infantry camps and he was restless to do more.

Everyone in our small town was absorbed in the war effort: Ned, our landlord, was in camp with the home guard, protecting the beaches with cardboard guns. My mother hoarded eggs and butter and made endless food parcels for her nephews and sons of friends. My sister, Sybil, now a member of the Women's Auxiliary Air Force, spent her days scrubbing airplanes in the freezing cold of the airport twenty miles from home, scrubbing and polishing with chapped hands. Dad replaced a traffic cop and passed the evenings directing the traffic at one of the city's busiest corners. Dad is not a calm person at the best of times and it was inevitable that Tom would get involved in one of Dad's nightly traffic snarls. I remember standing by the safety zone one evening watching the fun.

Dad had paused to wave to me, forgetting that a wave of the hand has extra significance when performed by a guardian of the traffic; the result of his fatherly gesture was havoc. Brakes screeched, mudguards bumped each other, drivers swore, Dad blew his whistle and waved his arms, his red face rapidly becoming purple. Then who should come along but Tom at the wheel of the gleaming white car which he drove for weddings. Tom couldn't resist sticking his head out of the window and indulging in some choice sarcasm. Although Dad did not actually break a blood vessel, I am sure his circulatory system was considerably loosened up that night.

In all tension, I was the lucky one. I could sit at home with Tiger beside me and add to a fast growing pile of woolies, all hand-knitted and threaded with blue ribbon; I felt certain we would have a son.

One evening towards the end of July, I stayed inside by the fire reading an Ellery Queen mystery and feeling rather peculiar. When Tom came in after his taxi rounds, I kept on stubbornly reading my thriller (it was *The Spanish Cape Mystery*), walking up and down the room in the approved fashion and wondering what was going to happen to me and if it would happen before I found out the identity of the murderer. Early in the morning I rang Mother to report progress.

"Go back to bed, it will be a day or two yet. You sound much too cheerful to be worrying me now. Just have a nice cup of tea and go to sleep."

I might have sounded so but I certainly wasn't feeling cheerful, and it was only after several calls to the nursing home that I could convince them that something should be done about me. Tom drove me to the hospital, then went off to a lecture. He was rather surprised when in the middle of a dissertation on the neural system, half an hour later, the professor stopped and wrote on the blackboard: "Happy Birthday, Tom Davis Junior!" But he was not to be Tom Davis; we called him John Cordy after my grandfather.

Tom and I thought John a marvel of perfection, even though a little thin. He weighed just four and a half pounds, a neat parcel of skin stretched over bone. Whenever I saw him during his first two weeks in the hospital, he was wrapped up in shawls with only his head peeping over the top, but his face looked fine to me. So eventually I returned home bearing my streamlined heir in triumph.

Tiger, his nose out of joint, accepted the appearance of John at first with suspicion, then with resignation. When I asked him to sit beside the pram and keep guard, he would sigh, raise his eyes to heaven and stick by his post, obviously hoping that canine passers-by would not think him a sissy. He had to carry my basket when I had both hands pushing my go-cart, but he gained mild revenge for my division of affection when I took him down to the beach for a run and a little showing off. If he saw a large crowd of onlookers hanging over the esplanade enjoying the salt air, he would imitate the circus greyhounds in the high jumps — over my back — then suddenly pretend to miss his footing and throw his full weight on me, landing me face down in the damp sand. Then he would pretend to be looking at a seagull. As usual when he was being obnoxious, Tiger really didn't mean it. After John's arrival he became more and more attached to me. He didn't disappear any more; during the baby's sleeping hours he would not leave me for an instant, even sometimes turning his nose up at Tom.

Tom was now in his last year of medical training. He kept steadily on passing his examinations though I admit I lived in constant dread of his flunking. If he said, "Lyd, it will be all right," once he said it a hundred times, but I continued to worry. Tom's class work came to an end in November of 1943, and ahead of him lay two years of interneship as a house surgeon. But this meant the breakup of our friendly group, and Mother threw open her house for one last party with Tom and the boys. Now they would separate in different directions all bound for different hospitals in New Zealand. Tom and I would be heading for Auckland, but this was the last meeting of the "Davis Club," as we had come to think of it, and our gaiety was not unmixed with sentiment at the parting ahead.

Win was in tears as the time came for our departure; she had come to look upon John as her own, and great affection had sprung up between us all. And we ourselves were heavy at heart because we had to leave without Tiger.

Tiger was settling down to staid and responsible middle age when the blow fell. We had no warning: it came with shocking suddenness as is the case with so many dog lovers. I heard a scratching at the door and when I opened it there he was on the mat, his ears down and his shoulders twitching.

I knew something was very wrong, but with Tom away at the hospital I was uncertain what to do. Fortunately John was asleep and, asking Win to look after him, I called Tiger, intending to take him down to the druggist who was an experienced veterinarian. But we had not gone a hundred yards when Tiger suddenly threw himself into the air and collapsed in a most distressing spasm. It looked to me like strychnine poisoning. There was no question of moving so large a dog into a taxicab, so I stopped the first van that came by and the sympathetic driver agreed to help me take Tiger the five miles to the animal hospital. He suffered agonies when we touched him, but with the aid of several kindly passers-by we lifted him onto the back of the van. The driver tried to avoid bumping his passenger, but each jerk of the truck brought on a fresh spasm. As I talked to him, Tiger seemed to say, "I know you are doing your best, but please hurry."

At the end of that nightmare drive, we could not risk shifting the dog again, but administered an emetic as he lay on the van. While he rested I ran to the hospital to fetch Tom and borrowed my father's car to bring our patient home again. Two days later, before Tiger had had sufficient time to regain his strength, we found him lying in the garden; the poisoner had been at work again, this time successfully.

It is a tribute to Tiger that every detective in the city laid aside his work in an effort to trace the poisoner. We found that, in addition to our dog, no less than eighteen others in our neighborhood had been destroyed in the same way.

Some people think they are doing humanity a kindness in removing dogs that they regard as pests. Perhaps if they could see the suffering they inflict and share the lonely gap left by the loss of an almost human friend, they would be less hasty. There can never be another Tiger. We were a silent, stricken household as we prepared to leave Dunedin.

Those two years in the Auckland hospital were a maturing time for Tom. For the first year he was required to live in the hospital quarters, and John and I found a small house in the neighborhood where he could join us when he was off duty. It was a time of pinching, scraping, and stretching ends to their last limits to make them meet. I took in a boarder, I knitted for neighbors, I grew vegetables and sold them at market, I even scouted through secondhand shops picking up bargains I could sell later at a profit. But Tom's legacy was now in the care of a new trustee who had discovered that Tom was eligible to receive a monthly allowance for his graduate studies. There was a clause in the will stipulating that the only way the capital could be drawn on was for educational purposes. Tom's allowance supplemented by the three pounds fifteen a week which he received as a house surgeon enabled us to squeak by. Somehow the rent was always paid and our plates always full. I was beginning to believe Tom when he assured me that "the Lord will provide." It seemed that the Lord occasionally needed a bit of help, but we managed.

By December 1945 Tom at last was a fully accredited Doctor in Medicine, and before Christmas to the delight of both

of us he received word of the appointment for which he had
been working so long.

My sixteen years away from the Cook Islands, in boarding
school, medical school, and finally as a house surgeon, had all
been pointed toward the day when I might become a medical
officer to the Cook Islands. This was the unchanged ambition
I had had as a boy, and my graduate studies and indeed my
extracurricular activities were aimed with this one professional goal in mind. I also dreamed of some day making a
memorable ocean voyage, but I knew that my work must
come first.

I had been trained as a physician and a surgeon and now
held degrees in both subjects; I had studied the administration of small hospitals and watched how they worked, the
principles involved, the economics of their operation. To
further my education I spent three months at Seacliff Hospital, a hospital for mental diseases, where as junior medical
officer I had supervision of some seven hundred female patients; it was valuable experience that I gained there, and I
was deeply touched when on my departure my ladies presented me with a blue silk necktie which they had knitted
for me on the co-operative basis. That tie was long enough
to tie round my neck and twice round my waist. Some of it
was knitted loosely, some tightly, some purl, some plain, and
the more confident of my patients had evidently taken the
opportunity to do some lamentably unsuccessful fancy
stitches. One could almost diagnose the patient's mental state
by studying the various rows of that tie. I wore it with pride.

In all this long span, I had been back to the Islands for a
one-month visit, in the summer of 1933. I left the Islands a

boy of eleven and went back for my one and only leave when I was fourteen. Mary came with me and together we had six weeks at home. All during my years in New Zealand I had lived for the day when I should see little Rarotonga again. I longed for the atmosphere, the food I had been brought up on, the freedom of the Island life, the nearness of the sea, the Island songs. It was the most wonderful month I had ever spent in my life. Mother received us with open arms and the people showed their affection. That was still the heyday of prosperity and the Islanders went out of their way to see that we were entertained every day and every evening. As a college student it was impossible for me to return: I was too hard up. But never did I forget the *rukau,* taro tops, done with chicken or pork; the delicious raw fish prepared with fresh coconut cream, limes, and chili; the delectable native sauces which take up to five days to ferment; pork and chicken flavored with strong scalded coconut cream and eaten until I could hold no more. I thought of the warm, tranquil lagoons, of the predawn showers which washed the Islands for the coming day; I remembered the joy of fishing from outriggers in the open sea. Now at the age of twenty-seven I was eager for my second home-coming.

I had served two full years in Auckland as house surgeon and physician when one morning I saw in the newspaper a small advertisement asking for applicants to serve as medical officer for the Cook Islands. Of course I applied at once, and since the Dominion of New Zealand was responsible for the administration of the Cook Islands I addressed my letter to the Department of Island Territories in Wellington. A month passed with no acknowledgment whatever, and I was at first eager, then puzzled, then resigned. Then the advertisement appeared for a second time. Again I applied. This time I was noticed — and received a definite refusal. I have never known the reason for this and I certainly didn't understand it at the time. Perhaps my youth counted against me; perhaps it was reasoned that no Cook Islander had served in a senior administrative capacity before and this was no time to begin.

Shortly after my second rejection the Director of Health for New Zealand paid a visit to the hospital in which I was employed. It was his responsibility to fill the overseas position that I wanted so badly. In his talks with my own superintendent, Dr. Gilberd, he was apparently persuaded that I was eligible. It was Dr. Gilberd himself who called me to his office to tell me the news that I would soon be chosen as a medical officer to the Cook Islands. When I broke in to tell him that I had already applied twice and been turned down without explanation, he was surprised but reassuring. "There is every chance now; no other candidate has your qualifications," he said. "You're going to be reconsidered."

Within three days in came an application form and a letter beginning, "Dear Dr. Davis: You have been appointed Medical Officer to the . . ."

The salary and allowances were adequate to support us in a tropical territory, though they were not nearly as large as I could have expected had I gone into private practice. (It was rumored that the patients with whom I had come in contact during my hospital work had gotten up a petition to have me go into private practice with an assured income of several thousand pounds. Senior doctors who had taken an interest in me, particularly Mr. Douglass Robb, New Zealand's most famous surgeon, tried to dissuade me from going to this remote service where the opportunities would be so few and where, they warned me, I might expect to be faced with endless frustration. They seemed to be quite certain that once I

settled in the Pacific Islands that would be the end of me —
professionally at least. However, I knew that this was what I
really wanted to do, and I told them that they need have no
fear that I would allow myself to vegetate in matters of
medicine.

My medical kit consisted of a stethoscope, a percussion hammer, and a sphygmomanometer. I had been told that I would
find the other necessary instruments in the hospital equipment on the Islands. I had no clothes suitable for the tropics
— darn few possessions, but plenty of hopes. Lydia, of course,
took charge of the packing.

The 1600-mile shift from temperate New Zealand to tropical Rarotonga might have involved Tom and me in a major
packing operation, but our first years of marriage had resulted
in the acquisition of remarkably few possessions. True, a number of impressive chattels had passed through our hands, but
few had ever stayed there. Tom's precious motorcycle, Hurry
Up, I had sold for ten pounds to a shady character who tapped
on the back door after admiring the old girl as she sat parked
in the street. I did this without Tom's knowledge and expected to be murdered for it; however, Hurry Up having
served her purpose, he didn't seem to mind. The old Austin
we had exchanged for an equally ancient though more sporty-
looking Morris, but in order to pay the freight to ship this
to Rarotonga I was forced to sell my pinto. The arrival of an
irate landlady waving that most embarrassing of objects, an
unpaid bill, wrote *finis* to the ownership of virtually everything salable we possessed. My fur coat I sold to the highest
bidder and with the proceeds bought sufficient tropical clothes
for us to make a passable arrival in our new home.

At the end of all this plotting and planning, into the holds of the government steamer went four modest packing cases. I found that a much-repeated catty remark made in the Pacific Islands is "Poof, she arrived with two cases and left with twenty." Pardon me, but I arrived with four and left with fifty-seven, and I'm proud of it.

I felt no regret at parting with my belongings so ignominiously, I was much too excited by our new prospects. Only when I was reduced to selling the piano did I feel a twinge of guilt. I knew only too well what my Mother's reaction would be when she heard that I had sold her wedding present to me; she would have been glad to give me money had she known I needed it so badly. Fortunately she did not know.

I said my good-bys to Mother and Father by long-distance telephone. Mother wished me happiness in my new home; Dad, on the other hand, who had years before toured the Pacific Islands, was not overly optimistic.

"Remember that Tom's people are not like us. You will be living among strangers who will be in no hurry to accept you, if indeed they ever do. If you can't get along with them, I know you will find some way to forget about them. If you ever want us, we're not too far away, and we'll always get to you somehow."

CHAPTER IV

Return to Rarotonga

THE three of us were on deck together as we approached Rarotonga in the early morning light. Tom had given me his binoculars and through them I could see a skyline unlike anything I had known at home: mountain peaks like towers plunged down sheer to purple valleys and cave-pocked rock faces. It seemed incredible that such a tiny speck of land should have had a birth so stormy. And here was my first glimpse of a lagoon. Pinkish-brown coral jutted from the royal blue fathoms of the true ocean, guarding the shallow turquoise waters rippling onto the yellow beaches. Beyond the beach rose a sheer wall of green, a harsh shade of emerald that I was to grow to recognize as the color badge of our home. Opposite the only rift in the encircling reef, the red roofs of the government offices peeped through the trees.

Almost before the steamer had anchored, tiny outrigger canoes came streaking alongside, the energetic paddlers talking in a strange tongue, their light skins and fine features, slender build and wavy black hair proclaimed them descendants of a race far from primitive. But they were noisy! They shouted, waved, laughed at the top of their voices and emitted streams of guttural dialect: truly Rarotongan language is the

German of the Pacific. They swarmed aboard, all so excited
to see Tom come home they forgot that I was a stranger and
that I might be a little shy of the back slapping, the hand
shaking and the curious appraisal of their eyes.

"*Kiaora' ana!* May you live!"

Following the canoes came the shipping company launch
towing a string of huge black lighters laden with laborers
ready to handle the cargo, for it was not possible for our large
ship to moor alongside the wharf in the shallow water inside
the reef. Disregarding the heavy swell, the stevedores shouting, giggling as if they would die of mirth, ignored the lad-
ders, hitched odd pieces of rope to the railing and monkeyed
over the side like a gang of pirates.

Some wore shirtwaists that obviously belonged to their
wives. All wore trousers, not the colorful red and white *pareu*
I had seen photographed in geographic magazines, but long
trousers with one leg rolled up and one rolled down; those
favoring shorts had been doing some fancy work with the
scissors. On their heads were either wreaths of flowers, which
Tom told me were called *ei,* or else a peculiar hat of woven
straw, the brim about half an inch wide and the crown soar-
ing up to a good six inches. These hats had bands of shells or
fresh flowers and every man without a hat had a gardenia
tucked behind his ear, quaint preparation for a day's work.
Most of the men were tattooed with hearts, ships, and "I LOVE
MARY." Full-rigged ships sailed on many a breast.

We and our belongings were loaded aboard the launch;
we waved farewell to the ship and headed for the wharf, the
crowds of natives waiting to greet us straining their necks
for a better view. I felt scared.

Here they were. Tom's mother, just as I had imagined her,
holding herself with a poise and dignity that set her apart.

She was a tall woman and she wore the mixture of native and
European dress that all the Rarotongan women favored — a
garment of Mother Hubbard style and atop her head a deli-
cately woven bamboo hat. Her face was square-jawed with
heavy-lidded eyes and firm-set lips. She seemed to be smiling
for this occasion, but the reserve I had expected was only too
clearly an integral part of her character, impossible to conceal.
In her whole appearance — her lustrous black hair, dark olive
skin and singularly unpright carriage — she was all Polynesian; if her father and her husband had been of another
race, it was clear that she ignored it.

She welcomed me in English, placed both arms around me,
kissed me on either cheek, then she hung around my neck a
deep red *ei* made of frangipani. I responded as best I could.
I was dismayed at the utter foreignness of this display. If Tom
had had time to explain which people were relations of his it
might have helped, but he was caught up in the welcome and
I had to adjust to this new life by myself. The garlands of
flowers now piled high on my neck felt strange, hot and over-
bearing. Did these people really mean all this?

That landing in Rarotonga seemed all flowers, hundreds of
people were wearing flowers instead of hats, flowers instead
of necklaces, and flowers instead of bracelets. I had so many
wreaths I had to crane my neck to see what was going on
around me. Tom's mother introduced me to dozens and
dozens of elderly folk who were "Your Auntie, Uncle Willy
from Titikaveka, Aunt Jane from Matavera," and "Tom's
sister Nane, his little nephew Henry, his daughter Mary."
Seeing my confusion, she took a minute to explain that these
were all people she had adopted into her home, so I breathed
again. I had always thought of Tom's mother as an only child
of an only child but already I was learning the island custom

of borrowing other people's children and ever after regarding them as one's own. Tom had warned me that there would be a lot of kissing and that, following the old custom, this would include hands and feet, so I accepted this calmly.

Not so John. The strangers kissed and kissed him, lifting him up and loading his small neck with piles of heavily

scented flowers. John has always hated to be handled and he struggled out of their grasp and ran to me crying. It was hardly my fault that my three-year-old son could not bear to be touched by elderly people, yet I felt I was being accused.

Before driving to Tom's home where his mother had prepared a welcoming feast for us, I wished to send a cable telling my parents that we had arrived safely. At the post office when I reached into my purse to pay for the message I came up with one miserable sixpenny bit, the sum total of my remaining cash. My mother-in-law, who paid the balance, decided then and there that I was not a "good manager."

Then came a short drive in the family Ford, a drive so lovely that I forgot my personal problems in wonder at the natural gaiety of this magic Island that was to be our home.

The roads were carpeted thick with flowers. The length of white coral was now quite buried under the fallen petals, scarlet and purple. On either side the huge gnarled trunks of the flame trees in full summer glory fanned to meeting high overhead, their blossoms competing in riotous color with parasite bougainvillaea that burst from their centers. Christmas lilies reared from between the boulders, I could hardly stop myself from jumping from the car to gather armfuls of these precious blooms that I had known only as hothouse treasures. And the hibiscus! I had never seen these lovely things before. As I oh-ed and ah-ed, Tom's mother only laughed.

"Those are weeds here. You'll feel differently when you find them in your own garden."

The garden of Tom's old home left me speechless. Grandpa Harries had brought to Rarotonga plants from all over the world and under loving green thumbs they still flourished. Thirty-four shades of hibiscus sprawled and tumbled beside tennis courts outlined with flame trees. In neat beds roses flowered as they had in England together with freak tropical blooms from South America, India, and the islands of Melanesia.

I was reluctant to leave this dreamworld but now John again caught my attention. On the veranda of the old house stood a tiny old lady chanting a traditional welcome to us strangers. She was dressed in flowing white robes and her

fluttering old hands and quavering voice gave an atmosphere
of eeriness to our entrance to the house where Tom had spent
his boyhood. Pulling away from me, little John walked
straight up to her and kissed her. This was the sole releasing
moment in that endless day of apprehension.

Then we sat down to the feast. Suckling pigs roasted whole;
tropical fish cooked in native ovens; lovely sticky poi made
from banana, breadfruit and paw-paw, gray-flaky taro cut in
circular slices, floury on the inside with hard brown crusts
at the edges; bowls of raw prawns soused in fresh lime juice
and coconut cream; golden piles of curried goat heaped round
with fluffy rice; tiny dishes of sea eggs; platters of sliced
breadfruit fried brown in rich coconut oil; baked ripe bananas
and boiled green ones; fritters made from the fat of sea slugs;
purple-stained plates of boiled sea snail; salads made from
custard apple, mangoes and those weirdly sweet tropical
fruits; and lastly, a signal of true Polynesian courtesy, roast
chickens, potatoes, and little green peas for the European
guests who might not care for native food.

What food! Food and more food, and all on the table at
one time, all beautifully served and decorated! I didn't know
what anything was but determined to try the lot if capacity
allowed, but first I had to learn how to eat with the fingers.
This isn't so easy. Although Tom showed me how much coconut sauce I should start off with, I was soon doing the wrong
thing again. It is polite as well as a good system to take only
one kind of dish at a time. I took a piece of everything, but
when I reached for a second helping, I realized the mistake.
I should have kept one hand clean, but now I was coconut
sauce and pork up to both elbows, needing assistance to keep
my plate full. My capacity for servings running into double
figures at least made a good impression with Tom's mother

who explained that in the Islands you are no good at all if you cannot keep up with the family at mealtimes. She obviously thought it a pity I was so thin, perhaps this might correct itself in time.

After the dinner I would have liked to go into a digestive stupor and brood, but not Tom. He had decided to waste no more time. He wanted to see the Island. What had been going through his mind he can tell you better than I.

For me this had been a day of very mixed emotions. I was up at daybreak, and as we approached Rarotonga and came within sight of Ikurangi, the highest peak of all, where I used to hunt flying fox and snare wild fowl, I felt surging through me the nostalgia of one who had been long away and was now coming home. As we approached the landing, the offshore breeze brought us the scent of frangipani and *tiare maori* beloved by every South Sea Islander.

Mother was the first to greet us, and she came towards me with both hands outstretched. I saw at once that she had not changed. She was a little thinner perhaps, but her hair was just as dark and her face as unlined as when I had last seen her twelve years before. She had the same proud bearing and her face had lost none of that determination so characteristic of her. Although her welcoming kiss was warm, I knew by her eyes that her opinion of me was still guarded.

Formally and graciously she turned to welcome Lydia to whom she spoke in English, and only after this ceremony did she reveal a grandmother's feeling as she stooped and picked up little John. She lifted him up to gaze straight in his eyes before she kissed him. John who was rather awed by her took it like a little man, and while for an instant we four were caught up in the intimacy of this reunion I was aware of the genuine emotion of those in the background, for to the Polynesian a welcome is as serious and as much a matter of tears as a farewell. Here were relatives of my mother with *eis* of frangipani and gardenia on their arms, waiting turn to bedeck us and welcome us to Rarotonga.

"It's Tom Taote come back to us," they shouted. *Taote* means "doctor," and from then on I was "Tom Taote" or "Doctor Tom." I was deeply touched by this welcome and yet made a little uneasy too, for I seemed to detect in the people, not our family circle, a feeling of restraint. Was it a mistrust of me because I had come back in a different status? Was it the long-time mistrust of civil servants? I couldn't tell.

But I began to pick up some clues to this after the feast when there were five short speeches in our honor: the first three were by chiefs, members of our clan, then the Doctor spoke, the medico whom I was relieving, and after him another European.

Listening carefully to both natives and Europeans I was able to get my first glimmerings of the curious attitude toward me I had noticed earlier in the day. Everyone was glad to see me return to Rarotonga; the words were genuine in which they expressed the hope that I would be able to help the people, but the speakers also made it clear that since I was still a young man I would be best advised to listen to their counsel before attempting any innovations on my own. With a minimum of tact the Doctor whom I was relieving intimated that my medical knowledge could hardly be sufficient for the post I was now to fill. These were "the Islands" and those who lived there had developed their own way of doing things. I sensed an underlying friction between the two races and that each side was wondering whether I would line up with them.

This ingenuous welcome, with the openly expressed doubts about my ability as a doctor, hurt my pride. I suspected that there was a touchy situation here which would require careful handling, and in my response to my mother and her guests I

restricted myself to a brief "thank you" and an appreciation of the welcome.

The day had faded into late afternoon when I excused myself. I was eager to take Lydia and John on the twenty-four-mile drive around the Island to show them the places of my childhood.

That drive was a depressing one. The reality was even worse than what I had heard. I found that the banana plantations had completely disappeared and there was little evidence of replanting of any kind; the European-type houses with their corrugated iron roofs, of which the owners were once so proud, were now covered over with coconut thatch, or were empty shells of limestone walls with native shacks, poorly

kept, snuggled in behind them; the villages were unkempt
and the general appearance was one of dejection. What had
happened? What had become of the *au vaine*, the group of
women who were the conscience of the community, and who
in the past had insisted on village and house cleanliness? What
were the *ariki* (the high chiefs) doing? It was obvious that
the European administration and the local leaders were out of
touch and equally obvious that the depression and the cutting
off of shipping during the war had destroyed the well-being
of Rarotonga. Now I began to understand the general resentment in the speeches at the feast and I felt sorry that I
had come so close to losing my temper. I resolved that for the
next six months I would do my work, keep my eyes open —
and say nothing.

When I presented myself to the Resident Commissioner
on the following morning, I wondered what kind of welcome
I should meet. I remembered the Commissioner from my
childhood when he had been a very popular junior official
and very kind to me. I expected something more than a formal welcome and was hopeful that he might give me a real
incentive for my medical work on the Island. Instead I saw
that he had aged; I felt a hint of patronage in the words he
said to me, and I must say I came away from his office dismayed.

Troubled that seniority and heavy responsibilities should
have so changed my old friend, I went on to the hospital to
keep my appointment with the retiring Doctor. He was to
show me both the general hospital and the sanatorium, and
this he did with a flourish.

First he presented me to the matron and then the three of
us toured the general hospital which was designed for thirty-
two beds. From the outside it looked like a jungle: a beautiful
jungle, it is true, but scarcely hygienic when one remembers

that mosquitoes are the carriers of one of our worst diseases, filariasis. Creepers, huge trees, tangled masses of flowering shrubs, and a crazy quilt of flowerbeds cropped up every-where. Our inspection of the handful of patients reduced me to silence. There were fifteen of them, almost all, according to the good Doctor, suffering from filariasis. As he led me from bed to bed, I could see — it was all too clear — that some of them were suffering from untreated pneumonia, from tuberculosis, or suppurating tuberculosis of the bone. Surely a T.B. hip would be hard to confuse with a filarial abscess!

While we were making the rounds, the Doctor said to me, "Tom, we are very lucky here. We have no cancer, no rheu-matic fever, no poliomyelitis, not even mumps!" His com-placency shook me. I could hardly believe that these diseases did not exist in the Islands; if they did exist, but were being diagnosed under the label of filariasis, I realized that little or nothing would be done for the cure of the patients. There is no specific treatment for filariasis.

The dispensary consisted of a murky and dirty room next to the doctor's office; its shelves were laden with dust-coated bottles of medicines and lotions which at a glance seemed obsolete.

In contrast to all this I was much cheered in my first im-pression of Matron Hawkes. It seemed to me that she was a hard-working conscientious woman trying to make up for the inefficiency of others. She chattered incessantly as she showed me through her hospital.

On that inspection I offered her no comment though my mind was exploding with plans for correction. The patients were obviously very sick people. Examination of their charts confirmed the fact that Matron took a dim view of the mod-ern drugs. I asked her whether sulfa compounds and peni-cillin therapy were ever tried.

"Oh, no native responds to these newfangled sulfa drugs, and as for penicillin, Doctor, you'll soon find out whether or not you can get a native to let you stick a needle into him. He'd rather die."

That didn't sound right. I couldn't remember natives being afraid of anything. Perhaps they had changed.

In the wards I stumbled over whole families of the patients' relatives. They had set up their homes in the hospital and were squatting beside each bed, patting and fondling their ailing ones and chattering incessantly during what should have been the rest period. I gently inquired if these retainers were essential in the hospitalization of patients.

"Dr. Davis, you can't expect eight young native girls to cope with all the work here. Our native nurses think of nothing but their boy friends, it's no use my trying to teach them anything. I'd rather do the job myself and these old folks are rather helpful, you know. They bring along food and cook it up in the kitchen. I wouldn't be without my patients' families for the world. If it wasn't for them we would never have a patient in the hospital. It's the Island way of doing things you'll soon get used to."

I swatted away a few of the flies that were swarming round food crumbs left by a fond auntie and flicked an ancient cigarette butt over the edge of the veranda. A look outside revealed that I wasn't the only one using the garden as a rubbish dump; orange skins, banana peels, and old papers already covered the ground, and I suspected that the garden was also doing duty as a sputum mug for anyone who passed by.

"It's no use your peering at that mess, Dr. Davis. I spend all day picking up after everyone. There's rubbish tins everywhere, but you'll never persuade them to use them. Now come and look at my flowerbeds."

"If you don't mind, Matron, I'd like to see the theater," I interjected.

"Oh, you don't want to see that. We never do any surgery here, the tropics, you know. Everything goes septic no matter what you do, and then with all this filaria about it's not safe to do an operation because of the complications you're likely to meet."

By the time Matron had paused for breath I had found the operating theater myself. Calcimine-flaking walls and rough concrete floors told their own tale of poor asepsis. There was no sterilizer, no special lighting and less than a minimum of rust-damaged instruments and broken sterilizing drums. I was going to be busy here.

"Have we any X-ray facilities?" I asked.

"Now you won't have to bother about that. We always get one of the schoolteachers to do all our X-rays, as many as ten a week. He hasn't been doing them for a long time now though, I believe there's a short circuit somewhere in the machine. It's been giving our man a lot of shocks, so we stopped using it."

Experimentally I pulled the switch and came to lying on my back on the other side of the room. As kindly Matron dusted me off, she muttered firm things about young doctors meddling with machines. But as I picked myself up, I could understand why they had no diagnosis. Yet without proper X-ray, how could you make a diagnosis or even attempt to cope with the scourge of the Pacific, T.B.?

"Can you take me to the laboratory?" I asked the Matron.

"Laboratory? There is no laboratory. We don't need that here. I do any of the urinary tests that are necessary. Now, what more do you want?"

So I thought to myself: no cancer, no rheumatic fever, no

poliomyelitis, not even mumps. With this observation, my tour of the hospital came to an end.

Our next stop was to be the sanatorium, a distance of four miles from the main hospital. As he drove me over, the Doctor, who must have been aware of some of my unexpressed criticism, began to speak with irritation of the witch doctors, as if by so doing he could transfer my unexpressed blame to them, and on the Islanders for going to them.

"Tom," he said, "you haven't any idea how many of these people, including even some of the Europeans, take their families to the witch doctors. Oh, sure, they know there is a law against such practice, but they go right on breaking it. We do our best to break it up; if we catch one of the witch doctors, we fine him or lock him up. But try as we may, there is precious little we can do." This is one of the stubbornest problems the Medical Department has to deal with.

We both lapsed into silence as we approached the new sanatorium which had been completed only this year in an area known as Black Rock, five miles from the main village of Avarua. The deep pools cradled in these rocks which gave the district its name had been a favorite swimming hole in my boyhood, but like every other Islander I avoided the towering brush-covered heights which were now the site of the sanatorium. To all of us native children this place was haunted. Legend had it that from the tallest rock dead souls took their departure from the Island; the Koutu, the plateau on the crest, had in times past been the coronation ground for the Tinomana kings, and sacred to their spirits.

When the news reached me in New Zealand that the sanatorium was going up on this spot I assumed that the natives had overcome their old superstitions, but now I saw differently. There stood the hospital, a thirty-six bed establishment, a sound up-to-date building, of wood and cement; we entered and I was introduced to the staff of nine nurses, the cooks, orderlies, and groundsmen. But there was not a single patient: not a bed was occupied.

Both the Doctor and the sister-in-charge were reticent to explain the state of affairs, and I did not press the point. I had been taught that the Polynesian had a low resistance to T.B. This was fact, and add to it their natural reluctance to approach Black Rock and what you had was a pretty grim prospect. I knew that we could not wave away the curse of this place until we had arrested the disease here, yet I suspected that we must have a rather high incidence of fatal cases to deal with. It looked like a white elephant. By European standards I could hardly blame officialdom for selecting such a site, perched up on the hill above the western point of the Island. The view from the patient's bedside is superb. At the foot of the hill the orange and copra plantations march neatly to the edge of the white road, taro swamps making great splashes of shadowed green beside the thatch-roofed houses. On the sea side of the road are the wild hibiscus and the cypresslike ironwood trees, lining the coral beach at the edge of the lagoon, while beyond the dark line of the reef the Pacific stretches endlessly sparkling. Here, high above the heat of sea level, the air is always cool and fresh, an ideal environment — if it had not been haunted.

Equipment for the new hospital was encouragingly good. Architecturally the hospital was modern and well designed for the tropics. I hesitated to say that it would be much too small to cope with the Islanders who would require treatment. With nothing but empty beds before me now, I preferred to keep my apprehensions quiet. I went home to help Lydia unpack.

The Hospital and the Home

THE outgoing Doctor and I arranged the change-over in record time. The same steamer that brought us to Rarotonga carried him away.

On my first day in charge I went over to the hospital at 8 A.M. to have a quick look at the patients. In the tropics everything starts early and by this time the hospital should have been clean. But it wasn't: I found cigarette butts on the floor, unmade beds, unwashed enamel, dirty dishes, and general havoc. I said nothing; it seemed fairer to charge off this state of affairs to the excitement over the Doctor's departure. When at last I caught up to Matron, I asked her to accompany me while I examined a patient whom I had noticed on my previous inspection of the wards.

"Poor old Mrs. Teariki. It's no use you worrying over her, Doctor Davis, she's been sick for weeks and getting worse every day. She won't last the night, poor old soul, so there's nothing we can do now. Come along, it's time for outpatients."

I had different ideas about Mrs. Teariki, and with the mental reservation that we would get to her soon I obediently followed the Matron to my office which was next to the clinic. There I was surprised to see a sizable crowd already waiting for me.

This was cheering. I began to think that the stories I had

heard of people refusing hospital treatment might after all be an exaggeration. When I had seated myself at my desk, I had another surprise. Matron installed herself firmly by my side, in her hand a small pink booklet, which I took to be outpatients' records of some kind. Here at last was efficiency.

"Ready to begin, Doctor?" said Matron rustling starchily.

"Let 'em come," I replied.

"Come in, whoever got here first. Doctor's a busy man, no dawdling there."

Perhaps after all my reputation as a doctor had preceded me.

"Good morning, what can I do for you?" I asked.

In reply I got the one word, "*pamati.*"

Matron was writing busily in her little pink book. She tore out a page and placed it before me.

"Sign here, Doctor," she said, pushing a pen into my hand.

I didn't know what *pamati* meant, so to cover my ignorance of this mysterious symptom, I picked up the slip of paper and here is what I read:

I hereby certify that Uti requires 1 bottle of whiskey for G. H. P.

Signed _____

Medical Officer

Turning to Matron I asked, "What's all this about?"

Her reply was lengthy, and full of detail, the upshot being that my duties during outpatient clinic time were to consist mainly of dishing out liquor permits. Now I understood the meaning of *pamati*, it must be the Rarotongan version of *permit*. The Rarotongan elders, no doubt influenced by missionaries, have declared the Cook Islands a "dry area"; a man can get an honest drink only with a medical prescription from the Medical Officer. "G.H.P." was the well- and often-used term

for "General Health Purposes." This arrangement meant that
I, as the Medical Officer, became the sole and autocratic con-
troller of liquor for the whole of the Cook Islands!

Matron informed me that the European residents received
regular monthly liquor allowances on the presentation of a
card at the liquor bond store which was under the direction
of the Customs officer. Should the Europeans exhaust their allowance before the end of the month, they then applied for
"specials." Every man in the medical profession knows that al-
coholic liquor has no medicinal qualities. However, Doctor's
pamati and *specials* seemed to be the only means by which
liquor could be procured in the territory.

I was astounded at the crowds packed outside the office door
and window and I must have shown my amazement.

"Oh, Doctor, this is nothing. Wait until Saturday. We really get a crowd before the week ends."

While this was going on, the Assistant Medical Practitioners, my native assistants, had been sitting on the veranda outside the office, chatting with the customers and apparently
keeping them well amused.

One hour later, the pink booklet was very much thinner,
and I had finished my first outpatients' clinic, with one solitary bona fide patient. He wanted cough medicine, he needed
it according to his own diagnosis—and he did.

"Now, Matron," I said, "I'd like you to set up a blood transfusion for Mrs. Teariki. Let me know when you're ready."

"Blood? Blood, you say? Really, Doctor Davis, what next?
You can't give blood transfusions to natives. Where will you
get the blood from? There's no blood bank in the Islands. Natives think they'll fall down dead if you take blood off. Even
if you can find a donor, how do you think you're going to get
a needle into Mrs. Teariki? Please remember, you're in the Is-

lands now. It's a pity, but Mrs. Teariki will have to die. Her illness is so complicated by filariasis that blood won't do her any good."

"Matron, let me have a word. If the natives think they'll drop dead from loss of a pint of blood, we've got to teach them that they won't — and islands or no islands, we're not

going to let Mrs. Teariki die because of her ignorance of medicine. You go ahead and set up; I'll find the blood."

Matron was flustered. "Doctor, we haven't the apparatus. There's never been a blood transfusion in this hospital."

"Well, in that case, we'll make one."

Matron suddenly got a glint in her eye and immediately became noisily and spectacularly enthusiastic. Even though she did not hold out much hope of finding a blood donor, her proficiency at "making-do" contrivances was unquestionable.

"Just you tell me what you need, and I'll dig it up from somewhere."

In a few minutes she proudly laid before me everything we needed; a rubber suction bulb from the back of a dispensary drawer — not quite perished, and still serviceable; a clean bottle and cork from Matron's private bathroom; a miraculous length of glass tubing, some questionable rubber tubing, and an assortment of hypodermic needles in various stages of sharpness. Fortunately we had found some powdered sodium citrate in the dispensary. We were ready to go.

"Now, Matron, you've got blood and I've got blood."

Matron sighed. "In that case it'll have to be me, you'll have to give the transfusion."

"No, we won't do it that way. This is too good an opportunity to teach the people that it won't harm them to give their blood. I don't mind sticking a needle into myself, but this time we'll let someone else be the donor."

With the makeshift apparatus, I could see I would be busy keeping things going.

Luck was with me, for I noticed an elderly native, a friend of my family's, preparing to leave the hospital after visiting a patient. One of the nurses had given him a garbled account of what I was up to; he was curious to know more. I asked him where I might find someone willing to give their blood, and carefully explained to him that I would need several volunteers as the blood had to be matched with that of the patient. He was so interested that he assured me that if I would wait another half-hour he would bring me as many blood donors as I needed.

He was as good as his word, for he went straight down to the local cinema, stopped the performance, and demanded volunteers in a dramatic plea from the center of the stage. In a matter of minutes almost the entire audience shifted from the picture theater to the hospital veranda, the overflow milling over Matron's precious flowerbeds and jostling for a position in the front of the queue. For once Matron forgot to scream at the vandals in her garden, she even forgot to bring order to the queue.

I cross-matched several volunteers before I found a suitable one. None of them seemed to mind having their thumbs punctured, and the man whose type was suitable was loud in his praises of the painlessness of the operation.

I estimated nearly two hundred volunteers on my veranda that night. The dramatic arrival of this crowd somewhat dispelled the anxiety of Mrs. Teariki's family, nevertheless there were still black looks directed at me. The transfusion was a success, and the sight of Mrs. Teariki next day, sitting at her open window and drinking cups of tea for all to see, dissipated all future aversion to blood transfusions or transfusions of any kind, even though this was "the Islands"!

Before retiring that night, I filed requisitions for regular blood transfusion apparatus, and liver compound for patients suffering from pernicious anemia.

⚬~✕~⚬

As the wife of a seafaring doctor I am used to living with a minimum of furniture. Included in the contract for employment of medical officers in the Cook Islands was the clause that we would "be provided with free quarters, free heavy furniture, floor coverings and constant maintenance of these by the local Public Works Department."

Tom and I had hardly stepped ashore at Rarotonga when we were informed that our house was not yet ready for occupancy and that, until it was, we would have to put up at the one and only hotel, commonly and insultingly referred to as the *whare*, the Maori word for a native shack. I made it plain that we wished to move as quickly as possible, and we did.

The outside of our bungalow was impressive, in fact the architectural genius who designed the house seemed to have been convinced that the average temperature would be around 110° in the shade instead of a moderate 72°. One roof would have been sufficient, two at a pinch in case we had a heat wave, but our house had four ceilings, each bigger and better than the last. This amounted to rather a large area to be covered with paint, and for many years there had never been that much paint to spare. The result was a dappled effect bordering on the antique and embellished by numberless patches of raw corrugated iron that had been hammered on to shut out the incoming weather.

The island dweller who possesses a room that lets in the daylight and breeze while excluding the heat of the sun is fortunate indeed, for in Rarotonga all the Government houses are completely surrounded by ten- or fifteen-foot wide verandas, whose sloping hoods, thoughtfully provided against those rare occasions when the rain might blow in, completely obstruct the view, the sun, and most of the fresh air. And so we lived on the veranda, treating the inside rooms as parlors or corridors. Although the lower walls were of good solid draft-resisting limestone, the whimsical designer constructed all the upper walls of fine wooden trellising. The house admitted drafts, dead leaves, rain, spiders, centipedes, and odd callers of the rodent and crustacean families, all into eternal gloom.

We lived in that house for nearly seven years, and we never knew which was the front door. The walled-off section of veranda that was obviously intended as a lounge had as its only access a route which passed the sanitary installations while a large and solid post (its use still remains a mystery) reared itself in the center of the floor. So the lounge became the bedroom and we continued to dodge the post, meeting it only when the electric power failed or our host had mistaken the gin for water when mixing a rum punch. The doors on the front of the house led into bedrooms, those on the side into Tom's study; at the back, into the kitchen; therefore callers could take their choice, certain of marching into an intimate Davis family scene whichever they opened.

The dining room extended along the rear of the house for a distance of some forty feet. We felt that this was rather large for eating quarters but were thankful for such scope when it became evident that the table must be moved every time it rained. As is common to all homes in the Pacific, the bathroom and adjacent offices opened directly off the dining room but we soon took this for granted and, lest we be considered too "different," did not bother to conceal the door with curtains. The best feature of the house was that the cooking premises were semidetached and what my eye did not see my heart was too lazy to grieve over. The retainers might leave the pots unscrubbed, forget to use their handkerchiefs and smash dishes to their heart's content, the cockroaches might reign supreme and the canned goods disappear over the back fence. I would never know.

In the matter of furniture and floor coverings, our contract seemed to have exaggerated. We did have a complete dining room suite of good quality thanks to the fact that it had been bought by the previous occupant of the house when he could no longer stand taking his meals from Government-provided boxwood. The few remaining pieces of furniture looked as if they had been brought over to Rarotonga by the first missionaries. Floor coverings consisted of one mat, the

center of which had fallen victim to rats or cockroaches —
anyway, something had eaten it.

I sat in the middle of this large bare house wondering what
to do next. I didn't wonder long. Hadn't Tom's predecessor,
the retiring medical officer, left just that day, and wasn't his
house empty now? It must hold furniture, but first I had best
try the honest way.

I drove down to the Resident Commissioner's office, introduced myself and politely requested that I might be supplied
with adequate furniture.

"We do not notice any requests for equipment from the
wives of Government officials. If Dr. Davis cares to make a
list of his requirements by filling in the correct form of requisition (in triplicate) this will be forwarded to New Zealand,
after my approval of course, and in due time the articles requested will be purchased and delivered by the Government
steamer." The Commissioner paused for breath. "Good morning, Mrs. Davis, it's been nice meeting you."

Closing his office door with a brisk bang, I drove straight
back to the retiring Doctor's house, picked the frail locks and
removed everything not actually cemented down. I didn't feel
guilty about it, because I knew quite well that we were now
at the beginning of the hurricane season and could expect no
more ships from New Zealand for three or four months. I
could not continue to live in the hotel for that period and
rather suspected that officialdom, arguing that Tom was a
Cook Islander, had quietly decided to ignore the housing
clauses of his contract and quietly edge him into living with
his family. Other Islanders in the service of the local administration were living under these conditions, I determined that
we would not. As it turned out, when the old Doctor's house
was eventually occupied, the new tenant applied my meth-

ods to the house on the other side, thus continuing a vicious circle convenient to all until the day when every house is occupied.

I should have known that I couldn't do anything on this small Island without everyone knowing of it five minutes later and it was not long before I received my first visitor. It was Matron Hawkes, accompanied by two native girls.

"Well, Mrs. Davis," she said, her eyes darting over the, to her, familiar furniture. "I see you've made a good start. Got yourself plenty of furniture from next door, that's the way, can't expect the Government to run after you. I'm so glad you're going to get settled quickly. Dr. Davis has just told me that you've had some nursing experience in New Zealand, isn't that lucky? We'll find plenty to keep you busy here, doctors' wives in the Islands have no time for tea parties, or any of this social nonsense." This suited me, I couldn't imagine anything worse than an island tea party.

"There's the Child Welfare organization for you to help with. Babies, you know. The old Doctor's wife always captained a Girl Guide Group, you'll do the same." Heavens, Rarotongan Guides! I'd try. "And then, of course, we have a nurses' club, teach them to sew and embroider, keeps them away from the boys. Do you sew, Mrs. Davis? I must say you don't look as if you do."

I can't help the way I look. I went up in Matron's estimation when I told her that I could sew, embroider, knit, and even crochet.

"Well, you sound ideal, even though you seem too young. You've no idea the trouble I have here. New Zealand sends me one trained nurse after another. They look at the palm trees, and sigh for the romance of the South Seas, then when they find the competition from the native girls too much, they take the first steamer home. I can always do with a district nurse, you'll be ideal. As soon as you are settled, and that won't be long by the look of things, I'll take you round to introduce you to the mothers, they'll be so pleased that the Doctor's wife is going to help them."

I doubted whether the mothers would be delighted, but I kept on saying, "Yes, I'll be glad to help." At least helping the Matron might serve to keep my mind off my in-laws.

Throughout all this chatter, the two native girls had been standing in the background listening hard. Now Matron remembered.

"Oh, yes, I nearly forgot. These two girls came to me just this morning, they wanted to be nurses, but I thought you might like them as housegirls, particularly," she added significantly, "as they're not related to your husband's family."

Now with this qualification, I heartily agreed. Tom's mother had already recommended several girls to me, but inquiry revealed they were all close relations and would be certain to keep my mother-in-law informed of all that went on in my house.

"This is Tere," said Matron, pushing her forward, "and this is Poko. They've never worked for a European before, so see what you can do with them. I've sent for some men to unpack your boxes, and the girls will push the furniture into the right places. While they're doing that, just you come over and have a nice cup of tea with me."

Matron might be a fast talker, but she was already proving herself a doer and an ally.

Tere and Poko are still good friends of mine. Tere volunteered to be the cook. She was just eighteen years old, short and thickset and rather ugly. She had the broadest and flattest feet I've ever seen. I couldn't help noticing them for she was so shy of a white woman that whenever I spoke to her she would rub one foot against the other, standing on one leg like a stork and tearing her handkerchief to shreds. If there was a post or an object handy, she would crouch behind this and conduct the conversation with her head poking round the edge.

She had never done any cooking, apart from using a native oven in her village home, but when closer inspection of the kitchen revealed that our stove would never get up enough heat even to fry an egg this was no drawback to her capabilities as a cook. She happily retired to a corner of the garden and reverted to the primitive.

She took a long-handled shovel and dug a large shallow pit which she lined with basaltic rocks. Tere did not know they were basaltic, but she did know that it is not the coral rocks from the beaches that will hold in heat but the black stones from the creeks high up in the hills. Beside the pit she piled a reserve of stones, some old mats and some flattened sheets of iron; she was careful that the site of her outdoor kitchen was near a grove of banana palms. She explained the system as she went along.

"Make the hole in the ground. Nice and clean, *manea tikai*, no dirt on our food. Put in stones, hot them with fire from coconut husks, just like the charcoal we use in the laundry irons. Wrap the *kai* in banana leaves, that keeps it away from smoke. Put these *purau* leaves on top, then some more hot stones. Nice and sunny today so I put the mat on top. If it rains we put this old roof over it. Throw some dirt on and, finished! We come back in an hour or two."

That is all there is to cooking in a native oven. There is no washing up of pots and pans, no stoking of fires or anxious peering in the oven door. Pop the food in and forget about it is the way it is done in the Islands and I soon found that there is no dish that cannot be cooked to perfection in this way, even sponge cakes and pies were taken out done to a turn.

Poko, on the other hand, admitted that she was the world's worst cook and would take charge of the laundry. She was older than Tere and showed Negro blood in her dark skin and molded features. Her attraction to the opposite sex had resulted in two children but no husband. She explained that this was no fault of hers as she was the daughter of the village chieftain and her boy friends had never met with her family's approval. She would have to remain single until she could find a man of high social standing with extensive lands. In the meantime, Mother looked after the children and no one worried about Poko's lack of a wedding ring. This is a common situation in the Islands. Parental control is strong, especially in the selection of a suitable husband, and grandchildren are always welcome in any family. When they grow up, they help in the plantations; the question of whether or not they were born in wedlock does not alter their capacity for work. The girls marry their choice (or, more often, choices) in the eyes of God and, until they find a mate who comes up to the family requirements and enough chickens for a suitable feast, someone else looks after the children.

So, in her hesitant English, Poko explained it all to me and told me not to look shocked, and "Could I please have another bar of soap?"

That request is one to be heard daily in Rarotonga. Statistics show that Rarotongans have the highest per capita consumption of soap in the world. They are always washing something. If it is not their clothes, their houses or their possessions, it is themselves. Everyone has a minimum of two soapy daily showers and the average bath rate for infants is around six dunkings between sunrise and sunset; the very fussy mothers probably sneak in a couple of extra ones during the night. This custom is not as beneficial as at first one might think. Constant lathering removes all the natural oils from the skin, and unless coconut oil is used to replace this children break out in unpleasant skin complaints. European

children are almost always covered with sores; their white skins show every spot to the offended eye of the nursemaids, so they are scrubbed all the more.

Poko lathered up bar after bar of soap and beat hell out of Tom's best shirts with a log she had selected from the woodpile. She squatted on a mat and did the ironing down on the floor. If she noticed one speck of grime on our clothes, she would order us to change, then whisk everything out to the tub and have it washed, dried, ironed, and ready next morning. I remember Poko with a great deal of sentiment, she was a treasure I never replaced, for she eventually left for New Zealand, there to become head laundress in the Wellington hospital. No less than twenty-seven washerwomen came and went in my employ. Most of them ran home in horror when they found pieces of people's insides splattered on Tom's clothes (it was too hot for him to wear an apron in the operating theater) ; the others couldn't face the mountain of laundry that our small family would accumulate each week.

At the end of that first day in our home, I seemed to have made excellent progress. My small collection of possessions had been unpacked, each one admired by the girls and the packers, its value and history carefully detailed for their information, and each tenderly placed by Tere in the place where, I thought, it would look its worst. The two girls seemed to possess the strength of horses, they tossed the heavy furniture around as if it were matchwood, scrubbed everything scrubbable, and still seemed as fresh as daisies. Next, they hung all our clothes in the wardrobe, they examined my few dresses minutely, for quality, cut, and fabric. (Later I noticed exact copies blossoming all over the island.) It had been a good day, but then I had a visit from my mother-in-law.

"Where did you get those two girls?" was her first remark.

"Matron found them for me. They've been doing a grand job. Look how well we've got along, we can sleep here tonight. I'd never have managed on my own." I said all this rather fast in the hopes that I could stem off any more questions.

I needn't have worried, my mother-in-law was already out in the kitchen, treating the two girls to a flood of Rarotongan, of which of course I couldn't understand a word.

Tere was hiding behind a cupboard again, but whatever it was my mother-in-law was saying was obviously not dismaying Poko. Her lips set, she answered what seemed to be an endless questionnaire in brisk monosyllables. Towards the end of the tirade, Tere made the mistake of wiping her nose with the back of her hand. Even I could understand the shower of shame this brought down on her.

"Never mind the girls, Mother, come and look at all the fine furniture I found." I eased my mother-in-law away from the kitchen premises, trying to reassure poor Tere, now in tears, with a sympathetic look.

Tom's mother nodded in approval — that is, until she came to the small room that I had set aside as a study for Tom.

"Now that looks familiar," she murmured, eying the large deal table we had installed as a workbench. "I lent one like that to the old Doctor's wife nearly three years ago and never got it back. Now I remember, I scrawled my name on the bottom of it. Hold my bag while I have a look underneath."

I stood helplessly by while this elderly lady got down on her hands and knees to peer under the heavy table.

"Just as I thought," she announced, dusting herself off. "Look for yourself, my name under it. I'll just get the truck and take it up to the house."

"But I got it for Tom. It's for him to work on. There isn't another anywhere. Surely you won't take it away now?"

It was no use, my mother-in-law was already out the door, not without having the last word.

"I'll send you down another cook in the morning. Get rid of that Tere."

Well! Poor little Tere, so frightened, and probably so tired after her first day's work! Tere would stay. When Tom came home that evening I met him on the veranda, prepared to deliver some ultimatums about mothers-in-law interfering with matters that should not concern them. But when I saw Tom's face, worried and exhausted, I changed my mind. I might have problems in my small domain, but I could tell that the day had not been easy for him.

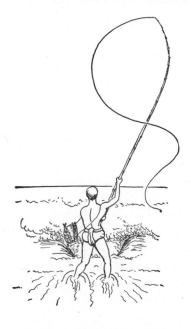

CHAPTER VI

The Island Way

EVEN Tom observed that I had made a good beginning indoors, so I turned my attention to the garden. Mosquitoes covered the Island in clouds, their bites resulting, to newcomers like ourselves, in painful septic ulcers. I remember that first year when I had no less than twenty-six septic bites on my legs. Everyone knew vaguely that these pests bred close to the houses, but no one made any effort to find or destroy the breeding places. The particular brand of mosquito that carries the disease of filariasis, so prevalent in all the Islands, likes to live and enlarge its family in small discarded con-

tainers easily concealed by profusely flowering tropical creepers and low bushes. Our garden was a mass of creepers beneath which lay old meat tins, jars, coconut shells and a
veritable mountain of empty bottles left behind by the last
occupant. To protect the more exotic plants an endless maze
of hedges had been planted. Here the insects sat down for a
little rest before attacking their next victim. As a mosquito
paradise, our garden was no worse than anyone else's, but I
had to agree with Tom that we should set the example in the
matter of practical mosquito control.

Tom threw himself into the improvement of the grounds.
He cannot distinguish a hydrangea from a pansy; I should
have known something would happen. But I was not prepared
when Tere rushed in with her eyes nearly out of her head and
those flat feet of hers rubbing one another off her legs.

"Come quickly, all the bad men are here. The men from the
jail are all over the garden. They've got big knives and chop
down everything. Come, come, I'm frightened!"

Prisoner and criminal are words synonymous in my mind,
and the specimens now swarming all over the garden didn't
look like angels. The lovely pink bougainvillaea that had
climbed and twisted over the pergola lay prostrate across the
path. Half the pergola was already chopped into pieces and
a band of wild-looking characters armed with machetes were
working on the other half.

I rushed up to the biggest and fiercest. "Stop, stop!" I
yelled. "What do you think you're doing? Go away! Go home,
go back to prison if you like but leave my garden alone!"

The huge man stared at me as if I'd been some unpleasant
kind of insect. "Dr. Tom says cut. We cut."

"I don't care what Dr. Tom says, you leave those hedges
where they are and — get your great flat feet off my lilies!"

"Don't speak English," he replied. "Dr. Tom tell us cut, we cut. Don't understand *you*."

Now along came an elderly native of great personal neatness and charm. He had been resting in the shade of the flame trees, but seeing my distress he rose to my aid. This must be the guard. Perhaps I could get some sense out of him, and what a wonderful command of English he had!

"Now, now, Mrs. Tom. There's no need to be alarmed. Dr. Tom spoke to us this morning about those troublesome mosquitoes. He explained to us how they have their babies in those old tins under the trees close to the house. I know the trees are old and very beautiful, but we must do what Dr. Tom tells us. The boys don't mean any harm."

Here was a good source of information.

"If these boys are such fine fellows, why are they in prison?" I asked.

"Well you see, it's the beer. They like to make a little brew now and again, so much cheaper than bond liquor, and our native fruits make wonderful beer I can tell you. The missionaries and the police think it's bad for them, but the boys enjoy themselves. And of course a lot of the lads are in prison because of the girls."

"But how on earth could girls put them in jail?"

"They make love to them. That's against the law here, but then young people have their own thoughts on these matters and they can't help being caught. They find it more fun than going to Scout parades or Bible class. And, jail isn't such a bad place. The lads can visit their families in the daytime; as long as they come back at night to sleep, the police don't mind. The food is good too, plenty of beef and taro and they don't have to pay for it. It helps to get the roads mended when we have the prison full."

"Very interesting," I said. "Will you excuse me, I think Tere wants something."

Tere had been hissing round a corner for some minutes. Now she had caught my attention and showed signs of tears.

"Do you know who that man is?" she asked.

"I suppose he's the jailer. Isn't he?"

"He's no jailer, he's a schoolteacher doing seven years' hard labor for marrying with his pupils. You make him get out of our house. My father a deacon at the mission. If he knew the kind of friends my Mummy's making he tell me to go straight home!"

At the end of a week, the gang had finished clearing the garden. At first the lawns looked very bare but the relief from further mosquito bites more than compensated for the lack of flowering shrubs. With the garden under control, I turned my attention towards having the house painted and repaired . . . and found why white women in the tropics are wrinkled.

The greatest source of annoyance and frustration to any dweller in the tropics whose husband is in the employ of the British Government, be it in the Pacific Islands or any other outpost of our Empire, is the Public Works Department. Tourists consider it an occupational disease that we rant and rave over the shortcomings of this local body. I say, "Rave on, ladies. It won't do you any good, but it certainly makes you feel better."

Although the architects who designed our houses may have been slightly off the beam, on the whole they left behind them sturdy monuments. But as the years went by the occupants never seemed to get around to attending to the minor repairs. The reason for this is usually termed "tropicalitis," more correctly diagnosed "worms." So if Junior swings once too often on the front door and the hinges, already pure rust, can no longer stand the strain, we happily use another door until that too drops off. The remedy for all this, as per the original contract, is or should be the Public Works Department.

They should be called the Public Works Sports Association for they have converted toil into a game. They make the rules as they go along and, as they keep them strictly secret from the attacking side, the householder, they cannot lose. So they sit in the shade beating time with a monkey wrench while they harmonize their club song. It goes like this, "Next week, Mum, we'll do it next week."

After a year or two of close but unsuccessful plugging, Mum bows to the winning side and lets the house descend round her ears.

I had previously become acquainted with Rule One. I lost that round in the Commissioner's office when I asked for the furniture we had been promised.

Here is the root of the trouble. All requests to P.W.D. must come from the husbands, or more correctly the officers. But the officer, so he says, is too busy with matters of state and hasn't a moment to spare for trifles like leaky roofs, dripping taps, burst drains and broken furniture; he can't run the house and the hospital too; he'll ring P.W.D. next week; he can't see any urgency in all this fuss, and anyway "I'm busy."

In my case, I reminded Tom of the great skill in household repairs he had so ably demonstrated in our less palmy days when we couldn't afford to pay anyone to work for us.

"Household repairs are a task for minions" was his lofty reply as he disappeared in the direction of the hospital, his haven of refuge.

When, after a lot of nagging and persuasion, a carpenter

did cross my threshold, I had the impression that "now everything will be fixed." Mistake. The game was still going on.

The carpenter drank several cups of tea, emptied the cake tin, lit our last cigarette, clucked his tongue when the roof leaked down the back of his neck (he was sitting in the strategic spot), then toured the house with a ruler and notebook. His inspection finished, he climbed onto his truck, backed into the lily bed, skidded over the newly rolled tennis court and disappeared back to the Public Works yard, where I have no doubt that he spent an amusing afternoon telling his teammates of his easy victory.

Now the game was in full swing. Mum has written a letter to the Commissioner and induced an officer to sign it. The Commissioner informs the officer that he should apply to the proper department, in triplicate, and that being Senior Officer he has only to ask to have anything his heart desires. This brings us back to the starting point and Round Two begins. Over a period of years there were rare occasions when the visiting carpenter stayed a few days. Then I would find myself the proud possessor of perhaps half a cupboard, an unhinged door, a shelf or two. Always before the work was finished, when the house was sprinkled with bent nails, pieces of odd timber and a pool of sawdust, our friend disappeared, taking with him all of his tools and some of mine too. I was then told that someone else had been asking for a cupboard for the past two years, it was their turn now. Any complaints should be addressed to the department concerned (in triplicate).

As a result of this apparently universal British system of house maintenance for Government officers, it is unwise to lean on anything and sometimes fatal to subside suddenly onto any piece of furniture. The Islander adjusts himself to prevailing conditions and, although his gingerly movements about his own house may seem eccentric to a visitor, after a year or two of dodging the unsteady and uncertain, insecurity becomes a part of life, and tire tape and string household necessities. I later adopted the system of paying an independent carpenter to do most of the work, but with what glee did I remove the cupboards and shelves on the day when I finally left our house. How bare and deserted the rooms looked when I had sold the furniture I had bought myself. It may have taken me seven years, but that day I think I scored in my long game with the P.W.D.

But in our first weeks in Rarotonga I could not expect to know all the rules. Now, in the beginning, I was foolishly dispensing hot tea and biscuits and giving the opposition a hand with the work. I thought I was setting an example; I know now I was just making a fool of myself.

After the round of welcoming feasts had subsided, we dropped back to the staple diet of Europeans in Rarotonga: bully beef, tinned peas and *kumera*. I had supposed that fish would be plentiful in this part of the world, instead it was a rare luxury. The natives had overdone the use of poison roots to kill their fish and now the lagoons were depleted, the native fishermen catching barely sufficient for their own families. Small quantities of fresh meat were imported from New Zealand and stored in a Government-owned freezing plant. The electrical installations for this were worn and outdated; six years of war had allowed no improvements to be made anywhere on the Island, consequently the freezer frequently broke down with accompanying waste, so that each steamer brought only enough supplies to last three or four days. After that we went back to can again.

The only native food that was plentiful to Europeans was fruit. Oranges, lemons, bananas, custard apples, and mangoes grew wild, but our source of protein continued to come out of a can. The summer weather was hot and depressing, rain threatened but never fell, hanging low over the mountains and making the air on the beach levels stifling. Now that we had cleared the garden, a cool breeze reached our veranda, but the rest of the Island was stifling. My legs with their running sores were giving me endless trouble, there were as yet no drugs in supply that could heal them quickly, and John too was beginning to scratch.

Tom was working night and day to cope with the increasing demand for medical attention. Patients came to the house, disturbing our nights with requests which were often ridiculous in their simplicity, but we were touched by their trust in Tom. Now that the house was comfortable and the girls, Tere and Poko, both proved to be good servants, there was no reason why I should not help Matron in the district nursing. It was useless for me to consider joining the permanent hospital staff; since I had banged his office door so briskly, the Resident Commissioner had made it obvious that he did not like me. He didn't seem to like Tom much either and showed open disapproval of my taking over the secretarial duties at the hospital. Someone had to do it though, and there seemed to be a ton of paper work to get through. I was not finding life in the South Sea Islands as idyllic as I had been led to believe.

We had come to Rarotonga right in the middle of the rainy season. Tom had often spoken of "ten-minute tropical downpours," but it seemed to me the ten minutes proved to stretch into two or three weeks, pause in a suffocating blanket of humidity, then start again. However, in the years to come I was to find that, apart from the December to March months (and even then the temperature never climbed above 92), the climate was as nearly perfect as we could wish for. From April to September the days were cool and sunny for weeks on end, the only rain that disturbed us came for an hour or two in the evenings, cleared the air, and kept our surroundings cool and green; for the remaining months the trade winds blew onto the Island, peculiarly steady, as if a giant electric fan had been switched on far out to sea, bringing no gusts, no storms.

I have always hated cold weather, and while other New Zealanders on Rarotonga longed for a brisk, frosty day, my only regret was that at no time that we lived on the Island could I look out the window and see the gold and haze of an autumn morning. Wherever I turned there was always the harsh green that I now know is the color badge of all the tropics. That green was broken only by the glare of the flowers, for it seems that the world here likes only red and yellow blooms. The restfulness of blue or lavender is a rarity and pastel shades too shy to compete.

Hurricane season had begun, officially that is, although during those first weeks the weather behaved normally enough. The sun blazed or merely simmered behind moist clouds, we sweltered and peered at the horizon hoping for a breeze and a breath of fresh air. The season is always declared open on the first of December, closed on the first of April. Should the weather misbehave at any date outside those laid down by the authorities, the Islanders call it a typhoon, cyclone, or an act of God, but never, never, a "hurricane."

During the storm season steamer communication with the Island ceases. In theory the stores lay in sufficient stock of the necessities of life to tide the residents over until shipping resumes its normal routine. But we soon discovered that in practice during "the season" everyone laboriously saved cigarette butts, unrolled them, baked the damp and smelly contents in the oven, then rolled the residue up again into "race horses," saving the butts of these to start all over again. Dry groceries become a seething mass of weevils and other foreign livestock but this did not make us gasp; we merely spread things out in the sun and watched the insects walk off. The providental few laid in a store of British staples (unvarying from Iceland to Central Africa — the Englishman can't get along without his tea, his flour, and his sugar, perhaps a raisin or two); these saving ones holed up in privacy and ate buns made from mold, determined never to admit that their stocks had gone bad on them.

The improvident, like ourselves, lived on native food; breadfruit fried in slices and spread with avocado pear took the place of buttered toast, and bananas and *kumera* took the place of everything else. The diet was tiresome but filling. I seemed to be getting used to what dear old Matron called "Island ways" very quickly. I rarely saw Tom who worked late in his office, our home conversation was reduced to "hullo" and "good-by." But from the enthusiastic remarks of the two housegirls who picked up the local gossip, I gathered that Tom was beginning to install a new order. He never had time to tell me of his plans then.

Lydia seemed to have settled her domestic affairs very quickly; but at the hospital my problems were far from solved. True, thanks to the spectacular recovery of Mrs. Teariki, I was not short of patients; but the medical staff, although busier than they had ever been before, were still disorganized and discouraged. The "blame it on the tropics" attitude is a stubborn thing to break down.

Here is how matters stood after three weeks of experimenting and consideration.

The Islanders would not accept injections despite the fact that curative and preventive medicine relies to a great extent on this treatment. Although driven underground by legislation, the witch doctors maintained a strong hold on the people. Surgery had a bad name. Infant mortality was high, very possibly much higher than the official figures showed because the death certificates in themselves were farcical. Only the European doctor could sign the certificate, whether or not he was familiar with the complaint of the deceased. Outer islands, where the assistant medical practitioners were in charge, were apparently not considered of sufficient importance to deserve the issue of death certificates or any other means of notifying the central medical department at Rarotonga of how the people fared. Major surgery and supervised midwifery were reserved for those who could afford to travel to New Zealand for hospitalization. The sanatorium obviously offered no practical answer to the tuberculosis problem. Filariasis affected a large proportion of the population; there was no attempt at mosquito control, and the hospital itself offered the worst possible example of sanitation. Equipment and facilities in the hospital were inadequate. Personnel was inadequate in number and there was no proper training of nurses, probably on the assumption that the girls would not respond. Most important of all, the Commissioner controlled the executive powers of the medical department and was known to be resistant to any change.

I spent one of my first afternoons examining the confidential records of the hospital personnel.

These records were extensive on the subject of the assistant medical practitioners. But surely the local staff could not be

so bad as these reports painted them! I had met only two
A.M.P.'s so far, the others were distributed throughout the
outer islands of the Cook group. These two were Tekao Tin-
erau and Tere Williams, both of whom had been educated at
New Zealand secondary schools, as I had been, and each of
whom had distinguished himself at the medical school in Fiji.
They were the sons of highly respected Rarotongan families.
Despite this background, the records reported that Tekao had
been periodically suspended from the Medical Department on
the grounds of misdemeanors including drunkenness. This
did not fit with my impression of the man.

Tekao was actually my cousin. He was then forty years
old and the senior of the A.M.P.'s. He looked like a chief.

When he met you, he bowed from the waist, clicked his heels
together and shook hands. He seemed taller than he really
was, so straight did he carry himself; he was handsome, always courteous with a gentility I have found in no other people. Eventually all my staff, Europeans as well as Islanders,

came to admire him. He was the Prince Charming of our circle. But that was not so at my arrival.

Since the average salary of the practitioners was around one hundred and fifty pounds a year, they were obliged to supplement their earnings by farming their own lands in their spare time; this made for insecurity but what made it worse was that they were not trusted. They were given no real responsibility or incentive. And thus a man like Tekao, after endless discouragement, became unsure of himself and lacking in confidence. I suspect that his case was typical of the others.

It all seemed a pretty dismal picture and the first thing I did was to "clean up" the hospital, instituting a regime which assured that by 8 A.M. the wards would be tidied. The patients applauded this innovation, showing their co-operation by bringing along their own ashtrays and for once using the correct receptacles rather than the garden for their garbage disposal. Cleaning up the garden, I knew, was going to be a slower job. How Matron loved her jungle; but insidiously at first, then more boldly, we pruned, thinned, then hacked until, retaining Matron's pet bushes, we had eliminated most of the mosquito breeders. Beyond that, Matron would not go, and I continued to drink my morning tea with a fern tickling the back of my neck.

After gentle though persistent questioning, I had found the reason for the natives' refusal of injections. It seemed that in the past the only injections given had been of morphine to moribund patients. I could hardly blame the families of the deceased for attributing the deaths of their loved ones to the insertion of that needle. I hoped that by administering all injections myself we might eventually overcome their reluctance, but I was finding it a nuisance having to turn out at three hourly intervals during the night to give a simple injection. I kept hoping that in time they would allow others to perform the operation. At least we had made a start here and no one had died as the result of or following an injection. As for infant mortality, we could not hope to lower this rate until we had a clearer definition of the cause of the present high figure.

The unpopularity of surgery and the inevitable sepsis that had in the past followed most operations were not in themselves serious problems. It did not take me long to trace the cause of the failure of surgery, for quite soon after my arrival I had my first surgical case. The patient was suffering from a strangulated hernia, and doubtless sought relief at the hospital not because he or his family thought that there was much hope but because he was in such great pain that he had no alternative. Although the operation was fairly straightforward, I found that three days later the wound was in a strongly septic condition. Unlike Matron, I did not blame the tropics. Instead, together we went back over the operation, step by step, until I found to my utter amazement that the swabs we had been using, the lint and the dressing sheets, were "Rarotongan sterile": that is, the swabs were new ones, they had not been dropped on the floor but had come straight out of the pack and then been carefully rolled in the nurses' fingers! So I took Matron and the nurses through a thorough course in the differentiation between "cleanliness" and "surgical cleanliness," and hoped for better things in the next operation.

Again I was lucky, for this time a European was admitted with an emergency appendectomy. Before starting the operation I announced loudly and clearly that this man would be out of the hospital in seven days' time — that is, if the theater staff obeyed the rules I had recently taught them. And in true

Rarotongan fashion it was only a few hours before most of the Islanders heard of my prediction. During the operation I checked the asepsis thoroughly; sure enough, my patient was on his feet in four days, back at work in the prophesied time, his wound clean and himself a practical object lesson in what good asepsis can do.

I did not expect to equip the theater with any involved apparatus. If the Rarotonga hospital was to be used as a training ground for the A.M.P.'s going to the outer islands, I intended to keep the gear as simple as possible so that these men would be able to familiarize themselves with its use, and use it by themselves in the more isolated islands.

My first major session with our Commissioner was a lengthy one in which I discussed maintenance of hospital, increase of staff and additional drug supply. I was fully aware that our administrator was in need of health education just as much as the people if he were ever to consent to my requisitions.

The efficiency of any medical department can be gauged by figures; death certificates will tell their own story if nothing else does. But the registered death figures that the Commissioner quoted me as an indication of the successful operation of my department in the past were, I knew, unreliable, and I took the opportunity of stressing the shortcomings of the existing system. "The medical department has been adequate, spending money on it now and hiring more useless natives to help won't improve things" did not seem a very reasonable answer to my requests. My requisition for drugs was not well received, but after a detailed explanation of the miraculous properties of penicillin and sulfa drugs and my introduction of the pointed remark that the Commissioner's own life might be lost if we did not procure these immediately, there went, to my delight, a radiogram to New Zealand ordering these stores to be flown in immediately. Then he came back to the unreliability of our system of death registration: it plainly worried him. He had spent his life at figures, and he liked them correct. He agreed to allow me the services of the Registrar of the Court, Lionel Trenn, in working out a more efficient system.

Lionel proved ingenious. He devised a certificate, applicable in all islands of the group, based on the international standard. Unless the certificate was correctly signed and in the hands of the proper departments, a man could not be buried. Now at last I would have an accurate indication of the death rate and its causes.

At least I had my drugs and a brand-new type of death certificate. Progress indeed, under the circumstances. That interview ended on a peculiar note. I think the Commissioner intended to be fatherly, I hope he did, for he told me that I was overworking. He had gained the impression (correctly) that I was overly concerned about the health of the Islanders. He advised me that, as I would always be fully protected against any charges of negligence, all this worry was unnecessary, and that it would please him to see me more on the tennis court or at the various social gatherings that were taking place on the Island. He patted me on the shoulders kindly as he led me to the door: "Take it easy now, Tom, and we'll all get along fine."

As it seemed that I was to have no additional assistance, I worked out a roster of duty for the A.M.P.'s, telling them that what they did in their off-duty hours was entirely their own business. I gave them each "*pamati*" with a warning not to quaff my "medicine" in duty hours. Tere Williams was to take care of medical patients, Tekao of the surgical, and I promised them that I would take every opportunity to demonstrate modern methods to them so that they could assume more and more responsibility in their individual fields. They seemed to take a new lease of life, spending most of their off-duty hours sitting in my office brushing up from my textbooks. I took every opportunity to invite them and their wives over to my house, and I think they appreciated being treated as doctors rather than as hospital chore men as they had been in the past.

Already our department had the use of radio to and from the outer islands to enable the A.M.P.'s to ask the medical officer's advice on patients whose condition was causing them concern. I wanted more than this. I wanted regular monthly epidemiological reports, and to this end concocted a code. With the ready co-operation of the radio superintendent this code was immediately put into use, giving me all the information wanted in Rarotonga, in New Zealand, or by the Director of Pacific Medical Services in Fiji.

My intentions regarding witch doctors involved a long-term plan. I felt that if, by our increased efficiency in the department, we could prove to the people that we could do a better and quicker curative job than their own doctors, then they would choose to come straight to us; perhaps it might be even possible to use the witch doctors by encouraging them to report patients to us.

All improvements depended on the co-operation of the Resident Commissioner, and I felt I wasn't going to get too much there. However, there was a court of last appeal.

It is customary for the head of each administrative department to turn in a monthly report on his activities. This report goes to the Commissioner, in quadruplicate of course; one copy is signed and kept in his files, one goes to the Pacific Medical Service in Fiji, one stays in the hospital files and the last one goes off to the Department of Island Territories in New Zealand. (I made five copies, one extra for myself.) Perusal of past monthly reports made dreary reading. They consisted of a short list of patients, both out and in (seemingly these were the same each month), followed by a list of the tea parties and other small gaieties in which the Medical Department had played a part. I resolved that my reports, at least for these first months, would be more detailed than this. I taught the A.M.P.'s how to make full case histories and insisted that these be kept on each patient who came to the hospital. I radioed the A.M.P.'s in the outer islands and instructed them to do the same. Slowly and laboriously I described the entire Medical Department, each of its staff members and each of its patients. I followed this with a lengthy, in fact very lengthy, account of its shortcomings, and finished my tome with a minute description of our requirements and my suggestions as to improvement. I sent this in to the Commissioner at the end of that first month, then waited.

The explosion was not long in coming.

"This is the Commissioner," said an angry voice through the telephone. "Will you please come to my office immediately? Immediately, do you hear?"

I was there in two minutes.

The administrator flung down the heavy sheaf of Lydia's laborious typing.

"And what, may I ask, is the meaning of this? Are you writing a book already?"

"My monthly report, sir," I replied, my fingers crossed but still looking him straight in the eye.

"Report, you call it! You have the temerity to stand there and call this — this — criticism of your own department, a report? Take it way and write another."

"I'm sorry, sir, but that is my report for the month of December. I have no intention of changing it or of retracting my statements. In fact the increased numbers in our patient turnover, which you will find at the back of the report, already show that this improvement was necessary."

"Who cares what they show?" shouted the Commissioner, banging his fist on the desk. "Do you flatter yourself that anyone's going to take the time to read all this screed? Even if I do sign it, which I won't, it will go straight into a pigeonhole and stay there. No one in our government, or in Fiji either, has the time to go through all this drivel."

"I think they will, sir; in fact, I am sure they will. I have tried to make it clear in the report that I have no ambition to turn the Rarotonga hospital into Guy's or the Lahey Clinic; the improvements are only those which in my opinion are consistent with the size of this territory. Whether you sign this report or not is up to you. My department is bound to submit a report of the month's work. That is it and there will be no other."

"All right, all right, Tom. You think you know everything. I'll sign it all right, but you may as well pack your belongings now, you'll be on the next steamer out of here. You'll see. Good morning."

CHAPTER VII

Hurricane

ON those few occasions when Tom blew off steam, it seemed to me that our troubles were man-made. Then Nature took a hand.

At 2 A.M. one morning a runner burst into our bedroom, shook us awake, and with a torch shining in our faces thrust into our hands an emergency notice. The meteorological station announced that a hurricane would be upon us in five hours' time . . . get ready!

Tom had experienced hurricanes as a child, but was rather vague as to just what should be done now to afford protection from a storm which might well bring with it a tidal wave that could wash right through the house. In any case, the hospital and patients there were his first consideration. He disappeared across the lawn, fast becoming a lake in teeming rain, shouting something about "putting shutters up."

Tere and Poko were not much help. They strolled outside, examined the sky and sea, and announced that there would be no hurricane. Poko cited her authority: "Center of banana palms not curled down, no more wind."

I have more regard for modern science than what the center of the banana palm might signify and after a good deal of yelling I persuaded the girls to tie things down.

My total experience of hurricanes had been derived from the Nordhoff and Hall film where I watched Jon Hall tie

Dorothy Lamour to a coconut tree and then wait for the world to descend round his ears. Hollywood always saw to it that it did. But this storm wasn't according to script. The hurricane was nowhere near our Island yet, but the rain was coming down in sheets and a wind which didn't seem more than thirty miles an hour was whipping the coconut palms

this way and that, sending down a shower of heavy nuts. Coconut trees were good things to keep away from. When one palm at the edge of the beach took off from its roots and whipped right onto the lawn in front of me, I felt it a good thing Miss Lamour was not tied onto that one.

All the veranda round our house was provided with heavy storm shutters, most impressive until one came to use them and found that twelve months' disuse had rusted away the hinges and, instead of clipping neatly into place, the heavy boards crashed loose to the floor. Doors and windows were the same. Islanders never shut their houses so one does not notice the condition of things until an emergency arises. However, assistance was on the way: a gang of natives appeared bearing hammers, nails and bags of hinges. Soon nails were being banged into odd sheets of old iron, hinges thrown onto shutters and padlocks onto doors. Loose pieces of iron roofing were covered with the heavy green leaves of the coconut palms and it was no time at all before our friends trotted off to the next house, assuring us that all would be well and that they would come again during the storm. They seemed no more worried than our two girls.

At the prophesied time — 7 A.M. — the wind strengthened towards the promised hurricane force. A tinkle of light bulbs on the veranda reminded me of the one precaution we had forgotten but Poko and Tere still sat calmly, doing a little sewing and chanting at intervals, "No more wind." Down at the edge of the garden we could see the lagoon. The sky was almost obliterated by sheets of white foam tearing over the reef, pouring across the shallow lagoon and racing far up the sandy beach onto the liana that crawled over the grass beneath the ironwood trees. Had I known then that the next time I saw a hurricane sea I should not be sitting in a sheltered veranda but instead peering through the hatchway of a tiny sailing ship, I should probably have stood under the most insecure coconut tree I could find and prayed for Nature to do its worst.

Bang! Another palm crashed onto the lawn, this time taking off a piece of roof as it went.

Tere and Poko could stand it no longer. They threw down their sewing and sprang into action.

"Come on, Mummy. Let's get those nuts before the sea takes them away."

Remembering Hollywood crouching in the village church and praying for deliverance I gasped, "You know Dr. Tom said we were to stay inside the house."

"No-o-o-o-o more wind. Come on. We gather the nuts, then look for hermit crabs." Poko was already wrapping John in his raincoat while Tere was arming herself with plaited coconut baskets to collect the spoils. Suspecting that Tom might be doing the same thing, I bundled up in a waterproof and joined the expedition.

This was hardly a full-scale hurricane, maybe Poko was right after all, for the wind never passed above sixty miles an hour.

Now I had my first insight into the Polynesian character. Everywhere in the village palms had fallen, fruit had dropped from the trees and gardens were laid flat. *Kumera* patches on the edge of the beaches were washed out, taro swamps on the higher land flooded out of existence. Tidal waves, the major danger of this subhurricane wind, had washed over the roads leaving piles of sand and coral boulders. No wheeled vehicles could move, yet everywhere there was activity, cheerfulness and an unselfish show of good sense. Old and young alike were loaded down with baskets of fallen fruit and nuts. The green coconut leaves had been collected and were now weighing down the thatched roofs of native houses. Fallen trees and limbs were gathered and dragged away to dry out for firewood. Bananas, breadfruit and oranges were being picked up almost as fast as they hit the ground; paw-paw too was gathered in before wandering livestock could eat it. Although the storm was still raging, the younger and stronger men were already wrestling the boulders from off the roads; when an extra-large wave piled over the beach, they climbed on the fences and waited until it went away. Wind and rain had brought unusual cold but everyone was too busy to notice it. The women sat over the cooking fires making ready the ovens for communal meals. The children swarmed over the beaches collecting stranded fish and hermit crabs that had been washed out of their holes. They would eat well tonight.

On this occasion Rarotonga was receiving only the edge of the storm, the center having moved further north, but I had no doubt that even in the severest hurricane these people would have been no less provident.

A storm such as this would be followed by lean times for the Island people. A year's work in their gardens was now gone for nothing, but nowhere did I see a long face or hear a complaint of the hopelessness of life. Today they would salvage all they could, tomorrow they would start again. Behind them lay generations of disaster, of famine and want, yet they kept on laughing, and their laughter rang true. Without apparent calculation, even the tiniest toddler avoided a coconut palm still holding fruit, knowing that wave tearing over the land must also run back again; easily they judged the safe moment to chase down to the lagoon and collect the fish. Just a foot or two ahead of gigantic waves, the children scampered onto the fences, their arms laden with harlequin reef fish. Others borrowed canoes and paddled over what had been dry land. With hibiscus sticks threaded with sennit, they fished for hermit crabs. It looked at first glance like play, but I realized that their work was as serious as that of the grownups. Food would be short from now on.

I met Tom in the main street. He was gathering crabs with the children. At the hospital the only worry was for the patients who would keep hopping out of bed and running out into the rain to join in the work. Matron was coping and enjoying every minute of it. The fact that a tidal wave had washed right to the hospital wall and covered her garden, always her pride and joy, delighted her. Now she could get that yard tidied up for good and all. She sent me a note de-

manding my lawn mower urgently. Not until I saw the state
of her lawns did I appreciate the joke. It would take weeks to
clear the sand and coral. I realized how lucky we were. Our
house stood opposite a break in the reef created by a fresh-
water outlet, the backwash here was too strong for any wave
to threaten us. I kept my lawn mower but lent her the prison
gang instead.

To an onlooker, the activity and cheerfulness of the villagers
made the storm seem like a holiday. It showed me why the
people of the Pacific islands are branded as improvident, they
give no thought for tomorrow. Tomorrow may rob them of
their homes and their food. No one can guard against the fury
of nature, even this mild blow had caused untold damage to
the plantations. Staple foods were cut to a fraction in a matter of hours yet nowhere was there a sad face or a request
for assistance. When the wind dropped and the rains tapered
off to showers, the gardens were already on the way back to
neatness, the roads cleared. There had been no bulldozers or
tractors to help, only broad backs, willing hands and unselfish
hearts. No work was done without a prayer, a hymn and a
muttered request to a native deity. Every Islander worked for
the public, for his neighbors and relations, and only then for
himself. When the day was done the people collected down on
the beach while a native pastor offered up a prayer of thanks
for the help from heaven.

Paradise

THE hospital in Rarotonga was becoming almost too popular. Tom seemed to be doing more than the usual amount of shouting and slamming of doors that he should have shut quietly. However, he *was* getting his drugs; the storerooms were filling up with neat cartons, the dispensary shelves with newly labeled bottles and jars. His lengthy reports were agony for both of us. He would prowl up and down his office declaiming while I searched frantically for the right verb, stuck in the carbon paper wrong-side to, and then, when I thought the report was completed, was ordered to do the whole thing over again.

Young John settled down to the island life with almost alarming speed: within a month of our arrival in Rarotonga, he had completely discarded the use of knives and forks and the wearing of trousers. He concentrated hard on attaining the same skin tone as the small-scale Rarotongan "gang" into which he had been initiated. At games we noticed that too often he was allowed to be the undeserved winner, but in the lagoons he proved that he could hold his own without having to be favored. Even when he was once swept over the coral and to the ocean outside the reef, he remembered what Tom had told him, and trod water until rescue, in the form of a canoe, came to him.

With other Europeans on the Island we had no more than a

nodding acquaintance, nor did we realize that we were innocently violating the age-old rules of society as laid down by white men in the Pacific. I was paying the girls twice what everyone else thought they were worth, giving them too many days off, and actually driving them to their home villages in our own car. This annoyed my mother-in-law more than

anyone else, and my relations with her cooled to distant politeness. Tom was so busy he always seemed cross and distracted. Patients were being discharged from the hospital as early as possible in their convalescence so that their beds might be available for more serious cases, and it seemed essential that I take over the district nursing to keep an eye on the returnees.

Because I didn't have Tom's advantage of knowing the language, one of the hospital nurses came with me as interpreter. Ngapoko was one of the loveliest girls in Rarotonga, but despite her languid eyes she was all gaiety and gossip, telling me the family history of her neighbors, teasing Niiau (who drove our ambulance) because he was afraid of the ghosts of the patients who had died in the back of his vehicle, bringing me a fresh *ei* each morning and running over to the

house when the day's work was done to report progress of the
patients in whom she knew I was interested, then staying on
to teach me how to strum the guitar and sing the native songs.

Each morning we would load up bags and boxes with medicines, pills, and ointments. My nursing experience being
limited to the eighteen months' training in Dunedin, I confined myself to the well-known brands of drugs and did not
attempt any ambitious treatments. Each day I prayed that no
one along the route would decide to have a baby as we passed.
Ngapoko was unaware of my ignorance of midwifery.

To start the ambulance (the self-starter was broken) Ngapoko and I would get out and push, then race after it when
the engine caught and before Niiau disappeared round the
next bend. He didn't want to be left alone with the ghost car
and would poke his head out the window, yell, and pump the
useless brakes as hard as he could until we climbed aboard.
We asked the ghosts to shift over and off we'd go round the
twenty-four miles of road that would bring us back where
we started.

I never tired of that drive. Rarotonga holds a charm all its
own. On either side the bush was full of exotic blossoms as
well as great twisted limbs which sometimes had to be removed for further progress. Ngapoko and I did a lot of pushing and running. Nowhere was the road in good condition.
Heavy downpours and an occasional deluge from the sea
during hurricanes have washed away the surface while fallen
palm fronds and coconuts are a constant menace to anything
more streamlined than a Model T.

The houses are clustered in villages, the few isolated dwellings being merely temporary living places for the time when
there is work to be done on the plantations. For their native-
type houses, Rarotongans build of sticks from the wild hi-

biscus which grows in profusion along the beaches while they thatch with plaited fronds of the coconut palm. The result at a distance seems to be an attractive grass shack. But in reality the house is unhealthy and uneconomic. The thatching lasts for only two to three years, and stripping a bearing palm tree of its mature leaves obviously injures its productivity. In addition, the hibiscus sticks become infested with a worm which produces a continuous cloud of fine white dust. The house is cool to the point of chilliness during the winter; it is also dark and holds the damp so that when the family crowds in it becomes an incubator of ill-health.

Every home has its garden of flowers and vegetables, and these plots are well laid out and carefully tended. White coral paths lead to separate cooking houses and store sheds and even the family horse-cart has its own coconut home. Rarotongan bathrooms consist of a tap down by the road tastefully camouflaged by a breastwork of coconut mats or by sheets of rusty corrugated iron. The taps must be near the road in order to utilize the one-pipe Government water supply. Rarotongans seldom bother to turn off their taps, so each bathhouse has a clump of wet taro and a stately stand of canna lilies thriving in the overflow. As it would be unwise to leave precious mirrors so near the main road, bathroom furnishings include a carefully shined-up biscuit tin. This Father props against the breastwork, and with the lid open has a convenient and cheap shaving mirror. The evening bath has developed into something of a social occasion, affording opportunity for a chat with friends, a hail to passing vehicles or a business discussion of church donations.

Except for the main village at Avarua where are the Government offices and the main trading stores, the four large villages on the island, Matavera, Aorangi, Ngatangiia, and

Titikaveka, have been settled for a long time, and they show this in the beauty of their setting. The roads through the villages are lined with flamboyant trees which, in the summer months, stain the white road with brilliant petals. The trees are of a forgotten age and have been let grow as they will so that now their lichen-splashed limbs wreath outwards to support the pancake roofs of brown beanpods and feverish blossoms. Their gnarled roots spread for yards about the trunk forming comfortable armchairs for the evening loiterers. Here they rest their backs while they strum their guitars and sing of the deeds of their ancestors.

Whitewashed coral rocks mark each front path and between these are planted sprouts of the *ti* plant with its purple-stemmed scarlet leaves. All over the Pacific this plant is used as a wand by the witch doctors. Each garden has its own trees of frangipani, white, yellow, pink and red, and its sprawling jasmine bush, while in the place of honor is a carefully guarded *tiare maori*, the wild gardenia peculiar to Rarotonga and to Tahiti. Its white star blossoms will be picked in the evening and worn behind the ear of the feminine members of the household; the left ear if you are unattached but hopeful, the right if satisfied with your lover. The other scented flowers will go into *ei* for the head and neck, and the opened blossoms are tossed into large baskets where they decay and are squeezed to extract their perfume for the coconut oil. Only the tight buds are chosen for *ei*, each being carefully opened with a flick of a coconut rib, then threaded through the center of a strip of hibiscus bark.

Between the villages the road is edged with untrammeled bush, the plantations lying behind this natural shelter. Here and there among the orderly rows of orange, lemon or tomato plants, wilderness appears. These are the sacred places of ancient worship or sacrifice where the family or tribal gods are buried, or where the spirits come to dance at the time of the full moon. Even now, over a hundred years after the conversion of the people to Christian beliefs, no native will knowingly desecrate these grounds, for the curses of the old gods are still potent.

It seems typical of Rarotonga that wherever some effort is made at orderliness or design, there is a mischievously incongruous note. A neatly trimmed hibiscus hedge will break out in a riot of blossom. The grave of a favorite uncle looms up in a carefully tended front garden. Paths that have started out straight suddenly swerve to avoid the burial place of the family god. Front lawns of the more prosperous homes usually have a horse as a centerpiece, this is so much cheaper and less tiring than a lawn mower. That is Rarotonga.

For some years child welfare groups had been organized among the older women. Each village had elected one or two whose responsibility it was to check on the health of each native baby, weigh it once a week, and report to the district nurse when she made her rounds. These women also delivered the babies in the homes: down on the floor with the mother lying on a pandanus mat. Women midwives were something of an innovation, for traditionally in Polynesia that had always been the man's job. Fathers of first children stood by and watched the grandfathers demonstrate, and on the strength of this experience carried on from there. But now the grandmas were in charge.

So once a week the village mothers, grandmothers, and babies assembled at the meetinghouses awaiting my call. These meetinghouses were prosaically unattractive. Used mostly as centers for prayer meetings and Biblical discussion groups, the plain limestone buildings roofed with raw corrugated iron are monuments to the thoroughness of Christianization and the obliteration of native art. In the Maori districts in New Zealand such houses and the churches, too, are centers which preserve the traditional art forms; lavish carving, brightly stained lintels, and various representations of Maori gods make them the show places of surviving native culture. Yet here, in the heart of Polynesia, the only decoration was a bunch of paper roses stuck into a pickle bottle.

The ceilings and verandas of these meetinghouses were unlined and the summer sun beat on the iron unmercifully. All the babies wore *ei*, all the mothers and grandmothers wore *ei*, and of course Ngapoko and I wore them piled ten deep. The combination of babies, jasmine and gardenia was overpowering, and after I had added my seasoning of iodine, peppermint-flavored cough mixture and carbolic soap, weighing babies became a fragrant operation indeed.

The babies were beautiful. Their skins were pale gold, their hair more often auburn than black, their eyes always that deep, moist brown. They all cried at the top of their lungs. No wonder, for every mother took this opportunity to show her neighbors how well she clothed her child. Each baby was submerged in woolen bonnets, woolen mitts, and woolen bootees. Yards and yards of cream satin ribbon threatened to strangle the poor mites and they wept and roared as they struggled to free themselves from these entanglements in a temperature of 80 degrees!

Knowing that the clothing must weigh almost as much as the babies, we undressed them before popping them on the scales. Horrors! Almost every child was covered from head to foot with ugly sores.

"Do you bath your baby, Mum?" I asked, thinking, as all newcomers do, that skin afflictions are caused by dirt.

"Bath him all the time, Mrs. Tom. Six times every day, plenty of soap too, still sores. It doesn't matter."

When I suggested that the mothers cut down on the woolens and go easy on the soap for a day or two, they were shocked. When I asked them to put the babies down to crawl on the floor, they clutched them tighter to their bosoms and peered at me as if I had gone mad. No Rarotongan baby crawls on the floor. It sits on knees. Grandma's knee, Mum's knee, Auntie's, Dad's or the ever-ready knee of anyone else handy. Sit on the floor? Never! They told me that a favorite child is actually carried round long after it is able to walk. They had a name for these children, *tama ua*, lap child. Wasn't my own husband a lap child? Golly, was he?

The younger mothers started to look a little shifty-eyed, and I felt that as soon as Grandma's back was turned they might be willing to try the new system. The grandmas set their lips, and said, "We'll ask Dr. Tom first."

Yet apart from the heat rash, every child I saw on my first visit to the villages was in perfect condition. Surely there must be some sick babies in Rarotonga? The storms we had just endured had left behind an all-pervading damp, the hospital was filled with adults with chest complaints, the babies couldn't all be healthy. Where were the sick ones?

I made a list showing the name, age, and village of each baby I had seen, and from Lionel Trenn we secured the birth registry. We compared names, noting those I had not yet seen. Tom suggested that I devote the next week to going up into the valleys deep inland and finding what had become of these unseen infants.

The missing babies and the homes they lived in showed me a very different picture from that I had seen in the villages. Here in house after house I found sickness and despair, but a pride too fierce to allow the sufferers to ask for help, even from the hospital. Many of these families came from one of the fifteen outer islands of the Cook group. They had traveled south to Rarotonga to make their fortunes, now they lived on borrowed land with no rights to the produce of that land and with only an occasional job from the two hundred or so Europeans to provide money for their daily wants.

Some of these people were so poor they could not buy clothes fit to be worn to the meetinghouse. A miserable coconut basket nailed to the wall held a single precious outfit one person could wear to church; for the rest, rags would have to do. The floors of the houses were covered with fine coral gravel, on this the whole family slept with only a plaited pandanus mat to protect them from the damp. This is not the Polynesian way of living. Polynesians like beds with white sheets and thick piles of mattresses filled with local-grown kapok. If a man cannot afford to buy a European bed, he will build a raised platform, lace it with sennit, and make his own.

What use to tell the mothers that they must give milk to their children? They fed their babies with boiled water flavored with scraped sugar cane, even coconut water was a luxury. Bulging foreheads and wasted limbs told their own story, and I could see the parents were famished too.

I came closer to the truth about the unmarried mothers and their children. I found several girls who had been made so ashamed of their fall from virtue that they had taken their babies and hidden them in the bush, far from the scorn of the village deacons and overzealous missionaries. These children were in the worst condition of all. I remember one home where I found a one-and-a-half-pound premature baby lying naked on the bare coral floor. A very young mother lay on the far side of the room with her face to the wall. Unable to bear the jibes of an all-or-nothing religious teaching, she had run down to the edge of the lagoon and tried to throw herself over the reef. A passing fisherman had rescued her, and the baby had been born before she could reach her home again. We put the child on a pillow and rushed it into the hospital. (A year later this same child received first prize at the baby show and had the proudest mother on the Island.)

Where the sick children had healthy parents, we issued free milk to the village headwomen; where parents needed attention too, we collected ambulance loads and put them all into the hospital until they could get back on their own. We found work for the fathers in trading stores, for the mothers in private houses or at the hospital. When Matron ran out of cots, she top and tailed babies in the beds and at feeding times everyone gave a hand. We each had our favorite and it became a point of pride to see whose prodigy returned to normal in the quickest time.

Children and parents regained strength rapidly, none of them died, and soon even the grandmas began to agree that we might be talking sense with our newfangled system. As the bonnets and mittens disappeared, skins cleared to golden smoothness. The babies were still knee-sitters, but they didn't cry on weighing days. Now mothers who had earlier refused to allow me to dress wounds and sores lest I soil my hands did not hide their babies' ailments. They listened and watched carefully when we handed out ointments and bandages. We no longer had to tramp into the bush to find a sick child. Tom had sent out word that if anybody needed a doctor he had only to hang a white flag at the roadside and the doctor or A.M.P. would call on his daily round. White petticoats, pants, and old shirts were the signals we looked for under the trees, and those who were sick were soon receiving treatment.

They were quick to learn the names and uses of the new medicines!

"Not gentian violet, Mrs. Tom. Too messy. Better the mercurochrome and some iodide powder for Tangi's head. Glycerine ointment brings flies."

They took ointments away in empty meat tins and medicine in old pickle bottles. They sat on at the meetinghouses after we had left, arguing and discussing the merits of their different mixtures. The grandmas knew every sick baby in the village, they knew who was "expecting." When the qualified district nurse arrived from New Zealand, they were ready to listen to her advice and accept any change she might introduce. I could retire from the field and concentrate on growing some skin over the septic ulcers on my own legs.

Tom was pleased that we were making headway but he was increasingly disturbed by the poverty which was a contributing cause of so many of our maladies. He determined to make a closer inspection of the villages and see if he could get to the root of the trouble.

The conditions that I found in the villages indicated that something was very wrong in Rarotonga. I could remember no want existing in my boyhood, and my mother assured me that it had not existed. What then had brought about this decline? Perhaps a house-to-house survey could show me, so leaving the hospital to the care of the A.M.P.'s, I arranged a *tutaka*.

It had always been the custom to hold an annual inspection of the homes in each village, with a prize being awarded to the neatest house and grounds. I made it clear this time that I would make a personal inspection and that there would be

no prize, but that I wanted to see everything — houses, people, plantations, and any village developments that might be
in existence. Where there were no roads fit for the car, I expected to borrow a horse or go on foot.

In earlier years, most of the people lived in European-type
houses built of limestone. These were copied from the Government-owned homes, but their design had been modified

to suit native craftsmanship and more limited resources. The
buildings were oblong, cross ventilation being provided by
narrow doors and windows. The roofs were of iron, often unlined. Long-hanging eaves made the interiors dark, dank and
hot, and the walls held the moisture. Now most of these
houses were unoccupied. They stood roofless and falling to
pieces, sometimes housing only the relics of a truck or car.
These ruined buildings were not a sign of the laziness of their
owners; hurricanes had blown the roofs away and there had
not been the money to replace them. Beside these deserted
homes stood the traditional grass shacks, which, in Polynesia
at least, are not made of grass at all, but built and thatched
in the way Lydia has described.

The use of coconut leaves for thatching and the resulting damage to the palm had naturally resulted in reduction of copra production, of feed for the livestock, and of sprouting nuts with which to increase the coconut plantations. The palms that should have been thickly feathered with leaves and laden with green and yellow nuts now pointed skywards, witches' broomsticks of one or two yellowing leaves. The thatching projected low over the walls, shutting out sun and air; the coral floors were damp and relied only on the appetites of marauding ants for cleanliness. Too often one member of a family would be coughing blood, the younger folk living and sleeping beside those who long ago should have been in the sanatorium for treatment.

The gardens of these houses may have seemed attractive to the noncritical eye, but what I noted were low-hanging bushes of jasmine, planted close to the front door so that the young girls would not have far to walk to collect the flowers for the evening *ei* — so close that those who did the cooking had no problem to dispose of coconut shells and meat tins, and empty bottles. Lifting up the branches of these shrubs, what a collection of mosquito breeders I found! It was a perfect public demonstration, for the whole family would have to stand back as clouds of insects flew out of their hiding place. Before I left the compound, newly converted mosquito controllers would be chopping and pruning while their children dug holes to bury the accumulated rubbish of years.

The plantations too had changed radically. I remembered the ground covered with mangoes and oranges, acres of thickly planted banana palms, neat rows of sprouting coconuts. These were gone and now only a few gnarled old trees stood as survivors of the rotting stumps. Taro and *kumera*

patches still lay beside each house, but they held only enough
for family consumption. Polynesians are primarily agricul-
turists, their land is their wealth; now this land was weed
grown and barren.

Every village showed the same picture. Prosperity had vanished, yet I knew that the war had not touched these Islands.

At the completion of my *tutaka* I held a meeting with the
village elders, and then I had the explanation.

It was not war, hurricanes, or laziness that had caused the
deterioration. When I was a boy, each month brought a visit
from the mail steamer from San Francisco. These boats stayed
a couple of days, then sailed down to New Zealand laden with
island fruit. During the height of the fruit season, extra cargo
vessels came out from the mainland so that in all about 6000
tons of shipping came and went. Copra from the outer islands
of the group was brought to the main island by small trading
schooners and stored in the sheds in Rarotonga until steamer
space was available. In those days the plantations flourished,
landowners bought cars and trucks, built new houses, took
pride in their plantations, and fetched in native workers from
other islands in the group.

In 1935 the shipping company changed the steamer route,
heedless of the fact that the economy of Rarotonga would be
ruined without regular transportation for local produce. The
New Zealand Government tried to fill the gap with the purchase of a small vessel, the *Maui Pomare*, to run between
Rarotonga and Auckland, for it realized that the perishable
fruit was the natives' main source of income. But the *Maui*
proved to be an unlucky ship, continually laid up for repairs,
and continually delayed. Fruit would be picked and packed
only to be left rotting at the wharves. This happened so often
that in time few plantation owners bothered to continue their

cultivation. There had been no relief to this predicament during the war years or directly after.

The disappearance of the larger trees, such as the mango and chestnut, had been due to the mistake of an enthusiastic but misguided agricultural "expert" employed by the Government. This man had for many years worked in South Africa and was under the impression that the methods that had proved successful there would apply equally well to a South Sea island such as Rarotonga. He first asked, then ordered those on whose land these large trees grew, to chop them down immediately, even going to the lengths of ringing the offending giants with red paint and issuing notices that those landowners who did not comply with his orders would answer to the court. It was his theory that the great spreading roots of these trees robbed the land of its nourishment. The natives, on the other hand, knew that these roots shook and moved in the summer winds, loosening the soil as no plow could have done, and that the spreading shade gave shelter to low crops. Down came the trees and the low crops sizzled in the sun or were washed out in the rains.

This same man had also ordered the pruning of orange trees. Nature takes care of that in the Islands; if a tree needs pruning, the wind will very quickly pare down its branches with no assistance from man. Those trees clipped by hand died within a few weeks. Now the Government was spending large sums of money to assist the landowners in a replanting scheme. Huge nurseries were producing orange seedlings, bulldozers and specially trained men were being hired to help in the correct planting of the young trees while fertilizer was sold and sprays and equipment hired too. This vast program, carrying with it a guaranteed price for a guaranteed shipment in five years' time, was received by the growers with suspicion.

They felt they were being placed in debt deliberately, and they distrusted this well-intentioned program.

"Dr. Tom, they are bribing us. What use is the high price for our fruit if we have no fruit to sell? We must buy cases, pay for trucking, and try to pay back some of the debts we have incurred for replanting. When will the trees be our own again? Is it our fault that the ships no longer come? Is it our fault that now we have but a fraction of the oranges you remember? Can we believe that five years from now the trees will be bearing and the ships waiting to take our fruit away? We have heard those promises so often and been told that we were to blame for being lazy.

"They told us that the bananas from Samoa and Fiji are better than ours so we let our banana shoots die and kept only enough for our own families. Now they tell us that the Fijian banana is bad and the Samoans too busy making copra to export fruit. They say they need our bananas now. They allot us space on the *Maui Pomare*, then when the steamer comes, there is no space left. Why?

"We know that Rarotonga is not happy now. The Government means kindly towards us. They give us free education to fit us to live by your standards. But without the money, how can we? What use to teach our children the ways of the modern world? They end their school days discontented; they get so dissatisfied that they save up money and go to New Zealand. We don't blame them, but we are bitter that the brightest of our young people are gone. What will become of our race when only the weak are left?

"Your own department gives us free medicine. We do not want gifts. We, the chiefs, know that too many of our people are learning to accept something for nothing as their natural right. This is bad. Give us a voice in the control of our own land and its people. You, Dr. Tom, are one of us. Go and tell them, for the villagers are weary of misunderstanding. We do not speak your language well, but we have tried in the past to help our sons to your level. The boys go away and do not care to return. They feel that life here is too hopeless. You have chosen to return, be our voice."

"But you still have your lands," I said. "Can you not farm with the aid of your families without accepting Government assistance?"

"Yes, you have seen many acres unplanted," the old chief replied. "Before the missionaries and the white men came to our lands, the *ariki* and his council were the trustees for all the land. They did not own it themselves, but they saw to it that on the death of each occupant the sections were redistributed fairly. Our women never inherited land. The eldest son, if he was fit, was given the voice of decision in all matters pertaining to the use of that land. If he proved himself unworthy, then another son would be chosen to take his place. If the whole family proved improvident, the land might be taken away in its entirety. Our lands were our wealth in those days.

"Now, in the eyes of your Government the eldest son is always the authority. He it is who is consulted by the white men. His word — even if he is incompetent — is law. Today each son and each daughter takes a share in the lands, for nowadays women have an equal right with men in matters of inheritance. Because we often marry women from villages distant from our own, now each person has a right to ownership in stretches of land scattered all over the island. Let me tell you what happens.

"My son Tangi here planted tomatoes last year. He chose a sheltered piece of his land far inland at the foot of the mountains. He and his brother, Tuaivi, cleared that land by hand, they plowed it and planted it. There was no stream nearby, so morning and evening when the sun was lowest, they carried drums of water on their backs the full quarter of a mile to their plantation and watered each plant. For three full months my boys gave all their time to growing that fruit and in the evenings they planned how they would spend their money. The price for our tomatoes is good in New Zealand.

"Last year we were lucky, the ships arrived here just when the tomatoes were ready for picking: that does not happen very often. The boys had a boat waiting in the harbor, the tomatoes lay in cases at the edge of the road ready for the trucks to take them down to the wharf. And then . . .

"From the village of Aorangi, far at the other side of the island, came my two nephews, Nga and Tere, who demanded a half share in the profits. Their mother is my sister and according to the white man's law she is entitled to half my land. Her sons claimed that half the money from the sale of that fruit belonged to them. My boys asked the court to help them, but it was no use. They had been planting land that did not fully belong to them.

"This year none of my family will plant. Tangi is in the prison now. Rather than be robbed of his oranges he and the boys went up into the hills and made a tin of orange beer. They had one wonderful day and at the end of it went off to settle accounts in their own way. Nga is now in your hospital with a broken jaw and Tere is hiding in the mountains. We think that what Tangi did was just."

The old man's eyes twinkled as he finished his story. I admired his sense of humor when his situation seemed so hopeless.

He probably did not realize that he had described a very typical result of the superimposition of western culture onto that of a semiprimitive people. Disregard of differences in terrain and ignorance of the system of land tenure had produced this unhappy result. We know from Captain Cook's description of the Pacific Islands as he first saw them that they carried a population many times greater than they do in modern times. John Williams, the first missionary to visit the Cook Islands, pictures Rarotonga as an island wholly cultivated, terraced, and irrigated, yet today only one tenth of the arable land is under cultivation and everywhere is soil erosion and waste. The shelter trees which had been destroyed by the misguided Westerners had always been grown for two purposes: to produce food in time of famine and to provide protection from hurricanes. Their removal has increased the labor of planters and reduced food. But at the very root of the economic difficulties of the Islanders lay the misinterpretation of the ancient system of land tenure administered by the *ariki*.

The *ariki* was always the head of the clan, below him (all members of the same family) came the *rangatira*, below them, drawn from the common people by right of achievement, outstanding leadership, or ability in battle, came the *mataiaopo*. The *ariki* never held title to land any more than the White House belongs to the President. The *ariki* might be granted the use of a small area for his lifetime but as he habitually received a portion of the products of his clansmen, ownership as such was unimportant to him. The same rule applied to *rangatira* and *mataiaopo*. But foreign administrators, not appreciating the meaning of Polynesian trusteeship, granted outright ownership to the clan leaders, and, what was more, regarded these leaders as holding their position on an hereditary basis and not by virtue of ability.

At first these new conditions did not bother the Islanders, and the *taunga,* the priests of the ancient religion who might have objected, had lost their power. The fact that women could now own and inherit land probably pleased everyone at first, for now both sons and daughters would be assured of a right of ownership. Polynesians are perhaps too ready to accept innovation.

Shortly after the arrival of the first white men, an epidemic of some unidentified disease (probably dysentery) decimated the population to an appalling degree. Native historians tell today of burning the dead in lime pits when there were not enough healthy people to perform the traditional rites for the dead. The fact that land was now being divided into small and isolated pieces, each owned by separate individuals, did not begin to pinch until the population increased towards its former numbers; then the people awoke to the fact that they had accepted a new order of life disastrous to their living conditions in an isolated tropical island. Natives did not envisage the day when a white man would see in their Island a source of cotton, of coffee, of cocoa, and other strange products of which those born in Polynesia had never heard. The people were eager to grow those things which would bring money to enable them to live like white men, and it was only then that the division of land ownership became a matter of jealousy and dispute. I believe that it was at this point that European prestige began to dwindle.

The old man's explanations helped clarify the matters that had been so puzzling to me. But, much as I was interested in matters of local politics, the health situation was at present my first consideration.

"Before I leave you," I said, "there is one thing I would like to know. During my inspection of your villages I have found many sick people who have not come to the hospital. I know that these folk have been taking some kind of medicine and also been receiving massage. I want you to forget for a little while that I am a government official and remember that I am a Rarotongan. I know very well that you have your own doctors. White men call them 'witch doctors,' but I prefer to use the old word, *taunga*. Our Government has been hard on these men, imposing heavy fines and terms of imprisonment, but I feel that there may well be some aspects of their learning which might add to those things which have been discovered in the great laboratories of the outside world. Do not think that I am trying to trap you, for that would be wrong. Let the *taunga* come forward now for I promise that no harm will befall them."

At first there was a heavy silence in the group, and I knew that I was on delicate ground, but soon several men came forward. One man, apparently their leader, spoke for them. "Dr. Tom, we will trust you. Here is our best *taunga*, our *tumukorero*, our relater of legend, memory for our history, and the wisest of our doctors. He will tell you what you wish to know."

I don't think that this *taunga* was seriously afraid that I would report his activities. The court knew of them already, for I found that he was their main source of information regarding the genealogies so important in decisions on land matters. Officialdom had long turned a blind eye. The *taunga* was quite willing to divulge his secrets of medicine. I had hopes of analyzing the various native brews and extracting or isolating their curative elements, but unfortunately I was never able to procure sufficient laboratory equipment to do this. However, I still think that science would profit by such analyses, else why did certain skin afflictions clear up immediately when treated with banana juice and coconut milk? Everything in my dispensary failed in these cases. How could a heated mixture of chicken manure and sea water placed in a coconut shell and held close to the wound anesthetize the pain of the bite of a stonefish? These things are still a mystery for although the *taunga* knew they cured, he did not know why.

Of course the *taunga* were not always so successful. Initial treatment for any pain is always energetic massage, and massage wrongfully administered was causing me endless trouble in surgical cases. I was finding that surgery which normally could have been performed in ten minutes now kept me busy for hours separating the multitude of adhesions caused by incorrect massage.

I could hardly blame the Islanders for returning to the ministrations of the witch doctors. We Government doctors were snowed under and yet I had already observed how little scope my chief was willing to allow our assistants, the

A.M.P.'s, when they returned to their home territory after their schooling in Fiji. Why is it that doctors are so reluctant to delegate even the purely mechanical aspects of their work?

Misuse of trained personnel, in the form of A.M.P.'s and nurses, seemed to me to be the main reason for the inefficiency of the department. The Chief Medical Officer was attempting to handle medicine, surgery, public health, control of filaria, care of schoolchildren and administration of the General Hospital as well as of the cottage hospitals in the outer islands. This situation, I have since found, is not peculiar to the Cook Islands for throughout the world members of the medical and dental professions are ever reluctant to follow the example of business executives who do delegate great responsibilities in their organizations without any fear that their assistants will attain a superior status. If a medical officer allows his assistant to open an abscess, then suture a wound, then perform major surgery, it should be taken as evidence of his confidence in the younger man, not as a challenge to his own skill. In my mind, the aim of a medical officer should be to ensure that his auxiliary personnel can do these jobs as well as he can. Never, in watching the initiative and skill shown by my assistants, did I feel anything but pride, never did I feel that I was losing public prestige.

When officials observed that I was giving responsibility to young men who had previously been regarded as the ringleaders of the village drinking clubs, they could foresee nothing but disaster. I was reprimanded, but when the change in my A.M.P.'s became obvious even to the skeptics, they began to wonder if my system might not be sound after all.

I had an example for this conviction not far away. In Fiji Dr. Samuel M. Lambert, of the Rockefeller Foundation, had envisaged a school that would turn out doctors equal in qualification and skill to those graduating from the great schools of the world. He asked first for natives to be trained as vaccinators and from this modest beginning he persuaded the administrators of the various Pacific territories that their intelligent natives would make good medical material. The school went up: not on such a grand scale as Dr. Lambert had hoped for and one that, on his death, slipped somewhat below its original proficiency, yet Lambert's dream became a reality, and when Dr. Merrill Cruickshank, a Canadian with no previous experience in the Pacific, became Director of the Pacific Medical Service, centered in Fiji, he too caught the same vision. A new school is now being built to accommodate students and faculty of a number far larger than was originally planned. Dr. Lambert's foundation is growing daily, and it was fortunate for me that at the time I was in the Cook Islands I should have in Dr. Cruickshank a man so much in sympathy with my policy, so ready to encourage me in what I was trying to do.

In those early days of my employment in the Pacific, it was my dream that I could bring the A.M.P.'s and nurses to a standard where they would merit the expense of postgraduate instruction and would eventually win respect from both natives and white people alike, sufficient to earn them the full title of Doctor. I was honest enough then to admit that, when eventually I would leave the Cook group, much of what I had done would fall away, but, as in the case of Dr. Lambert, I felt sure something would remain: a stronger foundation for some new man with similar convictions to my own.

Emergency at Atiu

A DOCTOR needs the trust of his community. The reorganization of my department was slow work, made doubly so
by the lack of confidence in me so openly displayed by my
superiors. Consultation with patients took time, for at this
point I thought it worth while to explain symptoms and treatments in detail; I knew the Islanders would return to their
villages and repeat all I told them; this would be a start in
the matter of health education. European patients waiting
outside my office chided me for taking the time to draw dia-
grams for "ignorant natives who wouldn't understand a word
I was saying," but I did it anyway. The hospital was bulging

at the walls, for in addition to the streams of infants Lyd
kept bringing us I was amassing a long surgical list with beds
filled with patients suffering from chronic complaints long
neglected.

Matron, who could improvise with remarkable ingenuity,
was proving a staunch support. She conjured extra beds out
of thin air, often borrowing cots and sofas from the hotel to
accommodate extra patients. She watched her surgical asepsis
with an eagle eye, chased untidy patients to the garbage bins,
and all round harried and heckled each member of the staff.
She was always alert for the unexpected. There was no A.M.P.
resident on the outer island of Atiu, but from the rather vague
account of symptoms radioed in by the Resident Agent of
Atiu, I diagnosed an epidemic of meningitis. Those who were
skeptical pointed out that it was quite impossible for such a
disease to have hit an island that had had no contact with the
outside world for several months. I must be crazy.

But I still felt sure that I had guessed right. I knew that
the best method of treating the cases would be by the administration of penicillin which, thanks to the prompt action of the
Commissioner, I now had in good supply in Rarotonga. But
Atiu was over a hundred miles away across the ocean. How
to get the drug to the people? There was no steamer expected
for several months, no trading schooner available, even the
shipping company launches were hauled out of water until
the end of the hurricane season.

When the number of deaths reported in Atiu climbed to
eighteen, I could stand the uncertainty no longer. I went to
the Commissioner and urged that transport be arranged; I
said that it might be possible to use one of the launches if
nothing better offered. We compromised in the end. The Commissioner agreed to radio to New Zealand the details of the

situation and my insistent desire that help should be given.

The reply came back that if necessary the New Zealand Air Force would send a Catalina flying boat to take me to Atiu. This would involve great expense and there was a strong possibility that the plane would be unable to land in the open ocean outside Atiu, for that Island has no lagoon large or deep enough to accommodate a seaplane. If I did not consider it safe to go by launch, said the message, a ship would be sent immediately, but this would take days and the circumstances demanded instant action.

No question it would be hazardous to go by launch. The shipping company launches are small Diesel-powered vessels that ply between steamer and wharf in unloading operations: they had never traveled more than a quarter of a mile at one stretch and the only cover they offered was the small cabin over the engine. Still, I believed that if we planned carefully they could carry me and my penicillin the 120 miles to Atiu and return. I suggested to the Commissioner that if we borrowed two sets of sails from one of the racing canoes owned by the Europeans, loaded up the launch with extra fuel, water, and food, and asked for volunteers — if we worked around the clock — there was no reason why we could not leave in twenty-four hours' time.

News travels quickly in Rarotonga, and in an hour we had more than enough volunteer helpers. We were offered two sets of sails, and Ron Powell, an experienced craftsman, stepped masts on the little launch, making a ketch-rigged motor sailer of her, grossly undercanvased, I admit. The radio station gave us two-way radio and their best man to operate it; the shipping company gave us their engineer, the stores gave us fuel and the people loaded us with food. The only difficulty was in trying to find enough space for men and cargo. I did not

want to sail with more than four: Tere, my A.M.P., the engineer, and Fred Storey, a European born and bred in Rarotonga who knew all there was to know about navigation and
sailing, and myself. However, the Commissioner wanted us to
play safe and we sailed with seven aboard: an extra navigator,
an extra radio operator, and an extra engineer. Thank heavens
I did take Fred, for all our "extras" were soon complete
wrecks from seasickness.

The voyage to Atiu was hot and uncomfortable. We were
heading straight into an easterly wind which although light
created a heavy sea; the sails were not large enough to steady
our vessel, and the launch had never been intended for deep-
sea voyages. Tere, Fred and I perched atop the fuel drums and
munched chicken and sponge cakes, the others hung over the
side.

Within twenty-four hours I was able to radio Rarotonga:
"ARRIVED SAFELY, DIAGNOSIS OF MENINGITIS CONFIRMED." I
found a dozen patients in varying stages of the illness; the
worst cases were in the tiny dispensary with its four beds, the
others at home. At Atiu I had my first meeting with Bill
Allison, the Resident Agent, who fulfills the function of our
Resident Commissioner. Bill had been on Atiu several years,
he was energetic, well educated, and fanatically concerned
with the welfare of his native charges. Like other resident
agents, as I later found, he felt with some bitterness that the
outer islands were neglected and that the officials in Rarotonga were uninterested in any projects for improvement.
He told me that for years he had been striving to impress on
the Government the necessity for better communications with
the isolated islands of the Cook group.

I admired Allison's tenacity and could observe his success
with the people. Atiu had been known as one of the most

recalcitrant islands in the whole Pacific. From this tiny land were drawn the warriors of Polynesia, and the modern descendants of these people still show a dogged stubbornness — they can be led but never driven. Doubling as schoolteacher, Bill had persuaded them to erect their own public buildings while Helen Allison, his pretty wife, helped with their education and assisted and directed the native nurse who was their only source of medical assistance.

Our launch trip had quite convinced Bill that now his isolation was at an end, and he carried his enthusiasm to the point of envisaging the next step: an air service for Atiu — no more dangerous launch trips in hurricane season! Followed by an enthusiastic crowd of Atiuans, I was rushed to the top of the Island to give my approval to a piece of land they had chosen for an airfield. The Atiuans evidently would not be happy till they saw a plane land on their own little Island. After I left, they actually built their air strip, but it was never used, for on my return to Rarotonga the New Zealand government wrote in requesting plans for a suitable vessel to be used between the outer islands of the Cook group.

We had arrived back in Rarotonga all badly burned by sun and wind and exhausted from lack of sleep. Tere had stayed behind, but even without him there was not enough room for any of us to lie down. All aboard were now my friends for life, each one felt a firm satisfaction that he had been able to play a part in bringing relief to my patients. I returned to my work and had my reward a week later when a press sheet was tacked on the notice board of the Commissioner's office, reading, "Thanks to the prompt action of the Resident Commissioner of the Cook Islands in sending prompt medical aid to the people of Atiu, the epidemic of meningitis on this Island is now under control."

Nothing ever settles down in Rarotonga. Within the month one of my nurses at the sanatorium was admitted to the hospital with what looked suspiciously like poliomyelitis. As the sanatorium was now holding a full compliment of patients, I knew this could have serious consequences. The nurse was soon followed by a young man with the same symptoms, then another and another.

I had diagnosed meningitis where meningitis had no right to be, but when I reported to the Commissioner that we had infantile paralysis right here on our Island, it was more than he could bear. The disease was attacking young adults in the eighteen to twenty-five age group, indicating to me that perhaps this was not the first time the infection had touched the Island; I said as much and only added more fuel to the fire. The Commissioner lost no time in reporting my diagnosis to New Zealand, but his radio cast serious doubt on my findings, and the return radio informed us that a plane would bring Dr. James Buchanan, then Director of Pacific Medical Services, in Fiji, to visit our patients and incidentally see what I was up to this time.

I was not too worried about the inspection, for inquiry had revealed that several of the older folk on the island were crippled with an unnamed disease which had broken out in 1904 and again in 1926. A sailor had come to Manahiki, an atoll far to the north, and, suffering from disease, had been left behind by his ship. Others had taken the infection, and to me the results looked remarkably like the aftermath of poliomyelitis, so that when Dr. Buchanan stepped off the plane I was well armed with evidence pointing to an earlier visitation of the disease. Dr. Buchanan took about five minutes to confirm my diagnosis.

On that brief visit, Dr. Buchanan (he was subsequently

knighted and became the director of the British Colonial Medical Services) did a great deal for me. In Rarotonga he showed himself a past master at administrative leadership. He very quickly and tactfully implied that the Commissioner would do well not to interfere in things medical, but at the same time, far from lauding my successful diagnoses, he hinted that I had better learn to use tact with those in authority. I did not explain that I was devoid of tact only when a situation was costing lives, but had I done so, Dr. Buchanan would have had an answer for that one too.

I felt certain, after outlining my long-term policy with my Medical Department, that at last I had someone who approved of my methods, and I was left in no doubt as to the Englishman's opinion of me when, with seeming casualness, he suggested that I would be better off professionally, and of more use to him, if I left the Cook Islands and transferred to the British Colonial Medical Service. I assured him that I was grateful, but now that I had started something in the Cook Islands I wished to stay with it and finish it to my satisfaction.

The day Tom sailed off into the blue in that nasty crowded little launch he left to my care our local lunatic, Takake.

As mental disease is not common in the Pacific Islands, Rarotonga had only a small one-room building attached to the hospital where mentally sick people could be lodged. I suppose we were sorry for poor old Takake, for our eight-by-six asylum must have been rather cosy for anyone so on top of the world as he. He was a little old man who for a long time had been suffering from manic depression. Rarotonga tolerated his peculiarities, but when he developed the habit of helping himself to new bicycles from the stores, riding them a hundred yards, then tiring of the exertion of pedaling, abandoning them in the nearest ditch, the hospital was called in to curb his activities.

I rushed home from waving Tom good-by, to find Takake waiting at the gate. He shook my left hand, shook my right hand, then started all over again. He ushered me towards the kitchen and announced that from now on he would do all the cooking. Then he ran outside, grabbed the lawn mower and went tearing up and down the tennis court, shearing the grass in swirls and wobbles. After ten minutes of this he charged down the beach yelling that he was going to catch enough fish to feed the family for a year. He was back almost before he was gone. He had to do his washing. Before he finished sorting his garments, he changed his mind again and started weeding the garden. I gave up trying to follow the trend of his activities and, telling Tere to feed him when he became hungry, I went off to look at babies.

When I returned home at the end of the day's work, it was to find that Takake, in one of his frenzied sorties down to the lagoon, had collected two *aa*. These are particularly vicious-looking sea snakes, whose bite is something to be avoided. However, if fried fresh after being caught, they make very good eating, and Takake had commandeered my kitchen with the idea of cooking himself up a good dinner. Unaware of the eccentricities of our stove, he was now doing his best to set the place on fire, stuffing in bundles of paper, pouring on kerosene and petrol, and throwing a match at the blaze. When Tere shrieked at him to stop, he took his still-alive eels in either hand and threatened mayhem. Tere fled, and so did I, gathering up John, who had been fascinated by all the excitement.

Dashing out into the street, I stopped the first group of natives who came along and begged assistance. I was out of luck, for the news had come of the success of the Atiu expedition, and it had been the signal for celebration in the villages. The men had spent an hilarious afternoon drinking toasts to Dr. Tom, in orange beer.

"Come quickly," I panted. "There's a lunatic in my kitchen."

"Mrs. Tom, your husband's a great man. No one die any more now. Come have a beer." That was the only reply I could get.

The next group I tried were just as useless, so I dashed back to the house, threw John in the back of the car and prepared to find a European. Of course the car didn't start, so locking John in the garage I ran over to the hospital to enlist the help of our already overworked Matron. I found her in the kitchen, and who should she be arguing with but Takake. He had eventually realized that our stove would never cook his eels, and so had taken over the hospital cooking facilities, his only reply to Matron's remonstrances being some Anglo-Saxon swear words and a threat to push his eels down her neck if she came one step nearer. Scorning to use a frying pan, he had simply crammed his two four-foot eels into one small meat tin. The patients' dinners and the babies' formulas he had lightheartedly tossed off the stove onto the floor. A fried eel supper — or nothing.

Matron is not usually helpless, but this was a case where assistance was needed. I borrowed a hospital car and at last I found a native policeman, cold sober, and full of sympathy. When poor Takake had been removed by the scruff of his neck and the seat of his pants, Matron and I cleaned up the mess, secure in the knowledge that my charge was now in

more capable hands down at the prison. Over several cups of
tea, we clearly and colorfully expressed our opinions of doctors who sailed off into the blue in unseaworthy vessels and
left helpless women to control good-natured lunatics.

Forty-eight hours later the launch was back, and I could
see that Tom hadn't been on a pleasure cruise. Apart from
the seven men who traveled to Atiu, there had been many
others who had helped to make the venture a success. To ex-
press our appreciation of their work, I decided that the time
was right to give my first party.

I did not then know that no one gives a party during hurricane season, so I was somewhat surprised when the girls
asked me how it would be possible to get food enough to feed
the thirty guests, all of whom, having been confined to the
monotonous diet of bully beef and *kumera* for the past three
months, would be ravenous. However, the old ladies in the
villages, hearing of the purpose of the party, came up with
the last of their chickens and fruit, for by now nothing but
the best was good enough for Dr. Tom. One old dear actually
gave me a live pig. I should have known better but I didn't
tie it up properly, and the dawn of the party saw half the villagers, armed with sticks, axes, and machetes, chasing my fast-
disappearing pig up into the mountains; when they failed to
catch it, there were offers of more chickens to replace the
truant!

All the guests arrived in their best dresses and spotless linen
suits, but I noticed that their eyes kept straying towards the
dining room. When I announced that supper was ready I was
nearly trodden into the floor. Maybe Tom and I had been
working too hard to feel hungry, but no one else had. Sitting
in a corner fascinated, how I cursed that darn pig. I should
have thought that twenty-five chickens would be enough for

thirty people, but no hostess likes to see her guests scratching
their plates. They all said they'd had enough to eat, but I
wasn't sure. Years afterwards I was to be reminded of that
wonderful dinner I had turned on in the middle of the hurricane season . . . but once was enough.

It was a slow start but gradually we were finding our place
in the community. Dr. Buchanan's visit and his reassurance
of Tom brought relief, for all through those first months I
had been haunted by the thought of Tom's being dismissed
in disgrace.

My mother-in-law still did not approve of me nor of anything I did; the fact that I was voluntarily helping the Island mothers seemed to her a lack of dignity on my part
rather than a genuine wish to assist her people. I tried not to
be troubled by this uncomfortable relationship. Tom rarely
had time to visit his mother, and if John expressed a wish to
see his Granny I let him wander off on his own. With the
other European women on the Island, I seemed to have little
in common. My association with the hospital was very close,
for I was interested in the children I brought in, and as I was
acting as Tom's secretary I could not help but know how matters stood in the Medical Department; to me the deterioration
in the native culture was a subject of endless fascination and
every mail brought new books that Dad had searched out for
us, all on the subject of Polynesia.

When the Government asked that plans be drawn for a
suitable boat, the undertaking was placed in the hands of
Tom, Ron Powell and John Pratt, and the two latter became a part of the household. Ron, an Englishman, had taken
to the sea at an early age, sailing the Mediterranean, Atlantic,
the Caribbean and the Pacific in small vessels before settling
down in the Cook Islands. He had cherished a kind of Swiss

Family Robinson ambition that would take him to an all-Polynesian island where he could put into practice schemes he had dreamed of far away in England. He had chosen to go to Palmerston Atoll, in the north of the Cook group, and there had married Elizabeth Masters, the beautiful daughter of the family that lived on Palmerston. But in time Ron had found the island life less idyllic than he expected and had returned to settle in Rarotonga with his family.

"Here I am," he would say, "I've been everywhere and done everything, looked death in the eye more times than I care to remember, and look at me now. Running a curio shop with five daughters playing in the yard. Five daughters! Fathering girls is like a hurricane, it descends on me!"

John Pratt had known Ron in England, but they had gone their separate ways, always on the sea. John had invested his entire income in a dream boat, the *Vagus,* a forty-foot yacht which he intended to sail round the world. He had set off from England with a two-man crew who had jumped ship in New York. Undaunted, John sailed on alone, taking the all-time snail's record of eighty-two days from the Galapagos Islands in the east of the Pacific to the Marquesas group in the west. In Rarotonga, John and Ron had joined forces again, and sailed up to Suvarrow Atoll, there to anchor and sit out the hurricane season in the shelter of the atoll lagoon. It was a cruel fate that chose Suvarrow for the center of the year's hurricane. John lost his boat and with it all he possessed. Whereas when he had arrived on the *Vagus* he had been honored and feted in Rarotonga for his brave singlehanded passage across the vast Pacific, when he returned from Suvarrow without even shoes on his feet his reception was rather different. New Zealand does not see a man stuck, and John was immediately offered the position of "freezer man," a Gilbert

and Sullivan position involving the equitable distribution of
the rare shipments of meat, the delivery of ice (nine tenths of
which melted en route), and the effort of persuading the customers to pay their freezer bills occasionally. By profession,
John had been a commercial artist; as the local butcher, he
was still a good artist. We suspected that rather than carve
the steak, he tore it apart.

The combination of Tom, Ron and John, all artists, all experienced sailors and all very decided boat designers, made
our household a little unusual. Conversation was colorful.
Ron had a Cockney accent, John stuttered and Tom waved
his hands. Surrounded by a lifetime's accumulation of their
yachting magazines and personal designs, the three of them
lay on their stomachs on the veranda floor and argued about
sheers and chines. At intervals Tom would grab up his little
black bag and disappear for an hour or two, but the other
two bodies were always there to trip over. To date in four
short months, Rarotonga had offered me in-laws, prisoners,
hurricanes, babies, epidemics, lunatics and now sailors. What
next!

When this hurricane season had reduced us to impaling the
rich and yellowed remains of cigarettes on the ends of safety
pins for just one more gasp, a shout went up. The *Tiare
Taporo* was coming, back from the shelter of Tahiti, bringing with her tobacco, red and white *pareu* cloth, French perfume and, best of all, her skipper, Captain Andy Thompson.

The Lonely Islands

"WHERE'D I come fraam? Lady, wid an accent like dis where d'ya t'ink I came fraam. Brooklyn, New Yaark, dat's where and tank God I had de good sense to get out of it. When I was a kid of ten my old granddad said to me, he said . . . but, no, I ain't gonna tell you my life story, ya'll go away and write about me and by golly lady no one's gonna write my life history. Mumma, hey Mumma, ya fat old balloon, come out and meet some swell folks."

Andy and Mumma are the original mutual admiration society and rightly so, for Mumma's heart is as big as her body.

Rarotonga's acquisition of Andy Thompson remains a mystery. From our many talks with him, I gathered that he arrived in the Islands by sailing vessel after spending his youth as an apprentice on square-riggers sailing down the west coast of South America.

"I may look a bad guy, but I was only in de calaboose de onct. That was in Callao, but it was wort' it. Boy, what a night dat waz, and I ain't gonna tell ya how I got dere."

When Andy first arrived in Rarotonga he was employed as a supercargo, then as mate on a trading vessel owned by Boss

McKegg, a well-known businessman in the Pacific. While on
the island of Atiu, Andy met Ngarangi. I think he may by
now have forgotten her pretty name for I've never heard him
call her anything but Mumma. Andy made a good choice
here, for not only was Ngarangi one of the most beautiful
girls in the Islands, but she also had the good sense to own
land in Atiu, Rarotonga, Tahiti, and Raiatea, these last two
islands far away in the Society group. Andy knew that no
matter how long he might be away at sea, Mumma would be
kept too busy on her plantations to be up to any mischief in
his absence.

When they were first married, they came to Rarotonga and
rented a house far up in the bush. Andy couldn't afford to
pay much for a home and he got this one very cheap . . . it
was haunted.

"Jeez, I tell ya, I've been in some tough places, but I never
was so goddamn scared as I was in dat house. Dis fat old balloon here, she lies and snores all night, but me? How I suffered! I'd just be dozin' off, see, den whang, down would
come some gravel right onto the roof. I'm not all yaller, and
out I goes wid me torch. Nuttin' dere. Not a goddamn thing,
so back I goes to me bed. Just layin' down again, den wham!
Everyt'in' starts flyin' round de room. I got kinda used to it
after a time, but when I woke one night and felt a couple of
cold hands clutchin' me round de t'roat, I lit out of dere so
goddamn fast I didn't even wait for Mumma. Don' anyone
tell me dere's no such thing as ghosts. Me for a shack on de
beach after dat lot."

Andy was eventually promoted skipper of the trading company vessel *Tagua,* and each hurricane season he would sail
away to Tahiti, some seven hundred miles distant, there to
"rest" until it was safe to come south again.

"De only trading skipper game enough to keep a boat down here in de hurricane season was your old Granddad, Tom. I knew him when I first came, and what a guy he was. He could cuss me out in twenty languages. But he lent me books and he taught me a good taste for rum. I went to Tahiti first wid him. Boy! What a place dat used to be and what swell people dere. Europeans too, guys like Charlie Nordhoff, Jimmy Hall, Ropati Frisbie, Bambridge, and even dat Frenchman Le Tec dat sprays paint onto velvet den sells the pitchers to de folks back in de States. What de hell, dey'll buy anyt'ing back dere. I'll never forget dose parties we had in Papeete, must have been a good-lookin' guy in dose days. In fact, dey tell me I'm not bad-lookin' now."

It is hard to imagine how Andy looked when he was young and his present age is his own secret. He is short and stocky with a chest like a barrel (a very hairy barrel), and as he scorns to wear a shirt except on the most formal occasions the Thompson chest is a familiar sight in Rarotonga. The sandy hair on his bullethead is largely a memory now, but his piercing blue eyes and weather-beaten skin stamp him with the mark of the sea. The most striking thing about Andy's appearance is his teeth, solid gold every one of them, and as much a part of his personality as his Brooklyn accent.

As they prospered Andy and Mumma built a neat stone house in a secluded part of Rarotonga and there on the veranda they sit: one at each end of the long table, keeping an eye on the road and ready to welcome passers-by. Andy dispenses rum punch like a Fifth Avenue bartender. Limes, sugar, water, ice, and lots of rum, when mixed in the right proportions and imbibed by the uninitiated, provide Andy and Mumma with endless entertainment as they watch their guests slide beneath the table or weave off home on foot.

While Andy holds court before his punch jug, he dispenses a philosophy that could well be adopted by the discontented ones of this world.

"Over forty years I've lived in dese islands. And why? Because I like de people. Dese wonderful Polynesians, dey really know how to live. Dey don't hate one another, dey don't remember past insults. When they smile, dey mean it. Dey don't struggle and fight to make t'ings better for demselves. And dat's not because they're lazy either. Dey've got more troubles dan you and I ever thought of, but dey don't go around griping, dey know if dey live a decent life, look after der kids and share the little dey've got wid dere neighbors, dey'll be right to meet de Lord. And it don't matter much to dem which Lord it is either, God or der old friend Tangaroa, dey knows dere's someone up dere waiting for dem to account for demselves. Money? What do dey want wid money? Dat stuff's only for mugs like you and me to worry about. Kids is money to dem, money in de bank. When a man's got ten or twelve kids, he can sit back and let dem do de work, and if he doesn't have any of his own, why den, he borrows dem from his relations."

Andy and Mumma had four sons and a daughter of their own, but Mumma could not resist taking into her home any child that she considered was not receiving proper care from its own parents.

"Look at all dose brats out back. Every time I come home dere's a new face and Mumma rushin' round growin' more food while de neighbors' brats eat dere heads off. But, wat da hell, dey're sweet kids, dey all call me Poppa, I only wish Mumma'd keep dem long enough for dem to grow up and do a little work around here. But no, she likes dem little."

By the time we arrived Andy's three eldest sons, Tony,

Andy and Sam, were almost grown men and learning to be sailors like Poppa, while the littlest one, always referred to by Andy as "Jimmy de Rat," was still at school preparing to finish his education at a New Zealand college. Like all the children of mixed marriages, they were particularly handsome, and so polite that I began to look on John with shame.

"I've got five kids, Mumma had four of dem, but dat Jimmy de Rat, de trouble I had bringing him into de world. Ya see when de others were born I was smart enough to be out at sea, but when dat Jimmy was due to arrive, I timed it wrong. Jeez, I'll never have another kid. Mumma got up and worked in de garden next day, but I had to go to bed for two weeks before I got me strength back."

Andy's tales were numberless, he was fun to be with, and I promised myself that when the time came for Tom to take an extended tour of the outlying islands he and I would travel together on the *Tiare Taporo.*

At the end of six months the Medical Department seemed to have shaken down into running order. Despite the ghosts, the sanatorium was now running at capacity; the assistant medical practitioners were working competently and with incentive; a district nurse from New Zealand took care of the district work and a training schedule was well under way for the nurses. Tom was a little surprised to learn that an additional medical officer who would be senior to him had been appointed to the Cook Islands, but there was consolation in the thought that he would have more time to look after the interests of the more scattered islands in the group. This seemed a good time to make an inspection of the isolated atoll islands in the north. The more southerly islands were high and volcanic in formation, and, being closer to Rarotonga, could be visited several times each year by steamer and schooner, but the atolls, Manahiki, Puka Puka, and Palmerston, were so small and so far away from the port island they rarely received more than one visit from a copra-collecting schooner during the entire year. The atolls of Suvarrow and Nassau, though deserted, had been used as coast-watching stations during the Second World War, and the *Tiare Taporo* on this trip was to call at these and pick up residual supplies. According to Andy this would be the trip of a lifetime and he encouraged me to come and bring young John along too.

We were to sail on the day after the new Senior Medical Officer arrived, and on that day an incident occurred that I was to remember.

The new doctor had lunched with us. He seemed agreeable and professed to approve of Tom's innovations. Directly after lunch Tom received a call to attend the child of one of the European missionaries living in an outer village. As our bags were almost packed and the house ready to lock on the following day, I accompanied Tom for the drive to his case; fortunately John was spending that last day with his grandmother.

When we arrived at the patient's house, we learned that the missionary was away on a mission to an outer island and that his wife, distracted at the sudden illness of her eighteen-month-old child, had been frantically trying to reach the hospital by telephone since early morning. A quick examination showed that the child was desperately ill; while Tom did what he could, I drove back to the hospital for penicillin and oxygen. I knew the baby had contracted fulminating pneumonia for I had seen children in the hospital in Rarotonga with the same complaint. None of them had lived, two had actually died in my arms while in the ambulance. Of all illnesses in Rarotonga, whether of children or adults, this is the only one that gives the patient almost no chance against death, especially when it strikes the infants. By the time I got back to this baby it was too late.

Returning to the main village with the bereaved mother I held the little body in my arms and wondered why Death should claim this innocent: there could be no better-intentioned nor selfless people than these, yet the tragedy had happened, leaving a gap in their lives that would never be filled.

So many people long for the power to look into the future, but I thank God now that on that afternoon I knew only of the present and after doing what I could to help the mother I was able to go on with our preparations for the cruise that I had long dreamed of.

I am strictly a one-bag traveler. Tom, too. This means that we arrive in a strange place with the barest necessities, and time reveals what we have forgotten. Tom does his own packing. He will never admit that he forgets more odds and ends than I do, but I may put it on record that he has actually been known to forget the whole bag. Andy had warned us that the trip would take at least four weeks, and "Please bring along a little liquor, why, we might even want a drink one day." As I drink gin and Tom drinks whiskey, he refused to have his luggage cluttered with my bottled goods, and four imperial quart bottles take up a good deal of room. I did a very good packing job, nevertheless. The only essentials I forgot were a pair of sand shoes, John's pajamas, and, as usual, my powder puff.

On board the *Tiare Taporo* Andy was at the top of his form, pandemonium reigned. In ancient khaki shorts and battered topee he stood astride the cabin top bawling orders at crew and passengers alike in his peculiarly Brooklynesque version of the Rarotongan language. Andy knows that he is an able skipper with a good crew that is quite capable of casting off moorings and setting sail with no help from him, but he loves a panic, and if he can't find one readymade, it is but a matter of a moment to create one for himself. With nine European passengers — including the Resident Commissioner — to be stowed in the four-berth cabin, a native family of eight into the trade-room and over thirty Rarotongans traveling on deck, Andy had the makings of a testy situation.

"You passengers get below or put your feet where my crew won't fall over dem — and if ya ain't comin' on dis trip for Chrissake get ashore, if we get tru dis reef before dark it'll be one of God's miracles." He had a good two hours of daylight left, but the effect of his bawls was excellent. "Don't ask me where to put dat luggage. For Chrissake put ya suitcases on your bunks and sleep on dem. Shouldn't have any luggage. Waddya tink dis is, a tourist ship? Chuck ya bags below and sit on dem. . . . And you dere. Call yaselves sailors? Get goin' blast ya hides. *Uti, uti, puaka Maori.* Get on dat stern line and heave, ya dogs. Don't lean on it, ya ain't sick areya?"

His anxious blue eyes peered through the cabin hatch. "Hey youse down dere. Lay off dat likker till we cast off."

Not knowing where we were to sleep, I parked my suitcase out of the way and John and I sat down to appreciate the bedlam in the forward part of the ship. Natives traveling between islands usually go as "deck passengers." This means that they sleep wherever there is space and carry most of their own food with them. It is beyond my imagination how they can get any pleasure from sleeping curled up in a damp lifeboat under a moldy tarpaulin, but they like it this way — so much, in fact, that I still hold a furtive ambition to travel "deck" just once.

At the moment these passengers were sitting quietly. They had not yet found time to sort out the baskets of food, babies, bundles of bedding, pots de chambre, large wooden chests of clothing and sacks of coconuts that made up their luggage. Some of the women were already looking green around the gills, though we had not yet sailed; the rest awaited the inevitable.

Tied to the rail with eyes starting from their heads and their feathers in a disarray of pure terror, chickens squawked for freedom; overhead huge bunches of bananas swung from every available support, swaying with the harbor swell and bumping the heads of the unwary. Even if they were in the way, we would all be glad of them in a day or two.

Suddenly on order from Andy, the engine-room telegraph clanged and the whistle screamed. A native pastor who was traveling "deck" struggled to his feet.

"We will pray."

Now everyone was quiet as he recited the prayer which he had learned from the missionaries and then, more reverently, he ensured us a safe journey.

"Keep us safe, Tangaroa, father of the people. Let the soft winds you gave to our fathers carry us over your seas, let this white man's canoe be no less swift than those of our ancestors. Watch over the folk we leave behind that the cooking fires may be warm for our return."

"Amen," came the chorus; then our traveling companions lifted their voices, as they would do night and morning throughout the whole voyage, and sang the tunes they have known since time immemorial. In the excitement of anticipation they swayed their shoulders and grunted, the women took heart and in the confined space at their disposal rendered spirited versions of the hula. The young bloods rushed off to take turns at sounding the whistle. So we sailed away from Rarotonga in dignity.

"Well, Mrs. Tom," said Andy fixing me with a calculating eye. "Since you're the only white lady passenger this trip, I think it would be very fittin' if we opened our little cruise by drinkin' a toast from one of dose bottles I know ya've got tucked away in that bag of yours. S'a pity ya only like gin, but we can save our whiskey for after, hey fellas?"

"Andy, I'll bring out my gin after you've given me a bunk. No bunk, no gin."

Andy rubbed the hairs on his chest and smiled benevolently. "Dat seems fair enough. We're a little snug dis trip. Lemme see, thirty-six on deck and seventeen in de cabins. Dere's eight bunks, the lockers, the table, and of course, gentlemen, plenty of floor. But for de lady, we must have comfort. You men'll be like maggots on a cheese, but why worry? Dis way, Mrs. Tom, and bring young John along too, we'll fix ya up real swell."

Andy stepped for'ard three paces and ushered me to the door of the old trading-room, now converted to cabin-cum-ship's-store. With all the flourish appropriate to concealed lighting and velvet hangings, Andy introduced me to my "stateroom."

"Dere y'are, lady. I'm giving ya dat top bunk dere all to yaself. Just put young Johnny down at de bottom, stow ya suitcase under da pillow dere, and if ya remember to keep ya feet out of dose groceries ya'll be real snug."

Snug was hardly the word. The trade-room was already occupied by two adults and six children along with the appropriate amount of luggage. Into the spare space were crammed two large cases of potatoes and two of onions, three of canned

butter, four of milk, hundreds and hundreds of cans of bully
beef and ship's biscuits, bottles of sauce and jars of pickles,
packets of condiments, sacks of flour and oatmeal, tins of jam,
and all the other oddments of food that might be needed by
the swarm of passengers. The particular groceries to which
Andy was referring were a head of cheese and a side of bacon.
The cheese reposed above what was to be John's pillow, the
bacon was hung on a hook above the exact middle of our
bunk. Before the trip was ended I was to get to know these
dainties very well indeed.

While I was still considering the best stowage, Andy
popped in once again. "Oh, Mrs. Tom, here's Dr. Tom's luggage. I'm giving him dat bunk below ya, but he won't want
to be cluttered up any."

As Tom is large and the bunks on the schooner very narrow, I knew it was useless to argue, so grasping my bottle I
joined the men in the main cabin. On the *Tiare Taporo* no
one drinks at sea, festive occasions being confined to leaving
or entering harbor. It was a good idea to have a small party
this first evening, the passengers in the cabin would now have
an opportunity to look one another over, for we would be together for a long time.

The Commissioner was to make an inspection of the atolls.
He was miserable and uncomfortable as he was suffering from
a bad bout of boils; he was not impressed by his traveling
companions, particularly with Tom and me, but, knowing
that he was very fond of John, I hoped things might go
smoothly. The island of Puka Puka had been out of radio
contact with Rarotonga for some weeks, it was rumored that
the unpopular Resident Agent had been murdered by the natives, so among the passengers were two journalists, hoping
that the worst had happened. We had aboard a very distin-

guished Rarotongan pastor, Joseph Vati, secretary for the Seventh Day Adventist Mission in the Cook Islands. Because Joseph was too tall to fit onto a bunk, he occupied the locker beside the table; as he slept on top of the bread, he was perforce an early riser. The cook couldn't start breakfast when Joseph was sitting on the staff of life.

Thanks to Andy's management, everything was soon in order.

In the trade-room, a native schoolteacher and his brood were installed. The very pregnant mother took the lower bunk, her fourteen-year-old daughter the top one, and the rest of the family spread mats on the floor. The mother and daughter settled down to being seasick for the whole of the journey, while Father and the younger ones passed the time getting under the feet of any of the crew who wanted a ship's biscuit during the night watches. The whole family, despite their misery, were delightful cabin companions, always cheerful and eager to help one another.

Our first stop was to be Palmerston Island, four days' rough journey distant from Rarotonga, and I looked forward eagerly to seeing the members of the Marsters family, famous in the Pacific for having populated this tiny atoll, and incidentally for being the in-laws of Ron Powell. I knew that William Marsters, who had first settled Palmerston Island, had been one of the crew of a whaling vessel. He had married a woman from Penrhyn Island, to the north of the group, and had chosen to find for himself a deserted atoll where he could settle down and start a dynasty. Perhaps feeling that one wife would not be sufficient to mother the tribe he intended to start, he also took with him his sister-in-law, and as I later discovered he was accompanied by a Portuguese friend who had been a crewman on his ship. The Portuguese brought his native wife along too: if anyone had known that she was suffering from leprosy, the story of Palmerston Island might have been a happier one.

The Portuguese did not stay long, for William Marsters proved to be a martinet, but he was there long enough for his wife to spread the infection of her distressing disease. William begat many children by his wife and her sister, he ruled his Island as a stern patriarch, and left behind him a tradition to be carried on by his eldest son. The younger William Marsters, now at the head of his family, was a very old man. Many of his descendants, following their progenitor's love of the sea, had left their atoll home to become sailors in all ports of the world, and the Central Leper Hospital in Fiji was caring for far too many of the clan. There were some sixty-five people on the home Island when we called.

Palmerston Atoll was a low island as contrasted with high volcanic Rarotonga. It seemed barely to rise out of the sea, a mere heap of sand standing in the tight circle of coral reef. To reach the land we would have to cross over the top of this reef in the schooner's flat-bottomed shore boat, and so the excitement started.

"Mrs. Tom, for Chrissake watch yourself gettin' into that boat. Take no notice of dese guys here, when I say 'jump' you jump. Watch me give the word." Andy flattered me with personal attention.

Certainly, looking over the rail of the schooner, transshipping myself into the smaller boat appeared to be a major undertaking. The crew had already piled the craft high with food stores for the isolated atoll dwellers who had not seen a boat nor fresh stores for over a year. Sacks of flour and sugar filled the longboat. Anyone who wished to go ashore, and that was all of us, was invited to climb aboard and perch

on top. Where the schooner lay just outside the reef a heavy
swell was running: one second the longboat was level with
the rail, then she was twelve feet down in the trough.

"Stand back, the lady's comin'. Jump!" bellowed Andy.
Trustingly I jumped, missed the crest of the swell and
skinned my legs between the two vessels.

"Woops!" said Andy. "Sorry, maybe we should have waited
a little. You'll do better next time."

I knew that when traveling in the company of men a lone
white woman is well advised to ignore any small inconven-
ience; if she is at all vocal about her distress, she runs the risk
of not being invited again.

Andy handed Johnny down to me, and wedging both of
us between a couple of flour bags I sat tight and hoped for
the best. Tom, who revels in any project that may result in
loss of life or limb, took an oar with the crewmen. Through
my mind flashed the hundreds of gory stories of people who
had been tipped out of reef boats, swept onto the sharp coral,
whipped under the edge of the reef to disappear forever, or
left to swim out to sea as best they could. As the natives (and
Tom) rowed up to the coral, they sang and shouted, but when
we were close in to the breakers they suddenly fell silent,
their backs to danger and their eyes on Taiona, the man at the
tiller. Taiona has the reputation of being the best tillerman in
the Pacific, I might have known that we would be safe.

There must have been over twenty people in that boat
added to the weight of piles of stores, and yet Taiona alone
held the bows straight onto the reef, waiting for the right
wave to take us across. We have all heard the story of the seventh wave being the largest one, yet the Islanders tell us that
the waves pile up in multiples of three: it may be the third,
the sixth, or the ninth, never the seventh, which will be the

largest. Islanders do not cross a reef on the crest of the highest wave. They wait until that one has passed, then ride in immediately behind the next wave, sweeping over the coral with a safe depth of water beneath the boat.

Now Taiona had made his judgment. "*Aere atu!*" he shouted and we were off, everybody yelling again like mad

cowboys and the oarsmen straining every muscle in the delight of defying nature's barrier to the land. In a second we were in the shallow water of the lagoon, and now everyone got out onto the coral and pulled the boat, there was not sufficient depth to use the oars. We dodged round the coral mushrooms that rose every yard of the half-mile stretch of shallows.

All the Marsters family were down at the edge of the beach to meet us. I can't say they showed much enthusiasm, for conditions were not too happy on the Island and the presence of the Commissioner, whom they were now seeing for the first time, filled them with suspicion: nor did Tom's presence — the first doctor they had seen in many years — interest them much, for thanks to their isolation they seldom suffered the usual sicknesses, and a visiting schooner leaves in its wake an epidemic of coughs, colds, and influenza. I should add that there were no virulent cases of the leprosy which had haunted them in the past.

As the first white woman to visit Palmerston Island for eleven years, I guess I struck a lighter note. The children had seen white women only in picture books and the women were interested to see how I might be dressed. I am not a snappy dresser at the best of times, and my system of assembling my luggage does not improve the situation. This, combined with the fact that I had not bathed for four days, probably rendered me a disappointment; however, the Islanders could not know that I was a poor specimen of modern femininity.

To our delight we found that the people here spoke a language all of their own. William Marsters had originally come from Lancashire, and he insisted that his part-Polynesian family speak the language of their father. Now, more than a hundred years since the founding of the family, everyone by the name of Marsters spoke archaic seafaring English with an added dash of the South Seas.

"Mrs. Taam, woulds't lake to coom oop maowntin'? Ba goom, s'not a reel maowntin', I grant, but we scoop oot t'e swamp for t'e taro then pile up t'e scoopin's high in t'bush 'ere. T'e maowntin's not but six feet 'igh but 'tis a graand place when t'e winds blow. Coom h'aft 'ere and look you."

There was a small mound in the middle of the Island and beside it stretched the swamp which these folk had dug out by hand. Ron Powell, in his Swiss Family Robinson era, had

shown the people how to make wheelbarrows and shovels of
the ironwood. With the aid of a pit saw they had even fash-
ioned wooden wheels for the barrows and dug thousands of
tons of earth above a brackish spring to form a swamp where
wet taro could be grown to eke out their monotonous atoll
diet of fish and coconuts. Ron had shown them how to find
the underground springs and how to make a pump using
piping made of bamboo sticks. He may have tired of his atoll
life, but his lessons will always remain in the minds of the
Palmerston Islanders. One lad, evidently a hero worshiper of
the seafaring Ron, had even built his own boat, to European
design and complete with cabin, using only the resources of
the barren atolls. Now that his boat was ready for sea, his resentment burned deep. The Commissioner would not let him
run the risk of sailing to Rarotonga. The lad argued that his
boat was seaworthy and strongly built, he interpreted the re-
striction placed upon him as further evidence of the poor
esteem of Europeans for Polynesian industry.

The lad's resentment was evidently shared by all his family,
though with them it went deeper and for different reasons.
William Marsters, in order to gain complete domination of
his atoll home, has from the start leased his Island from the
Government, agreeing to pay a small yearly rental. Palmerston Atoll had proved to be always in danger from hurricanes.
As fast as new coconuts were planted, the seas swept over the
sand and washed them out, so that the people, relying for income solely on the sale of copra, were soon unable to pay the
rent for their home. The Government, understanding the
hardship involved, agreed to waive the rent until Palmerston
was again able to export copra. Now, when they were struggling to re-establish themselves economically, they were expected to pay arrears. They resented this bitterly. Every-

where on the Island we saw signs of the struggle for existence, and the tyrannical discipline imposed by the patriarch. Bread-fruit, paw-paw, and banana trees which do not readily grow on coral were fighting to survive in the sand. Bandages made of the bark of the coconut palms were tied carefully over trunk bruises while sticks of mahogany supported weak plants. Every second day the part of the atoll where the people had built their houses was swept for refuse and fallen debris to be piled round the roots of the precious plants to form a small oasis of soil in which they might grow. The Marsters family were tall and husky, the women as powerfully built as the men, for here everyone must work with his hands in order to exist.

We had hoped to stay a day or two with the Marsters family but an urgent radio message ordered the schooner to proceed to Manahiki Atoll, there to pick up an emergency medical case. Manahiki is famous throughout the world as the island of hats, mats, and the hula. The people of this atoll (it is said to be the most beautiful in the Pacific) are not of pure Polynesian blood for the blackbirders, slavers who carried off the natives to the Peruvian mines and the Queensland sugar plantations, and the ships carrying Asian laborers down to Australia, stopped by at Manahiki; they introduced exotic blood strains. Now you can always tell a Manahikian, he has a darker skin than his purer-blooded cousins while slant eyes and high cheekbones show his Oriental ancestors.

We intended to stop for just one hour, time for Tom to examine the patient and bring her aboard should it be necessary to shift her from the atoll. We crossed the reef with dignity, and while Tom discussed medical matters with the assistant medical practitioner stationed on Manahiki I wandered off in one direction and John in another. This proved to be a mistake, for I made my first (and last) acquaintance with palm toddy. The only gift that an islander can give is food, so at each house I passed, the people called me in to share their afternoon meal. Being still unfamiliar with their language, I smiled and smiled and ate and ate, courteously accepting the numerous coconut cups of what I thought was ordinary *nu*, the juice from the fresh nut. Tom tells me that I arrived at the clinic swaying in the breeze with a flower behind each ear. I kept telling him over and over that I had only been drinking *nu* but he thought otherwise.

"You've been sampling toddy. Go right back to the ship and cool off. When I finish here, I've got to see another patient," said Tom sternly and mysteriously.

Feeling rather sheepish, I weaved my way back to the beach to find that John and the other passengers had been ordered aboard. Along came Andy.

"Jeez, but dat toddy's swell stuff, 'specially when mixed with rum. What d'ya t'ink of it, Mrs. Tom, and where's Tom got to?"

Focusing Andy with effort I reported that Tom was seeing a sick man.

"He is, is he? I bet de man is Ben Ellis, and he ain't sick. Take my arm, madam, we too will pay a visit to Ben."

Supporting each other at an acute angle, Andy and I progressed back the way I had come. I knew that Ben Ellis was running a profitable pearl shell and copra business in Manahiki and that his hospitality was legend. See a patient, indeed!

Sure enough, there was Tom sitting in Ben's neat little house, a glamorous Balinese-looking girl rushing back and forth with supplies of rum and toddy. Andy and I joined the party to listen to Ben's story.

"We don't spend money here. What is there to buy? We

have sunshine, fruit and flowers, that is all we atoll people need. If we want entertainment, the boys bring out their drums and we dance all night, yet by your standards too we are rich. There's not a bed in Manahiki that doesn't have a box full of cash buried beneath it. The lagoon is full of pearl shell, the coconut trees laden with nuts ready for the copra making, and there's fish enough in these waters to feed many times the people we have here."

Andy insisted that I share a canoe with him for the return reef crossing, and to even the score of my independence of the morning he persisted in rocking the boat, splashing water over both of us. To my delight his precious cardboard solar topee floated off on a wave so there followed more dangerous maneuvering as he retrieved his most valued possession. In time we clambered aboard all in one piece. Our fellow passengers took one look at us and felt hurt.

"Don't feel sore, fellas," said Andy heartily. "Let the party continue, bring out a bottle and we'll sing 'Rosie O'Grady.' "

The Commissioner, who had spent a worrying morning trying to persuade the people of the Island to put their hoarded money into circulation, took a dim view of all this. The patient was aboard, installed in Tom's bunk, her servant and small son added to the occupants of the trade-room floor. John had found his way back on board, and Tom was in a mood for giving orders:

"Lyd, give the patient a shot of morphia, then go to bed. You've had enough for today. Andy and I are going to have a community sing." The other passengers broke out a tin of biscuits, filled their glasses, and to the strains of "Rosy O'Grady," sung slightly off key, we sailed away from Manahiki on the last leg of our journey to the island of Puka Puka.

Before visiting Puka Puka (and more than ever after seeing the Island and its people) I considered Robert Dean Frisbie's *The Book of Puka Puka* a classic in the literature of the South Seas. Frisbie could appreciate the melancholy and the lightheartedness of the island people. I had never met him and I doubted I ever should, for he had left the Cook group and was living in Samoa, seriously ill with the complaint that had dogged him all his life. But now perhaps I might meet Mrs. Bosun Bird and William the Heathen, see the house that Frisbie had built for himself and his family, and explore the fabulous beaches where the young people hid themselves to make love, away from the prying eyes of the Government Agent.

The white coral sand dappled with the shadows of the palms was Puka Puka just as Frisbie had painted it, straight off a picture post card. None of the ugliness of European innovation marred the villages here, neat pandanus houses lined the spotless road where no buggies, bicycles, or motor vehicles had ever passed.

To the disappointment of our journalists, the Resident Agent of Puka Puka was very much alive. Bearing aloft a large black umbrella he had paddled out to the schooner in a canoe flying the New Zealand flag. To my delight, accidentally on purpose, the paddlers knocked his umbrella out of his hand. They roared with laughter as they fished it out of the tide. They laughed at everything, particularly at me. Dr. Ernest Beaglehole with his wife had stayed a short time on the island twelve years before to study the people and write his *Ethnology of Puka Puka* (a tome too technical for me to appreciate). Since then the islanders had not laid eyes on a white woman: the adults thought I was a joke, the children something from the land of legend. As Tom and I in stately fashion proceeded along the single street on our way to the

Agent's house where we were to stay, every child in the village followed us, but we kept straight faces and tried to look like Empire Builders. The effect was rather marred when I stopped suddenly to tighten my shoelace and the entranced and staring children fell over the back of my neck and piled up in the rear, one on top of the other. John wandered into the first house and as usual made himself one of the family. A little farther, an old lady came out of her house to take a look at us: when she caught sight of me she fled screaming and slammed the door behind her. I've never had that effect on anyone before!

We were to stay eight days on the Island while the schooner loaded copra, the Commissioner straightened out local problems, and Tom caught up with a medical organization that was only too obviously nonexistent. The dispensing of drugs and medical attention had been taken over by the wife of the Agent. She was a Polynesian, though not of the Cook Islands, and fanatically religious, as was her husband. Her moral standards were quite incompatible with the happy tradition of the Puka Pukans. Strangely enough, although I openly argued her standards, and did nothing to return her hospitality, so much did I disapprove of her, that woman has always remained a good friend of mine. At least the sternness of her interpretation of Christianity has taught her to forgive. Now she made no effort to conceal her principles.

"These Puka Pukans don't deserve medicine, the heathens. The way they carry on in those love huts on the outer beaches, it isn't decent. Prison is the place for them! They think we think they're Christian because they sit on the beach and sing hymns all night. They're not singing, just covering up for the sinners in the bushes. We've stopped all that now, curfew keeps them in their houses after nine and the police see they stay there. If they're caught at their love-making, they can spend the next month or so making mats as a punishment, we can't fine them when they're too ignorant to earn the money to pay."

Where was the happy island Frisbie wrote about? Where the carefree tradition? The love huts lay broken on the sand, and though the natives still laughed I suspected that it was with relief that strangers had arrived who might sympathize with them in their oppression. Tom spent his first day, a Sunday, listening to the chiefs explain their difficulties. I wandered off to find some characters from the *Book*. William the Heathen was dead, but his family still flourished, his brother carrying on for the old sinner who had escaped Bully Hayes and lived to tell the tale. The brother looked me up and down, then walked right round me.

"Hmm," he said thoughtfully, scratching his chin. "A fine-looking young man like Dr. Tom could surely have married some pretty young girl." Such honesty discouraged me from further advances, and I preferred to follow Tom around rather than submit to further frankness. While Tom talked in a dialect quite incomprehensible to me, I drank coconuts, one after another. Soon I made a beeline for the one and only privy in Puka Puka; all the children had been waiting for this, and in my haste I had not noticed that about forty gaping small fry had followed me along the causeway over the water and to the building, the use of which, since it had no door, was obvious. I decided to beat a hasty retreat the long distance to the Agent's house and privacy. Thereafter, I drank only one coconut at a time.

The following day Tom began his clinics, asking me, not the Agent's wife, to assist him. The dispensary, the courtesy title given the tiny eight-by-four pandanus hut housing the

drug supply, was about five hundred yards from the house,
and the nearest heat supply for sterilizing instruments was
the Agent's cookhouse. After each patient had been attended
to, I had to toil all the way back to the cooking fire and boil
up again for the next. The temperature was around 90° in
the shade and the mosquitoes were thicker than I had ever
seen them. The fact that each insect carried filaria was evident
in the unsightly elephantiasis that distorted the limbs of nearly
every adult male on the Island. The women did not seem to
be victims of the deformity though they must have been carrying the disease. By my private theory, as the men of Puka
Puka left all the hard work to their women while they sat under the trees or occasionally went fishing, the women never
sat still long enough for the mosquitoes to bite them.

Yaws also was very prevalent here. The dispensary shelves
were piled high with cartons of neosalvarsan, a drug which
could have cured this uncomfortable and acutely infectious
disease. But neosalvarsan has to be given by intravenous injection, and no one on the Island knew how to administer one
so the drug lay in unopened cartons while the natives walked
on the outside of their feet to keep the open sores on the soles
off the sharp coral. Some of the sufferers were so covered
with hideous scar tissue that it was well-nigh impossible to
find a piece of clear skin to inject. Watching Tom jab
needles through the distorted flesh, I often had to get out for
air.

Many of the women complained of repeated miscarriage.
Working endlessly at the backbreaking job of weaving pandanus mats in punishment for making love on the outer
beaches is not healthy for pregnant women. The only drugs
that the Agent and his wife understood were Epsom salts and
aspirin; these they kept locked in their house to be dispensed

to deserving applicants. It was heartbreaking to hear Tom tell so many patients that nothing could be done for them, the illness had gone too far.

Though their hearts must have been heavy, each afternoon the people of the villages made a feast for all the visitors. We knew their food supply was limited, that in their efforts to increase copra export they had rationed their eating and drinking coconuts, yet they cheerfully killed off their precious pigs and chickens and worked all day through to honor us. As we ate, sitting on mats spread on the ground and using leaves for plates, they sang and danced with a rhythm and harmony peculiarly their own. Puka Pukans do not claim to be Cook Islanders although they are now included in the Cook group. Their history tells that they came from the Tokelau Islands far away towards Samoa, settling on the atolls of Puka Puka and Nassau, the latter an uninhabited island some forty miles away and now owned by the Government. A hurricane had hit Puka Puka at the end of the nineteenth century, creating such damage that after the storm had passed there were only fourteen Puka Pukans left alive out of nearly seven hundred. From these survivors had come the six hundred persons now trying to make a living on the Island. Because of inbreeding the modern Puka Pukan is slower of wit and movement. His isolation does little to improve his appreciation of Western methods. Frisbie taught the natives a little of civilization, it was not his fault that grown men passed their time playing marbles or weaving cowboy hats and carving guns out of wood. The Islanders were not so dull as not to realize that they were living under virtual dictatorship. By tradition they had once had a voice in their affairs, that had now been silenced by one man. They knew that their population was far too great for the land, but they made no move to distribute part of their people to Nassau. Was not Nassau theirs before the white men came?

The Commissioner was sympathetic towards them, but, and rightly so, it was not his policy to refuse public support of one of his agents. In private I have no doubt that he was very firm with this officer, but in public he was careful never to belittle him. He wanted the Islanders to rent Nassau. "Pay for our own Island" was the interpretation of this. At every feast the songs and dances told the legend of the days when Puka Pukans had lived on Nassau. The Islanders might well have saved their breaths, they were not understood.

We called briefly at Nassau after leaving Puka Puka, finding an island loaded with coconuts, natural taro swamps, wild pigs, everything a Puka Pukan wanted but couldn't pay for. As long as the small copra income had to be paid back to the Government in fines, there seemed no prospect of easing their need.

En route back to Rarotonga, we called again at Palmerston Island to pick up more copra. Old William Marsters and virtually every member of the family was afflicted with a severe cold, the infection we had brought on our first call. The old man was desperately ill, and the resentment of his people consequently greater than ever. I remember a husky girl who served us breakfast the morning after our arrival. I talked to her of the beautiful work the women did, weaving Panama hats and plaited belts. She took me into her home and showed me how the pandanus leaves are soaked in sea water, stripped of the green bark, bleached in the sun, divided into narrow widths, then placed over a block for weaving. She was friendly, pleasant and very intelligent. When I saw her again, six years later, she was a patient in the Central Leper Hospital, blind in both eyes.

We had been away from Rarotonga five weeks before we again sighted the home Island. Our landfalls had been full of interest but too often depressing, and to the Europeans aboard it must have seemed urgent that matters be corrected. Standing on the afterdeck with Rarotonga close in sight, Tom and the Resident Commissioner entered into a conversation that convinced me that Tom would not be a medical officer to the Cook Islands for much longer.

CHAPTER XI

Showdown

TOM: I went to these atolls to inspect the medical setup. There isn't any setup. All I've found in the dispensaries, if such those hutments could be called, are rows of bottles, labeled in Latin. Bottles from which the corks have never been pulled — they must have piled up over the years. Some of them contain the very things that would help make the people healthy. But no one there knows what's in the bottles or how to use them.

OFFICIAL: It's a remarkable thing that they don't know how to use them when the medical officer has been telling them how for the past twenty years.

TOM: Yes, telling them of Epsom salts and aspirin. These won't cure filariasis, yaws, hookworm and tuberculosis.

OFFICIAL: Now wait. I saw as many of them as you, Dr. Davis, and no one can deny they're a hefty-looking bunch of natives for anybody's money, plenty of food to eat, plenty of energy for their games and dancing, too.

TOM: Oh yes, they sing and dance, and they give you their last bite of food, but did you notice the way they walk? On the outside of their feet because the soles are so cracked open with neglected yaws they can't bear to put them to the ground. You laugh, and say, "We all know the Puka Pukans walk like crabs." So would you walk like a crab if the sole of your foot was open and bleeding. And they're hefty, are they? Did you roll up the trouser legs of the men and take a closer look at that heftiness? Let you try a native dance when your legs are three times their normal size because aspirin won't cure filaria.

OFFICIAL: Tom, those people have broken almost every law that we and the church have given them.

TOM: Sure, they've broken them, but did your men or the church ever stop to explain why those laws were imposed in the first place? What you regard as a breach of the law or as a breach of morals to them is just part of their natural behavior. Go ahead and fine them all you like, fining when the wrongdoer can't understand his crime won't stop what we call crime.

OFFICIAL: Your interest in the people of our atolls is touching, why not concentrate on Rarotonga first?

TOM: Because Rarotonga, though it may be the center of the Cook Islands, is not the whole of it. If the atoll people suffer and die, the fact that you can't see them doing it or why they are doing it makes them no less important.

OFFICIAL: Why do you suppose the Government has never disapproved of the state of the atolls?

TOM: Have they ever really known of it? Reading the past reports of the Medical Department before I left on this visit, I would never have guessed it. The atolls have been regarded as the outposts of this little empire, but that is no reason they should remain neglected.

OFFICIAL: Tom, you're supposed to be a doctor, not a reformer. But as far as I can see you're nothing but a troublemaker who sets himself up as an expert over others who have spent years studying the administration of the people. Young as you are and with no experience, you consider that you know best.

Tom: You can go on studying the people for the rest of your life and get no further ahead in the understanding of them, much less the curing of their ills.

Official: Ills, you call them? Show me one territory in the tropics that doesn't have yaws, or filariasis, or hookworm, or tuberculosis. Just show me one, everyone knows there's nothing to be done about that.

Tom: I can't show you one, that I'll admit. But I can show you the reports on research, the accounts of medical surveys, and the totals of money that are being spent every day of the year by people who, unlike you, think that something can be done. And I'm one of those people. See what was done with the yellow fever menace in Central America, and with the malarial mosquitoes that plagued our fighting men during the last war. Even here in the Cook Islands you know how we have reduced the number of lepers, and reduced it only because we were acutely aware of the problem. It won't be long before we're made aware of the poor health of the Cook Islanders too. They won't all suddenly drop dead in their tracks, but their rotting economy is helping ill health in every way, and that you won't be able to conceal or ignore forever, in fact it's my guess the day of reckoning isn't far away.

Official: No, and I have no doubt that you will play your part in bringing it nearer.

Tom: In spite of what you think of me, that won't be so, but when the day comes I'm going to listen, and if it is humanly possible I am going to help to make things better, whether that help be given purely as a medical man or as just another interested European.

Official: Our doctors, and all the others who have played a part in the administration of these Islands, have given the best they had to offer. If the natives have not prospered it's because they wouldn't understand our motives, and that is hardly our fault.

TOM: Another man answered that kind of statement better than I can. "The fault, dear Brutus, is not in our stars, but in ourselves."

CHAPTER XII

The Spark

THAT conversation was still rankling in my mind when I returned from the five weeks' visit to the northern islands. To my great disappointment I found that my new superior, the Senior Medical Officer, had installed a regime identical to the one which had so shocked me on my arrival. Once again undue economy was the order of the day. All authority was once again back in the hands of one man: the A.M.P.'s were permitted no part in the running of the hospital, and without sufficient drugs to take care of the people of the villages things were back where they started.

A quick trip round the southern islands of Mauke, Atiutaki and Mangaia showed me a picture even worse than in the north, for here tuberculosis, the result of the shattered economy, was an added menace. On the way I had selected young men from all these outer islands whom I hoped to train as dispensers and dressers so that they could return to their home islands with sufficient knowledge to care for their people as male orderlies. I had also loaded the decks of the *Tiare Taporo* with patients whom I knew needed immediate hospitalization.

My superior's attitude towards me had stiffened during my absence and he was now antagonistic to the point of belligerency. He grudgingly allowed me to resume charge of the operating theater, and said I might carry on the mosquito control program, although from its inception he had had no faith in it.

This was only a fraction of the work I wanted to do. But time did not hang heavy on my hands. A sense of responsibility towards the Islanders, the feeling that they were in some measure dependent on me, urged me to extend my house visits, day and night, at the request of patients' families, or wherever there was a rumor of distress. As a rule I was fortunate to get four hours' straight sleep. This all brought me closer to them, and now that I had the opportunity to talk out their personal and social problems I was able to avoid the frustration which might have arisen from the collapse of my constructive medical activity.

I was glad to have the chance to study their manifold difficulties, and my disgust at the methods of administration in the outer islands, resulting as it had in an outburst that might well cost me my position, made a reform program all the more urgent for me. I felt sure that my conclusions about the past medical administration had been correct and knew that I could not be deprived of my position without an open inquiry that would be all too revealing for the comfort of our administrators. I was unafraid of such an inquiry, and so I made no secret of my disapproval of current methods and welcomed to my house native leaders and those European officials who were willing to exchange their different points of view.

Some years earlier the natives had formed the Cook Islands Progressive Association and this had steadily gained in power. Rumor had it that the Association was being directed from New Zealand by Communist sympathizers with the aim of freeing the Cook Islanders from the administration of New Zealand. To oppose the Association the Government set up a

Union of its own which, of course, the members of the Association would not join.

The Association, which had originally been intended for the economic improvement of the Cook Islanders, was in fact following the pattern set by left-wing agitators in New Zealand. The improvement of an economy that must necessarily be founded on agricultural development is a long-range program, and 98 per cent of the Islanders were dependent on the soil for their economic security. Accordingly the leftist guides of the Association sought for a quicker, sharper focus for the discontent, and they found it in the most obvious way, wages. It was undeniable that the cost of living had risen since the war years and that the native wages had not increased in proportion. Only about 2 per cent of the natives received regular wages, and they were Government employees, trading-store hands, and wharf laborers. The latter, of course, made the best target for agitation. "Strike for more pay" was the direction. "We'll employ different laborers" was the Government's answer.

And so the ugly phrase, "scab labor," was heard on the Island, and when that phrase is heard, whether on a tiny Pacific island or in the largest seaport of the world, one can expect trouble; that is what the Communist directors of our Association were counting on. Shipping, which had become critically meager, now passed by rather than stop to pick up fruit and risk the delay caused by quarreling wharf factions. The Administration interpreted this refusal to work the ships as sheer ingratitude on the part of the regular stevedores; on the other hand the natives were willing to take any risk that might eventually result in a voice in their own affairs. The fire was laid, and only a small spark was needed to bring it to a blaze.

When members of the Association turned to me, I suggested that it would be expedient for them to join the new Government-controlled labor Union, gain control of it and so come into their own responsibility. But the natives were opposed to the Union which they feared would sell them down the river for an unsatisfactory settlement. So the community lined up in open antagonism: on the one hand, those loyal to the Association, on the other, those loyal to the Administration. The fact that the Association was being used as a tool by political agitators seemed no concern to the people. They did not understand the meaning of "communism." But word of this friction got back to New Zealand and before long we were being visited by newspapermen and sociologists, some of whom in their curiosity turned to me.

For my part I agreed with the Islanders' resentment against the Government's attitude, but I could not agree to their cooperating with Communist agitators who were using their discontent as a lever. I now had the ear of the people, and when they begged me to represent them I said I would if they would agree to lay aside their antagonism to the Government. With this in mind, I called on the Commissioner and suggested that I be allowed to take an active part in the reorganization of the Association. To my disgust, this brought nothing but intense disapproval. It was impressed upon me that I was primarily a medical officer, not a citizen who should take an interest in a "political situation." I was told that I was exaggerating and that there was no emergency. If I wished to remain in the service of the Government, I had best leave the people to their own salvation.

In the midst of this dilemma I began to listen to the reports of an Islander named Puia. He was older than I, and his family had long been servants of my mother's family and, according to Polynesian custom, this position gave him a right to advise or warn me if he thought I was not doing the right thing. When I first met him, Puia bluntly informed me that I was a little too big for my boots. Shortly after this, he visited me in my office and said just as bluntly that he had been wrong. His candor intrigued me and we formed a lasting friendship.

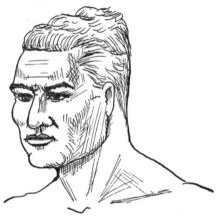

Puia was well loved and respected by his own people, but his insistence on fighting everyone's battles, both verbally and physically, did not endear him to those with whom he disagreed — and they were many.

It is difficult to tell what Puia looks like. One's first impression of him is of squareness; not above middle height, he is very powerfully built and the strength of his face is well in keeping. Ruggedness and aggressiveness are written all over him, but when one looks at his hands, square-palmed, fine-fingered and sensitive, one realizes more of the real man than one can read from his face. As he is an excellent talker, speaks reasonably good English and has been a light heavyweight boxing champion in his day, Puia invariably comes out on top in any argument. He proved to be a godsend to me, a reliable informant of the feelings of the younger people of the Island. Through Puia and the older men I really came to know the attitude of the people. I made up my mind to disregard the advice of the Administration and take an active part in native affairs.

I had made many friends among the European officials; even the Commissioner believed that I would be a good medical officer if only I would leave politics alone. The fact that I did not regard the present disturbance as "politics" troubled him not at all. Far away in New Zealand, disapproval of me was becoming only too evident, the current opinion there was that "Dr. Tom would be a nice guy if only," etcetera.

At this time, because she was expecting another child, Lyd was virtually immobilized. Bored with inactivity, she had decided to try her hand at writing magazine articles, a new departure for her but one at which she was successful. After what she had seen on our trip round the atolls and her close association with the present troubles, she was privately appalled at the risk I was running in sympathizing with what was to her a lost cause. As New Zealand editors were aware of my sympathies, they insisted on captioning her innocent articles with politically slanted titles, often giving them feature space. She now felt that because of me she too was being branded as a political agitator.

I had made up my mind that the Association must cease to be an organization directed only at improvement of labor conditions. Its first aim thus far had been to involve the Cook Islands in labor disputes when, for all to see, the land which in the Islands is the true source of prosperity and health still lay waste, neglected even more now that the owners were fully occupied in labor meetings. Agriculture, I argued again and again, must always be the basis of sound economy in the Islands, it was the foundation which assured them prosperity in the past. To back these words up I had to join the Association and take a leading position in its activities. At the risk of being branded a Communist agitator in the eyes of my Government, I did just that.

In truth, I was not at all sure just what a Communist really was, but felt sure I wasn't one. The reputation of the Association was so bad that I felt that Lyd and my friends might well be speaking the truth when they prophesied my dismissal, yet, as one who was at least in a part a Cook Islander by birth, I would have been ashamed to have acted otherwise.

As soon as it was known that I had been elected vice-president of the Association, officialdom set out to belittle me: they tried to discredit my medical skill, they held out on my liquor permits and on my gasoline allowance, and police were set to watch my house for any possible irregularity.

Matters came to a head when the next vessel arrived at the Island. Had the Government had its way, she would have been unloaded by members of the Union. But a leading official of the Association — and he was no Communist! — paddled out to the ship in a canoe, climbed aboard and put the case before the crew. The men sided with him and brought work to a standstill. But he was nabbed the moment he came ashore and taken to jail, charged with stealing a canoe; the fact that the canoe was village property and he himself part owner was ignored. Now the fire was really beginning to burn.

Officialdom made it still worse when next day they visited the ship in a body and persuaded the crew to co-operate with the Union in unloading the ship. This was the final spark for the Islanders. For ten years they had seen their European-type houses (of which they had once been so proud) go to ruin, their plantations of oranges and bananas revert to jungle for lack of shipping, and their own crude attempts to recover their economy hampered by lack of sympathy and understanding from those above. Now they had been divided into rival camps, and their anger was directed not only at the Administration but also at their own people who had joined the Union and taken their wages from them.

I knew they were angry, but I did not know that they were planning violence. Nor did they notify me, for they knew that I would try to stop them. But at eleven that evening my good friend, Fred Storey, shook me awake.

"Tom, for God's sake," he exclaimed, "get out of bed and do something. The Association is up in arms and really means business."

"Do you know what they are up to?" I asked.

"Yes," he said. "They are going after the Union members, and they'll beat them up. They'll release their own man from the jail. And if they are not stopped, they'll burn down the Commissioner's Residence. They really mean business. You've got to stop them."

The Rarotongan like all Polynesians is slow to anger (I know that myself), but once his anger is up he asks no quarter. If this came to blows, it could be a bloody and one-sided affair, for there were only 200 members of the Union whereas there were 4000 members listed in the Association, and the entire community was on their side.

Throwing on a dressing gown I drove down to where they were meeting. It was a turbulent mob of angry men and women gathered under the sharp radiance of a benzine lamp. I forced my way through them up to the veranda of a house and there under the light with my robe clutched around me I asked to be heard.

"Today," I said, "I'll admit that you've been outrageously provoked. I agree entirely with your feelings. For a long time now your economy has been wrecked. Today your living has been taken from you, and you've not had a fair hearing. I don't know whether this provocation has been deliberate or not, but I do know that if you go out and fight your own brother who happens to be on the other side, you are doing exactly what people you do not consider your friends hope you will do. The moment you begin to fight among yourselves, the moment you begin to fight among your own people, you have given them just cause to suppress you with the military force at their command. Do you honestly think that by burning down the house of your Government representative you will gain that assistance which I have been trying to get them to give you? Everything you intend to do now will prove that after all the Rarotongans are not kindly people but ingrates, and bad at the core."

"Bad?" growled a spokesman. "Of course we're bad. Haven't our administrators been telling us we're no good these many years past? All right, now we agree. We are no good, and we are not afraid to show how bad we are. Let us forget the things we know that will help us and our children. Rather would we forget the future and live on taro and fish again and be free as we were. We won't care then that people say we're bad. We'll be alone again and will not need to listen to them. And we don't want the assistance of people who have not given it to us in the past; we have no faith that they will give it to us in the future."

I pleaded with them to give me one more opportunity. "I have the power to bring these things you want so badly. You may not want them at this particular moment, but you will when you are calmer. New Zealand can be the market for

your goods; it can give your children the better education you
want. It can bring you better health. Give me the opportunity
to show you that this can come about peacefully even though
the road I take will often arouse your impatience, but give
me the opportunity."

Now they listened, wavered for a little, and then I had the
answer I had hoped to hear.

"Very well, what you have told us is perhaps after all the
right way. We will lay down our weapons because we believe
your word. But there is one thing we will not tolerate. Our
man must not remain in the prison. We shall go now and ask
that he be set free."

Under his leadership the mob — and I was glad to see that
they were unarmed — moved off in the direction of the Government offices. I went back to my car and drove home very
troubled in mind, and it was not until the following morning
that I heard what had happened. They had demanded to see
the Resident Commissioner and in answer to a telephone call
from his secretary he came down and faced them. The spokesman insisted that their man be released and spoke bitterly of
the injustice of his arrest; this came as a surprise to the commissioner for it transpired that he had not been informed by
the Chief of Police that the Islander had been imprisoned,
ostensibly for the theft of his canoe. He was no less disgusted
than the natives and acted promptly. He ordered the Chief of
Police to release the prisoner at once; he said publicly that he
was sorry this mistake had occurred and he urged the people
to go back to their homes.

The Commissioner told me later of his humiliation at having to make such a public disavowal of one of his own officers
at a time when the entire Administration needed his full support. But he was not in a mood to conciliate the members of

the Association and the atmosphere was still tense when within forty-eight hours a transport plane from New Zealand landed at Rarotonga and out marched eighteen of the largest military policemen, uniformed, fully armed, and obviously prepared to settle any trouble by force if necessary. Rarotonga was virtually under martial law, branded as a group of islands that had succumbed to the influence of Communism.

I was angry and I was worried. Here, in what we are pleased to call an enlightened age, was further evidence that the best means of settling misunderstanding is by the power of force rather than by intelligence. The police were ready to fight, so were the Islanders, the native women in particular had whipped themselves into a frenzy. Now they remembered the days when the Polynesians had not been a gentle people but warriors to the death. The show of arms proved to them that the only thing a European understands is force.

They came to me for advice, and I pointed out to them that it would be far better if they were to go out of their way to make friends with these police officers, invite them to their homes and teach them that the Cook Islanders were decent friendly people rather than a people so rebellious that they must be quelled by arms. It may have been difficult for them, but they promised to do their best.

I felt no qualms in continuing my attempt to influence the Association: the members were angry, sullen, and ashamed, but their enthusiasm for a co-operative society still prevailed. It was not very difficult to persuade them to disassociate themselves from the factions in New Zealand whose influence had proved so disastrous.

Then a new and unexpected channel opened for me. Roger Duff, a well-known New Zealand anthropologist who was actively interested in the situation in the Cook group, wrote

to a friend living in Rarotonga asking that he prepare a paper
on the Islands which could be presented to the Conference of
the Royal Society soon to be held in Wellington, New Zealand. Duff's friend immediately showed me the letter and suggested that I write the report. I had two weeks in which to
do it.

I was delighted to seize this opportunity of presenting the
truth of the situation as I saw it to a group of scientists and
inquirers whose evaluation of the facts would undoubtedly be
more unbiased than the newspaper reporters and Government
representatives who so far had been the only source of information to the New Zealand public of what was happening
to their tiny island possession. Calling my paper "Rarotonga
Today," I traced the current sociological degeneration back to
the days when, with the advent of the culture of white men,
the social system of the Islanders started to slough away. I
made no attempt to imply that the old ways were perfect,
but my résumé of present-day conditions — including the
poor housing, poor sanitation, inadequate education, uncertainty of land ownership, the lack of shipping facilities, the
poor nutrition, and, above all, the depressed mental outlook
that inevitably accompanied this state of economy — I hoped
would leave no doubt in the mind of the reader that an outburst such as the Cook Islanders had so recently taken part
in was inevitable. Lydia, who disapproved of the whole idea,
typed the manuscript and we sent it air mail.

Back by return post came an agitated letter from Duff sug-
gesting that if I did not tone down my statements I might be
involving myself in serious trouble. Duff was unaware that I
was already in sufficient trouble for a little more to make no
difference. I wrote him that I had simply been stating the
facts and let them speak for themselves. The paper was read

aloud in its entirety, and I was later told that it was the "sensation of the Conference." To those outside the medical profession who had been so ready to criticize my interest and activities in what seemed to be purely nonmedical matters, the realization came home that good economics do play an inescapably important part in the maintenance of good mental and physical health. Medical men, particularly those in the field of public health or in administrative positions, have always been aware of this truth, but that fact did not lessen the criticism that had descended on me.

Now that the members of so august a body as the Royal Society had shown sympathy with my reasoning, I hoped we would notice a change in the attitude of administrators generally towards the Cook Islanders and their problems.

I was no longer under a cloud because of my part in the Association, but this seemed to be my vulnerable year and it made me angry when I heard that I was being discredited because of my friendship with the native medicine men. There was talk that I too was dealing in "black magic." I could hardly blame officials for this interpretation as the medicine men had occasionally attributed to me supernatural powers that I knew only too well I did not possess. I felt a little foolish to be called to a case only to find that all that was expected of me was that I sit beside the patient and lay my hand on his brow. But I put up with this, for I had discovered that the medicine men were an invaluable liaison between my medicine and the public. In any community of the type found in the Cook Islands, the local medicine men always stand higher in the eyes of the people than the foreign doctor. These healers are intelligent men, and even today in the Islands they retain something of the status of the *taunga* of old, being respected as a source of native wisdom.

Because I listened to the medicine men, they willingly listened to all I told them of my methods, going back to the villages and repeating my lessons. I explained to them that some medicines could be taken by mouth, others it was necessary to inject directly into the body. I explained how vaccines and inoculations worked in the prevention of disease. They protested that in the past injections had been given and the patients died; I surmised that the injections had been forced on them only *in extremis*, and I said that today they were applied earlier and with real hope. I urged them to trust me. They said, "All right, but only if we are injected by you personally." Thus it took months to overcome this prejudice, but within the year they had gained enough faith to take injections from nurses and the assistant practitioners. This could never have been brought about without the missionary zeal of the medicine men.

So we broke down the fear of the sanatorium and the fear of autopsies; we built a spirit of co-operation rather than of antagonism between the medicine men and modern medicine, and above all we gave a new feeling of public confidence in the Fiji-trained assistant medical practioners. There were eight of them on duty throughout the Islands, natives all, and now at last they had the opportunity and incentive to use the modern methods with which I had been helping to indoctrinate them.

To insure good relations with the medicine men who saw that I was taking over a great deal of work which formerly had been in their hands, it was necessary to credit them with a commensurate amount of responsibility. This I could do by referring back to them psychological and psychiatric treatment in which field the medicine men excelled. Many a time I have listened to a medicine man interviewing a troubled patient and always I have been astounded at the effectiveness of his method, for he would talk not only to the stricken person but to his family, his wife, his parents, children (a participating audience of as many as ten relatives would be present), working right back to the patient's childhood and

digging, digging, until at last he brought aggravation to the surface.

We were also making slow, steady progress on another front. With the aid and direction of Mr. Walter Amos who had flown in from Fiji, we instituted a rigid program of mosquito control in the battle against filariasis. My chief considered this an unnecessary extravagance, but Mr. Amos and I continued to toil round the villages at night, lecturing the natives on the evils of careless rubbish disposal. Local Administration agreed that the whole program was unnecessary and would never prove of use in eliminating mosquitoes that had from time immemorial been part of the South Seas scenery: fortunately New Zealand's Prime Minister, ever a staunch supporter of aid to his Polynesian subjects, in support of us and the British Colonial Medical Service in Fiji, did not agree.

So Amos and I battled on, selecting boys and training them in field inspection and blood examination. Gradually every one in Rarotonga became overwhelmingly mosquito-conscious, to the extent that to have an empty tin lying in the garden was to court public disgrace. With breeding places cut to a minimum, the mosquitoes began to disappear, we hoped that filaria would go too, but it would take a long time and repeated surveys and blood tests before this could be ascertained. Our work was done on a grant of six hundred pounds a year.

The mosquito control program was at that time one of the projects for the benefit of the natives in force on the Island, and I was receiving wholehearted co-operation. This indicated to me that if the other departments would show interest and sympathy with the community, success in any other project that might be introduced would be assured. These came, as I hoped they would, but only gradually. Almost imperceptibly I noticed an awareness of native problems begin to rise in the administrators of other departments on the Islands. With the formation of a Legislative Council consisting of elected native members and nominated officials, there was open opportunity for the exchange of opinions. Natives' opinions were not always sympathetically received, but at least they were heard and recorded. Naturally, after so many years of silence in their own affairs, the natives were timid in expressing themselves at the beginning. Also they were not headlong in accepting my plan to convert the Association into a producers' co-operative. Although there were no further public demonstrations against the Administration, the main street of the village was always specked with clusters of serious-faced natives weighing the pros and cons. Association meetings were held almost daily now.

And at last the great day came. There had been a deal of

hammering and sawing going on at one particular part of the village street, and gradually a small office appeared, neatly painted but with no indication (at least not to those who were not in the know) of what the nature of this structure might be. Then one day every European official in Rarotonga, every trader, every white resident, and each member of each family, all were invited to a great feast. And there, large-lettered in black on a white board nailed across the top of the new building, ran the words, "OFFICES OF THE COOK ISLANDS PRODUCERS' CO-OPERATIVE SOCIETY."

That feast, the first of many in which the Co-op joined with the Administration in feting notable visitors to Raro-tonga, was, I thought, a very gracious gesture — and how different from that angry outbreak so narrowly avoided but a short time ago. When the leaders of the Co-op lifted the great roast pigs from the traditional ovens, the orator for the day said with a smile:

"Friends of the Co-operative Association: We wish to apologize to you and to our ancestors who are looking down on us today. If those ancestors were here in our place, it would not be pig that we would be serving you, for the greatest honor we can bestow on a guest to whom we wish to extend our friendship would be nothing so lowly as roast pig. Instead it would be roast man. And so we ask you to forget what you have seen, and go back to the past and pretend that today's gesture is higher than you know it to be in reality."

That feast in its way marked the beginning of a new era for us all. Our house was now full of comings and goings. Puia who now had encouraging reports was always waiting for me on my return home. His honesty, loyalty, wisdom and logic more than made up for any of his occasional lapses from so-briety and at that time he never made any vows to mend his ways. If he stumbled into private gardens during one of his little bouts, he did not intend to trespass, and when I paid his small fines he more than expressed his gratitude in the kindness and help he gave my household.

From the native medicine men I started a collection of songs, poems and legends, and translated them for Lyd to re-write for use in the local schools, a transcription she could easily do in the long days as she sat waiting for Timothy's arrival.

The policy of the Administration in improving native welfare had not changed overnight but we could all see and feel the difference. The Association had by this time been reorganized into a Co-operative Producers' Society aimed at a policy of economic improvement through agriculture. It had a long way to go but at least we had made a start. The next step towards mutual sympathy, perhaps stirred on by "Rarotonga Today," was when within the year the Government instituted scholarships to native children so that they might have an education in New Zealand that would fit them to return to positions presently filled by Europeans. Everything promised a turn for the betterment of the Islanders and my long period of uncertainty seemed at an end.

The military police were removed from Rarotonga, and I never will forget their leave-taking. They were well tanned, having spent most of their time sun-bathing on the beaches by the lagoons. Each of them had fallen in love, at least once, if not oftener, with the daughters of homes which had treated them in the time-honored custom of hospitality to guests. These men, who had come to Rarotonga with chins outthrust and revolvers at the ready, left with tears in their eyes, holding tightly to fragrant *ei* and the handmade gifts of the people they had learned to love.

CHAPTER XIII

The Cricket

TOM took me to the hospital on the expected date and delivered our second son. Timothy was everything he should be, the right size and the right sex. Most important of all, as I had imported a large stock of baby food several months before, he was happily consuming large quantities of milk out of bottles. The baby was healthy, so was I, and when the steamer brought letters from all over the world congratulating Tom on his Royal Society article "Rarotonga Today," which had been made into a pamphlet by the Polynesian Society and circulated to scientific societies, I even began to stop expecting my world to dissolve into ignominy and to believe that in supporting the Islanders Tom had made the right decision. Our house was always full of people and I now began to enjoy the arguments and discussions on the future of the Cook Islands, lasting far into the night.

John was overwhelmingly proud at the acquisition of a little brother; he could not wait for the day when he would be allowed to push the new pram along the main road. To John there had never been such a remarkable baby born into this world. Timothy straightway settled to the normal routine of baby life; sleeping peacefully and waking with the clock, he seemed the most ordinary of children.

Then it happened. Just fifteen days after he was born, I looked in on him in the afternoon as he lay in his cot. He was sleeping as soundly as usual, in half an hour it would be time for his evening meal. I tiptoed out of the room so that he would not be disturbed ahead of time.

I returned half an hour later to find him in convulsions with his face quite blue.

"Tom, Tom!" I called. "Come quickly, Timmy is ill."

Tom looked at the baby and gave me a thermometer. I held it under his arm, and, reading the mercury, saw to my horror that his temperature was 107 degrees.

Tom and I looked at each other in silence. I think each of us was remembering that day just a year before when I had held the still body of a neighbor's infant that only a few hours earlier had been alive and healthy.

"I'll go for penicillin and oxygen," Tom said. "Keep trying to get some kind of fluid into him. I'll be back as quickly as I can."

I held my baby close to me, convinced that he would not live for more than another half-hour. I knew that this was the fulminating pneumonia so fatal to children we had been trying to save in the tropics.

I sent one of the girls to fetch Tom's mother: she had been so proud of her new grandson. All the time I kept thinking that I ought to cable some word of warning to my parents. Meantime I sat holding Tim in my arms striving to be still for fear that some small movement might cause him shock or hemorrhage.

I did not have to wait long for Tom to return, and his mother arrived almost as soon as he did. For Timmy, every breath was becoming more harsh and labored, and I could no longer get him to take milk for he could not close his lips to suck. The girls brought me warm boiled water and as he gasped I kept dropping this on his lips.

My mother-in-law, who had run all the way from her house, was frightened.

"Give him to me, Lydia, and I'll rub him," she said holding out the small bottle of scented coconut oil she had brought with her, the only remedy she knew that might help a dying baby.

"No, Mother," Tom warned. "Don't disturb him, just let Lyd hold him still and keep on with the water. I think these injections will help better than any disturbance."

"Whatever you say, son. Thank God you learned to be a doctor." She laid aside her precious oil and set to work to help make the baby more comfortable.

The word of Timmy's illness spread quickly, and soon friends, neighbors, both Islanders and Europeans, and even those who had been critical of us, were gathering on our veranda standing by to give what help they might, or the condolence they dreaded. Timmy's cot was placed on the open veranda for the weather was hot and oppressive, and beneath the oxygen tent, improvised from cot sheets, he fought on for his life.

Tom had brought from the hospital a large tray covered with a dressing sheet. He told me that he was about to do a blood count on the baby and asked me personally to supervise the sterilization of the instruments he would need. Reluctantly I left the side of the cot and went out to the kitchen.

When I returned a few minutes later, Tom told me that he would not need the instruments I had made ready, and on looking at the baby I felt actually nauseated to see that into his chest Tom had inserted two coarse cannulas. Now an intravenous stand stood beside the cot, and through the cannulas trickled a saline mixture to give Timmy nourishment that he no longer had the strength to take by mouth. I realized why Tom had inveigled me out of the room, he knew that neither I nor any mother could have borne to see those thick needles inserted into such a tiny baby: how he brought himself to perform that operation on his own child I will never know.

Besides the intravenous drip of saline, we injected penicillin, morphine and other sedatives subcutaneously every three hours. Tom and I treated Tim in turns, every injection an agony to us, but we had to save his life! My mother-in-law and the three European nursing sisters from the hospital spelled each other sitting beside his cot, regulating the flow of oxygen, watching the drip.

At ten o'clock at night the electricity was turned off and we kept our watch by kerosene lamps. We had no refrigerator in which to keep the penicillin, and used a thermos flask filled with ice from the hospital refrigerator. There was not even an electric fan to cool the air. The four cylinders of oxygen, all we had in stock on the island, were without indicators. When we changed a cylinder we held our breaths for we had no way of knowing what their contents might be. The second cylinder we turned on proved to be empty, the other two stood ready, their exteriors no indication of their contents, grim like a threat of death.

Because I felt certain the baby could not live, I sent for the Protestant missionary asking him to perform baptism. It was a dismal ceremony. I could not shut out the memory of John's christening in the quiet church — lace-edged gown, the carved stone baptismal font, and above all the pride and congratulations that were ours for that day. And now there was only fear.

Even the missionary showed this as he hastily poured a little tap water into the top of a thermos bottle, blessed it briefly, then, for only a second, removed the oxygen mask to sprinkle a tiny drop on Timmy's forehead. This was no time for the selection of godparents. Tom's mother, my closest woman friend, Myra Wingfield, the wife of our dentist, the village chief, and the old medicine men were the only ones with us.

The words of encouragement given us by the pastor, "Now your child is in the hands and care of God," could not hide the good man's pity for what I could plainly see he regarded as the inevitable loss of our baby.

All day and all night the natives sat cross-legged on the lawn outside the veranda, silently hoping. In the evenings they left quietly to go to their meetinghouses and join in a prayer to save the life of a small child. For three whole days Timmy struggled on, gasping in air and oxygen that his congested lungs had barely room for. At noon on the fourth day I felt that now I must stop hoping, for life had gone. Breathing had ceased, there was no sign of a pulse, and when Tom removed the oxygen mask and turned off the saline he did not need to tell me the truth.

Tom left the room: he was experiencing, as was I, the first deep thrust of personal grief. I lifted the mosquito net over the cot and sat down to hold that cold and blue little hand just once more. Our friends had left the room, only my mother-in-law and I remained now. I raised my eyes from the still little body, and there on the net above me I saw a strange thing. A green cricket sat perched on the mesh; no ordinary cricket, but one bigger than I had ever imagined, a good seven inches in length. When I raised my hand to flick it away, it remained motionless, only its antennae moving gently. Then I saw the grandmother smile in her tears.

"That is a messenger of good tidings. Leave it be, perhaps it will stay a while. And look! Look at Timmy!"

I could not believe my eyes, for the baby was breathing again. We were watching a miracle. On each inspiration of breath, Timmy threw his arms out sideways, expanding his chest to gulp down a fraction more of life. In and out, jerkily as though being pulled by unseen hands, the frail arms threshed against the sides of the cot. Gradually the horrible darkness faded from his face, gradually the pulse in the neck returned and quivered to greater strength.

I looked around and saw Tom beside me. "It's all right, Lyd, a moment ago something told me it would be this way. He's going to live now we have known our own sorrow."

High up on the edge of the net, the giant cricket waved its antennae and my mother-in-law nodded her head, smiling now.

"The gods have brought our son back, the cricket will stay. Tomorrow we will make a feast of thanksgiving."

Although a power we could not understand was working a miracle for Timmy, we continued to give him all the help that modern medicine and the resources of our Island could provide. The injections and the constant watch by day and by night continued; sometimes it seemed that the baby lapsed again yet always he fought on, too weak even to cry but strong enough to hold onto his small shred of this world. The injections numbered seventy, then eighty, and after eighty-seven we stopped counting: we were afraid to keep count. Even if the baby came out of this illness, we could expect difficulties from those myriad skin punctures some of which, despite the constant check we were keeping on asepsis, would inevitably become septic in this humid weather.

The hospital staff brought over dressing trays so that we would be ready to meet this contingency. Yet four days after Tom regarded it as safe to discontinue treatment, there was not a single mark on the tiny body. Even the two deep wounds in the chest where the cannulas had been strapped had completely vanished. Timothy was emaciated and exhausted after two weeks of desperate illness, but his skin was as clear and unmarked as the day he was born.

Neither Tom nor I nor his mother had slept for weeks, snatching moments of rest that never lasted more than a half hour at a time. The girls from my kitchen had behaved magnificently. I had not been near them since the first day of the illness, yet all the way through they continued to serve regular meals and do all the marketing without troubling me for instructions. For myself, then and for weeks afterwards, I found it quite impossible to take solid food, existing only on myriad cups of tea. My mother-in-law and my friends brought us delicacies for those who were being so helpful, but I just couldn't swallow.

I felt so bitterly ashamed. All along I had doubted the wisdom of Tom's drastic medical treatment of the child. I had

not said as much but each change of drug, each new treatment, I thought would prove fatal, Tom's mistake. Fear of
inflicting some additional pain on the baby had reduced me
to the stage where I could not touch him. I had tried to give
the injections, but when my needle drew a drop of blood I
could not go on. Gnawing indecision as to whether or not I
should let my mother and father know that the baby was so
ill tortured me. This was not something on which I could ask
advice from either Tom or his mother, and I could not reach
a decision by myself. I kept on shrinking from the responsibility of shocking my family, yet all the time the prospect of
notifying them of Timmy's death loomed even larger in this
balance of decision. I felt desperately on my own and inadequate for this trial. Tom and his mother, and even people who
were almost strangers, were the ones making the decisions, I
was the one wringing my hands.

I tried hard to make up for what I considered my failure
by attending to the small things that I knew were almost unnecessary. I kept the cigarette box filled, the lamps burning,
the injections mixed, and the syringes sterilized.

When the baby started to recover, I felt more ashamed than
ever: ashamed that I had doubted Tom's judgment, yet with
all this there crept in a conviction that I would never need to
doubt again, would never need to make a decision as long as
Tom was with me. I felt almost as if I could now fold my
hands and sit back for the rest of our life together, but I also
knew that even though our family would be safe this was not
the end of jeopardy or danger.

I now shared the belief of the island people that some en-
tity we could not see was caring for our child, perhaps the
strength and sincerity of the emotions of these people had
played a greater part than we realized: in their hopes and

prayers lay a power of healing far stronger than any practical medical aid.

During those bitter days the unqualified generosity of heart shown us by residents on the Island, from some of whom we could have expected nothing, was an inspiration we shall never forget. The missionary, of whose methods of conversion we had openly disapproved, had baptized our child and expressed a belief in Timmy's recovery which he afterwards confessed he had never for a moment genuinely felt. The Resident Commissioner, who had been for so long at complete odds with us, could not have been kinder in this time of need. Each evening he too went down to the meetinghouse and sat with the natives to join his prayers with theirs. Years afterwards he put into words what I had been feeling when he told me, "Lyd, if it hadn't been for the prayers of the people that child would never have lived. I have never seen greater sincerity of worship and prayer than the Rarotongans showed at that dreadful time." Through his sympathy and helpfulness Tom and I came to a better understanding of this man whose directives had often seemed to us utterly wrong. So there began an interchange of ideas that was to result in a lasting friendship. But there was no healing the rift between Tom and the Senior Medical Officer.

Our native friends had proved themselves staunch beyond belief. Puia came and went in the sickroom, tiptoeing to the side of the cot, returning to the garden to report back to the natives waiting outside. The chief of our little village stayed in the house day and night, helping Tom with equipment and sterilizing instruments with an attention to detail that would have put many a trained nurse to shame. This good man would leave the room only when injections were given, he could not bear to see the baby hurt. The medicine men regulated the oxygen while Tom and I snatched a few minutes sleep, and I remember the gentleness with which they eased Timmy in his semi-sitting-up position. Myra Wingfield deserted her own delicate child to stay with me all the way through.

It wasn't easy for all these people to devote so much of their time to us for we were not the only ones in trouble. Early in Tim's convalescence an epidemic of whooping cough broke out in Rarotonga; there was an insufficient supply of drugs to treat the victims and the death rate amongst the young children shot up appallingly. We forget how virulent whooping cough can be under poor living conditions. Out of Rarotonga's total population of almost 6000, over 300 infants died, a ghastly record that stands as a grim reminder in the Government reports of the Cook Islands for 1947. Tom was out day and night and now it was our turn to comfort those who had comforted us.

During this crisis I came at last to understand my mother-in-law. She never rested, never slept, and was never out of reach of her grandson. Her faith and acquiescence in Tom's efforts amazed me, for it must have been hard for her to watch the apparent torture that was being inflicted on the tiny baby: yet never once did she question her son's actions. Yet her faith was wholly Polynesian. She was sure that as long as the cricket stayed Timmy would get well, and it did stay. For ten days it clung to the mesh of the mosquito net, an omen of good fortune to every Rarotongan that saw it. The natives would pop their heads over the open veranda and ask, "Is the cricket still there?" On being told that it was, they would go away relieved.

My mother-in-law's trust in native methods played an important part medically. When it was discovered that

Timmy was suffering from internal hemorrhage, she took a small piece of boiled calico, dipped it into a bowl of coconut cream and put it to his lips: this was the way her own mother had soothed painful tummyaches. This brought the baby relief and it gave him added nourishment and strength as he lay sucking the rich cream off the tiny piece of cloth.

For one whole month my mother-in-law stayed beside the child, and the strain of Tim's illness and lack of sleep left their indelible mark on her features. In the long afternoons she talked to me of her troubled life in a way that gave me greater insight into my own difficulties of adjustment to this island way of living.

She told me the story of her unhappy marriage, perhaps not appreciating the significance of her words and not knowing that those very things which had wrecked her life were the very ones that had produced my antagonism to her. She told me the story of the rich young girl who had met and married in New Zealand a man who had never been to the South Seas and who had no conception of what life there would hold for him. She told how, when she and her young husband came to Rarotonga, the impositions demanded by her family had proved intolerable to the stranger in the house, so much so that he had stayed only three weeks and then returned alone to New Zealand rather than make the attempt to fit into his wife's way of life, or to make a new way for himself.

She told how she had borne her first child alone, and then leaving her baby, Tom's sister Mary, had traveled back to New Zealand by herself to try again to persuade her husband to make the effort to adjust himself to a normal life with her. At this time she showed no animosity towards the man who had been so adamant in his refusal to live on the Island she loved. "Tom's father was a good man, Lydia, but I bore two children alone, with no home of my own as other women had. If I had been educated in New Zealand instead of Tahiti and had been more used to the ways of the city, things might have been different, but my father, although always promising that I should have the education that was my right, would not let me go away from him. I was his only child, and I cannot blame him. I could not make a home for Mary and Tom, and to me divorce seemed the best way."

I knew she would never understand how different was my outlook from hers; I only hoped that she might forgive me in making my life and that of her son so different and so separate from the one she had planned for us. Now I loved her people, but I did not think that I, or any other European, could ever come to understand them as she and Tom did, for that understanding is beyond a man of another race. I determined that, unlike my father-in-law, I would never give up the struggle but would see my marriage through, compromising by giving whatever concrete help I could when any Islander might need it, and should this help be misdirected or apparently unappreciated, I would try to avoid disappointment in the knowledge that I was doing my best at least as I saw it.

CHAPTER XIV

... And Cure My Own

IT is a sensitive matter to treat one's own flesh and blood, as every physician knows. During those days when Tim hovered between life and death I prescribed and performed all his treatment by myself. The moment I diagnosed the symptoms of fulminating pneumonia I went to the Senior Medical Officer, described what I was doing, and asked his advice. I found him lying down on his veranda sofa, and he seemed only mildly concerned. "Nothing serious," he said. "Give him small doses of tincture opii." He never once offered to cross the few yards to my house and examine our child.

Tim was then only fifteen days old, too young as yet to have roused deep emotion in me as his father. But as the days went on and despite my efforts the child made no progress, I found my feelings were involved and multiplying until the anticipation of giving still another injection into that heaving little body was agony to me. When I saw that fluid infusion was vital if Tim's life was to be prolonged, in despair I again went to my chief, told him of the type of infusion I thought best for so young a child and again asked his advice and help. His response was the same as before — more doses of tincture opii — although now my anguish over Tim's condition must have been only too obvious to him. When I left my chief and returned to the sickroom alone I knew that I would have to insert the giant cannulas into that tiny chest by myself, and I was filled with horror at what I had to do and with fury that another doctor, no matter what his personal feelings towards me might be, would offer no assistance.

The Resident Commissioner as soon as he had realized the gravity of the situation came straight to our house; his genuine sympathy went far to relieve the constraint there had been between us, and his offer to help us in any way possible touched Lydia and me.

Twenty-four hours after the saline infusion had been given, the last remedy I could think of, I could find no sign of pulse or breathing. The little face was blue and without a flicker of life. I went away to my study to be alone with my anger and humiliation. As many a father has done on the loss of his son, I railed at God. I thought I had done everything that could be done, yet I had been cursed with failure. Now for the first time I was learning the meaning of personal grief, and it was bitter.

And as I sat alone, trying to reason through my despair, as clearly as though a voice had spoken to me aloud, I knew that the test was over and that at that moment a miracle was being performed. As I approached the bedside again, I hardly needed to look at the baby to know that life was returning. I bent over him, observed that his breathing was noticeable, and when I put my stethoscope on his chest I could hear his little heart quite distinctly. At that moment I knew that as long as I could supply him with fluid by transfusion the chances of his recovery were good. But I also knew that I would have to continue these drastic measures for an indefinite period. I winced at the thought of having to use those large cannulas on such a frail little body and so indeed did my neighbors who remonstrated at the sight, and I feared for the period of sloughing and the scars that they would leave behind them when at last the time came to remove them. I can never explain how it happened, but only a few days after they were removed there was not a mark on Tim's skin.

Timmy was really beginning his convalescence and Lydia and I were catching up on our sleep, when out of the blue came the epidemic of whooping cough. Within a matter of days it was a serious threat to the whole Island for the adults were just as vulnerable to it as their children. While whooping cough is not in itself a serious complaint, the complications that go with it can be very serious indeed. The risk of pneumonia is always present and especially if there is an insufficiency of medical care and drugs. We suffered from both of these deficiencies in Rarotonga. The policy of economy shut off our supply of drugs and, to make things worse, the truant officers were ordered to see that the children were returned to school at the earliest possible moment. I went to my chief to protest against both these measures.

"Dr. Davis," he said, "merely because a few children on this Island have whooping cough is no reason for you to start handing out drugs right and left. It is the responsibility of the parents to look after the children, and the issue of drugs I have made available is quite sufficient to cope with the situation. I can assure you that the drugs you have are enough . . . and they're all you're going to get."

Since his reassurance did nothing to ease the situation, I called the assistant medical practitioners together for what was a council of war.

"What drugs have you got for these children?" I asked them.

"Only aspirin, Doctor, and it isn't enough for pneumonia. The penicillin has to be issued on the chief's signature, and

the next best thing, sulphadiazine, is locked in his office in
the hospital. We just can't get hold of any."

"In his office, eh?" I said. "Well, have you noticed that
when he goes off to his morning tea he doesn't always lock
the office? If the sulphadiazine is still in that cupboard, next
time he has his morning break we'll pick the lock and steal
the stuff. God knows, we need it."

The practitioners were a little shocked. "That's all very
well, Dr. Tom, but if we get caught stealing those drugs you
know it will be the end of things for us. We can't do it."

"Look, boys. We have to make a decision between ethics
and live children. When I was coming over to the hospital today, I saw a child on a bicycle so racked by that damned
whooping cough that he crashed off his bike and lay coughing
and vomiting in the dirt at the side of the road. The mothers
tell me that they must keep sending the children to their lessons before they're well because they're afraid of the truant
officers. If the kids are going to die in the ditches because we
can't get at that medicine, I'll welcome the scandal if I'm
caught stealing. There goes the old man for his morning tea.
You keep watch for me."

And so every day I performed my housebreaking. The loss
of the pills was never noticed because the chief never checked
the containers. Even so, the death rate among preschool and
school children was alarming. So alarming that good Lionel
Trenn, in his capacity as Registrar, was horrified at the rising
death rate, and in his agitation reported the true state of affairs to the Resident Commissioner.

The routine that followed would have been funny if it
had not been so pitiful. Of course the ruthless record of the
death figures was a matter that would be of concern to New
Zealand, and as such had to be reported to the mother coun-

try most carefully. The Commissioner, always a stickler in the wording of his radiograms to headquarters, used the word "excessive" in describing the death toll. The Senior Medical Officer pooh-poohed the use of that word "excessive." The Commissioner insisted that he was right. The doctor got redder and redder in the face. For two days the argument on the use or abuse of the English language continued, but the Commissioner was vindicated in the end. The word "excessive" did it.

New Zealand demanded of the Senior Medical Officer why the deaths had been "excessive"; he was reminded that medicine necessary in an emergency would be flown in by special plane if he so requested. Furthermore headquarters asked had not the required drugs been in good supply? Why had they not been used? (No one ever discovered that in part they had been used, if illegally, but by the time I took my desperate measures the damage had been done.)

Very shortly after that my chief resigned and left the Cook Islands for good: whether by request or by his own volition I was never to know. It was enough that he was out. His resignation roused in me no feelings of gratification, merely a sense of frustration at the months that had been wasted. It was too much to expect that I would be promoted to the position he vacated, and I was cheered when an older friend from medical school days, Pat Irwin, arrived to take up the position as my senior.

Pat was cheerful, hard-working, good-natured, and very, very fat. He intended to stay in the Cook Islands only as long as his present contract with the Government lasted, a further eighteen months. His wife was a hopeless cripple, and Pat was eager to take her back to New Zealand where she could find greater comfort and attention. Pat felt sure that he was acting only as a stopgap until I should be made chief, and accordingly he gave me *carte blanche*, working along with me to restore the Department which in the last twelve months had been so rudely disorganized. Pat's favorite occupation was drawing up fantastically long lists of hospital stores. God knows they were needed and, in view of the recent disaster, so much of which could be traced directly to medical economy, we were assured of receiving all we asked for. The storerooms went from the ridiculous to the sublime, the walls bulged and the surplus overflowed. Now the hospital was once more a place of cheerfulness and in the Medical Department a patient could be given a more effective cure for his ills than a couple of aspirin tablets.

Visitors

PAT IRWIN lost no time in restoring the standards of the hospital: he gave Tom every support in new projects, and since there were now two doctors working together in harmony the scope and the efficiency of the whole service improved. In off hours Pat was an ardent radio fan; when he was not signing stores lists, he was tapping his Morse key. He came and went at our house, borrowing radio tubes, getting his gear and Tom's in a hopeless muddle, but always cheerful and friendly with his assistant . . . that is, except for those times when the two of them were reduced to violence in an argument over the ownership of a certain radio condenser that had mysteriously walked across the lawn separating our two houses. Pat even joined with Tom in approving the activities of the natives who were by this time proudly displaying the sign "HEADQUARTERS COOK ISLANDS PRODUCERS' CO-OPERATIVE SOCIETY."

An experienced child nurse arrived in Rarotonga just in time to rescue Timmy from a relapse. Nurse Aulin bustled round the house, giving the baby her constant attention and working always to alleviate my fears for him. Despite Tom's certainty that Tim would get well, it was months before I believed that this was true.

Then came a friendly event which touched us closely — Robert Dean Frisbie and his family sailed in from Samoa. Being in frail health, he went to see Tom at once; and Tom took him home to meet me. He soon became a daily visitor to our house; he took a genuine interest in my feeble literary efforts and willingly spent hours instructing me in the work which was gradually holding my interest. Contrary to my expectations Tom and I found Frisbie good company.

In the days I knew him, this is what he looked like. He was a slender man, seeming much younger than his fifty years. He had the longest chin and the deepest-set eyes I have ever seen. I never saw him other than meticulously well dressed: he always wore American army issue khaki, a solar topee set well to one side of his head, distinguished polaroid glasses on his nose, and jutting from the corner of his mouth, a hazard to anyone who might bump into him suddenly, an eight-inch handmade bamboo cigarette holder. He said this was to keep the smoke out of his eyes when he was writing. I suspect he felt it lent him distinction. Frisbie rode everywhere by bicycle, he always carried a notebook in his pocket, and it was not unusual to find him sitting on his bike, propped against a handy coconut tree, jotting down one of his imperishable thoughts in his little black book.

"Go away," he would say if one stopped to say hello. "Can't you see I'm giving birth? Wait for me at the next coconut tree."

Frisbie was always accompanied by one of his children, if not by all four. Papa, Jakie, Florence (nicknamed Johnny), Elaine and Nga were very much of a family. He never missed a moving picture, running up colossal credit accounts with the local movie theater so that he and his entire brood could sit in the front row and lick ice-cream cones while they watched the uncertain and often interrupted running of Rarotongan movie projectors. The whole lot of them went five times a week: they would sit through the greatest trash and the only time I remember them walking out before "God Save the King" was the night a hurricane warning was flashed on the screen. Everyone else sat still, but Frisbie had not forgotten the horrors of the hurricane he had survived on Suvarrow Atoll, five years before.

In the midst of all this and to my great joy, Dad paid us a visit. Although I had never complained or discussed my troubles in my letters home, my mother's intuition had told her that life here was difficult for me to adjust to. Yet she preferred to remain in New Zealand knowing that my father would make sure that things were not too intolerable. I think her reluctance to make the long trip was founded mainly on her persistent nervousness with native people. I had told neither my mother or father of Timmy's illness; however, Dad alighted from the plane a very worried man. . . . I had not reckoned with the rapidity with which rumor travels in the South Seas. A member of the plane crew, acting in good faith no doubt, had told him in Fiji that the Davis baby was desperately ill.

Dad need not have worried. After Timmy's return visit from heaven one would have expected the child to have retained an ethereal quality, in fact the opposite was the case. All that infant thought of was food. He guzzled all day, gulped down double rations, burped, closed his eyes for five minutes then yelled that he was starving.

"For the twenty years I've looked after sick babies," said Nurse Aulin, "never have I struck one like this. Three weeks ago a skeleton, now a balloon."

"Yaaaaaa," bawled Timmy, "I haven't eaten for ten whole minutes."

Nurse shifted her bed into Timmy's room so that she could

keep feeding him all night. If she hadn't been so proud of her baby elephant she would no doubt have dropped in her tracks from lack of sleep. Because to the natives Timmy was a very special child, he had no lack of nursemaids and admirers and became a small king in his own right, a position which, in order to gain more food, he exploited to its fullest. We had given him the middle name of Ito, the name of Tom's great-grandfather who had been the last practicing Polynesian navigator. I doubted very much if Timmy would ever stop thinking of food long enough to pause to consider a noon sight.

Johnny was very proud of his brother. All through the long weeks of his illness when the house had been so silent, so full of strangers and so tense in atmosphere, he had quietly merged into the background, uncomplaining at the lack of attention and hoping as much as the adults that Tim would live. How well I remember him lining up a deputation of his small friends, ordering them to remove their shoes, and then leading them in single file to the side of the cot to look at his most cherished possession.

Even now, years later when Tim has grown to be more aggressive than John ever was, the elder still treats his brother as if he might break in half any minute. As long as John is with Timmy, I feel sure that all will be well.

Dad's arrival in our house was rather like Christmas day, his luggage seemed to be filled with gifts rather than clothes. He had even miraculously managed to sneak several bottles of Black Label Johnny Walker past the various customs officers he had met en route. But his prize offering was a large blue ring for me. The only finger it would fit was my engagement finger.

"Lydia," gasped my lady friends, "how marvelous of Tom to give you that wonderful sapphire."

I did not bother to correct them on the origin of my gem, but on reporting the remarks to Dad he shouted with glee.

"Sapphire! Since when do you think I'd buy you a sapphire as big as a pigeon's egg. It's a spinel but you needn't tell anyone that."

Now the truth is out. I haven't got a sapphire, only a spinel; but referring back to a certain day in a registrar's office in 1940, how could I have a sapphire, or even a small diamond?

It took Dad about five minutes to collect all the "island characters."

"A swell old gent," said Captain Andy, "dat Mr. Henderson. Sir, come to my veranda and we will proceed to discuss life."

"Very handsome man," said the natives. "Cuts his hair a funny way though."

Never was Dad so sensitive about his lack of hair: it wasn't his fault typhoid fever had robbed him of his locks.

Tom's study, never a peaceful nook nor yet a tidy one, soon resembled the private bar of a men's club; Nurse Aulin and I were allowed in only by special invitation. To add to the general confusion, came our friend Dr. Eric Bridgeman, the man who had brought medicine to the isolated tribes of the New Zealand Polynesians. Nurse brought her friends, Dad brought his, Bridgy added his collection, and Tom brought the whole Island. I tried hard to block my ears and write something that might bring a word of praise from Frisbie, also occupying Tom's study.

"Lyd," said Dad cheerfully, "you're living in a madhouse, but it's a pleasant one."

The elegant philosophy that seeped out the door of Tom's study to us three women held us spellbound. Frisbie, Andy,

Tom and Dad expounded far into the night on the best means of correcting the whole world. Dr. Bridgeman disagreed with everyone on principle, the rest sat open-mouthed and marveled at the wit and wisdom of the ringleaders.

Dad thought, as I had, that Tom's activities on behalf of the natives were risky, nevertheless he gave advice to Tom and the native leaders from his experience in matters of commerce, advice which was to prove invaluable. I knew that he would return to New Zealand and set my mother's heart at rest, perhaps show her that "the Islands" were not such a bad place after all.

Mysterious visitors in the employ of the Government still asked questions regarding Tom's interest in native affairs, but we were no longer uncertain of what our attitude to these people should be. We wined and dined them, gave special parties for them and disagreed when they suggested that Tom would be well advised to get on with his medicine and to mind his own business. Occasionally the combination of climate and alcohol unsealed their lips and they would "spill the beans" and quite openly tell Tom that as far as New Zealand was concerned they had inside information that he was on his way out of the Cook Islands. Myra Wingfield and her husband helped us in reducing these inquiring souls to maudlin frankness, taking particular pleasure in insuring that when they climbed aboard the plane out of Rarotonga they were sick, sad and sorry.

Our friends still expected the worst but Tom was convinced that very soon his superiors in New Zealand would come to the realization that not only he but the people of the Cook Islands, too, were working towards progress and deserved to have their actions approved by their Government.

With the change of medical officers, the hospital again became a very busy place. Natives formed queues outside Tom's office asking for surgical treatment and they were joined by Islanders from territories outside the Cook group. That is how I came to know Maria.

Maria had been living for many years in Tahiti. Once, suffering from ordinary toothache, she had visited the local dentist in Papeete and emerged from his office (her tooth extracted) with a complete paralysis of the left side of her face. The dentist had accidentally severed her facial nerve.

Now when the doctors of Tahiti suggested that she required removal of her appendix, Maria hastened down to Rarotonga to let Dr. Tom do the job. It proved that she required removal of her gall bladder, not her appendix, an operation that would entail a short period of convalescence; she would have to find somewhere to live until she was fit to return to Tahiti. Beds in the hospital were at a premium and she had no friends on our Island. Tom had long ago formed the habit of sending convalescent patients over to me so that he could keep an eye on them.

I already had a boy, Potiki, occupying the outside room — and what a nuisance he was. He was suffering from tuberculosis of the hip; each time we rested him sufficiently for the sinus to close up he would go off to a beer party, get drunk, fall off his bicycle and be back where he'd started. Poor Potiki, I had decided that he would be occupying the convalescent's room for the rest of his life but I had not reckoned with the strength of character of the new patient.

Maria made her entrance into our lives with a flourish. Other patients would come to the house very timidly, their meager possessions knotted up in a small *pareu* bundle, and obediently follow the rules as laid down by the housegirls.

Not so Maria. She commandeered the hospital ambulance and a couple of groundsmen to shift her vast collection of goods and chattels and, with a cigarette hanging out of the corner of her mouth, supervised the disposal of her boxes, bundles and parcels just where she wanted them. The fact that Potiki was already in possession of her room worried her not at all. She knew he had been disobeying doctor's orders and in short

shrift Potiki and his belongings were out in the street. As soon as things were arranged to her satisfaction, she came into the house to meet me and inspect the premises.

I stared at Maria in awe. She was about my own age and height but two and a half times as broad; her thick black hair was upswept in the latest Parisian style, a large hibiscus drooping coyly from her left ear. Her dress advertised the gaiety of fabulous Tahiti: gardenias, pineapples, breadfruit and canoes in red, yellow and shocking pink gamboled all over a royal blue silk background. And Maria wore high-heeled shoes. More than that, unlike any other native girl I had seen shod in this way, she didn't wobble when she walked, that is, her heels didn't, but the rest of her did, most noticeably. Maria was obviously "different."

"Who does your washing, Mrs. Tom?" she asked, looking me over critically.

"At the moment Nga is doing it, but we change laundresses every couple of weeks in this household, Maria."

"As soon as I'm well, we change that," she snapped.

She peered into every room, ran her finger along dusty ledges and snorted. When dinner was served, she inspected that, too, and in vile Rarotongan told the cook just what she thought of her. At first Maria was not strong enough to institute any of her reforms but it was not long before she took complete charge, assuming with me the same position Puia now held with Tom. It was almost impossible to converse with her. She spoke virtually no English and very little Rarotongan so we made do with my bad French, in which language she was very proficient, while Tom tried his tongue in Tahitian.

After Nurse Aulin returned to New Zealand, Maria chose Timmy a suitable nursemaid. She fired the cook, she fired the laundress, she fired the gardener, replacing them all with Rarotongans she considered more suitable. Instead of handing me the housekeeping money, Tom now handed it to her and she made it last twice as long as I could have done. She refused to accept regular wages, preferring that I keep her in tobacco and give her an occasional dress.

Having readjusted our household, Maria next turned her attention to the affairs of the Island. Because she had traveled widely in the small islands of the Pacific, she was known everywhere as "the Banana Tourist." If she tired of an island, she would pack up and try another. She had long ago divorced her husband, and being childless, was a free agent. In the evenings she would gather young people about her and teach them the songs she had collected and the legends she had learned from the islands the other girls had never seen;

fascinated with her stories, these youngsters preferred to learn and practice the new songs and dances rather than wander the streets. Maria was soon the choreographer for all the exhibition native dancing on Rarotonga.

However, on the rare occasions I wandered out to the kitchen to listen to the music, I was not always pleased at the company.

"Maria, you have some queer friends. Do you have to bring that girl Annette into my house?"

"Well, Mummy, I know you think Annette not 'nice,' but she very funny," was Maria's response.

"I'd like to know what's funny about the madam of the local brothel, I've got another word for her," I countered, feeling self-righteous.

"She tells stories. Listen to what she told us tonight.

"Each week she makes the tin of beer. For Rarotongans, one shilling a bottle: for white sailors, and the Government officials that visit the girls, two shillings the bottle. Costs her only three shillings to make one tin, she sells it for three pounds. Plenty of money there."

"Good heavens, isn't she afraid the police will catch her, it's against the law to brew beer here."

"Oh Mummy, she not scared the police. She tell me they nearly did catch her once. I tell you. One of the sailors get angry with his girl because she try to steal his money when he sleep. He goes to the police and tell him Annette make the beer. A friend of Annette's is in the police, so he tell her 'Hide the beer, we come looking for it today.' So she pull up some of the floor board, dig a hole under the house and put the beer there. She not pour it out, Mummy, waste of beer that way. Along comes the Chief of Police, that white man who's always angry. He say, 'Annette, are you making beer here?'

She look him right in the eye and say him, 'If you find beer, I make it; if you can't find it, I never make beer in my life.'

"He pull all the girl's lovely house to pieces, look under the beds, up in the roof, in all the cupboards. No beer. He get very angry to Annette, but she keep him stare in the eye. Then she look at his feet. La! La! He standing on the end of loose board and it start tip up. She say 'Have you look outside?' and off he run down the taro patch. Then she pull the bed over boards and cover with mat. She pray to our Holy Mother, 'Forgive me tell a lie.'

"He never find that beer, Mummy, and next time girls have sailors, Annette charge two times for that tin. Very special tin, that one."

As Maria was always willing to repeat Annette's "stories" to me I did nothing further about censoring the company she kept, for I learned that old Maria was proving very useful in rescuing young girls who, innocently or adventurously, strayed from the narrow path and decided to try the oldest profession. Maria delivered them safely home to their mothers before any damage was done. Prostitution in Rarotonga was not organized as Maria had known it in Tahiti, and I believe that she was instrumental in persuading Annette to send her young ladies to the hospital outpatient department for what she called "regular checks."

But Maria hated Puia. If Puia dared put his foot inside the kitchen door, she would either stamp on it or throw a saucepan at his head. She considered Tom's friendship and admiration for Puia sheer folly, and Puia bowed to her authority — which was strange for him who would not bow even to Tom's. I thoroughly agreed with her, for when he had been drinking Puia would barge into the house without any regard for convenience. No matter how important visitors might be, he would prop himself against the doorpost and launch into a long discussion with Tom in Rarotongan while my guests shuffled their feet and wondered what it was all about. And when he was sober and tinkering with a repair job, he sniffed. At ten-second intervals, he sniffed with never a lull until I could have screamed at him.

"Puia, for God's sake use a handkerchief, haven't you got one?"

"Got one, Lyd, but don't need to dirty it just now."

Puia was the only Rarotongan who called me Lyd. He did it to annoy me, I think.

Tom had deputized him to see that the land he had recently acquired was cleared and planted with citrus trees and coconuts; and I must admit that the work was being done with amazing speed and efficiency, yet Puia still irritated me and Tom's respect for him irritated me still more. I could tolerate this ugly smug member of the household only when he took his guitar and sang.

The tunes he played were of his own composition and the words were those of the old legends. I realized that if this man whom I now regarded as the bane of my life had been born into a different civilization he would have been respected as a great musician: that his knowledge and understanding of his own people were no thing of chance, but the result of a careful study of old customs and tradition. I too had to applaud Tom's choice of an intimate; my husband seemed to be proving himself most irritatingly correct and me most shamefacedly wrong. Yet Maria always agreed with me, right or wrong, and if she didn't would take endless trouble to explain her Polynesian viewpoint. Now, for the first time, she did not want to move on.

"I stay with you Mummy. Where you and John and my

own Timmy go, I go too, or else I wait till you come back to me. Now I belong to you and you and your family belong to me."

Belonging to Maria was not always easy. She was never familiar and always deferred to my judgment. Again and again I discharged her, to find a day or two later that I would have to search all over the Island and bring her back. She would drop whatever she was doing and with that crooked face of hers expressing more strongly than words which one of us had the most common sense, reinstall herself where she had started. The other white women wondered why I put up with such a martinet; when she marked time in their houses waiting for me to pocket my pride and bring her home again, she deliberately did as little work as possible, preferring to sit and smoke cigarettes and order the other servants around. No one believed me when I extolled her prowess as a cook. She wouldn't produce her French or Chinese specialties for anyone else, a tin of bully beef was enough.

The fact that I did not like tea parties, entertained medicine-men in my home and, worst of all, sometimes published articles in magazines and newspapers, did little to endear me to the other European women, while my staunch defense of Maria puzzled them even more.

"Why can't that Mrs. Davis behave herself, I think she's a little queer. Do you know that she's actually friendly with Robert Dean Frisbie, even has him in for meals, so I believe."

Frisbie's reputation in the Islands was hair-raising, but it is neither wise nor kind to judge a man by a reputation gleaned from gossip. I found that Frisbie's deliberate violation of all the laws of decent society had risen from his rage at the criticism and lack of appreciation of his work; few white men in the Pacific had the command of the English language that

Frisbie had, and he knew it; yet everyone he met was ready
and eager to point some small flaw they had found in his latest efforts. He was fond of saying "All the world's a little
queer but thee and me, and even thee's a little queer."

He had always been regarded as a misfit and an oddity. His
impatience with the attitude of others had resulted in a firm
conviction that everyone was against him; he would not give
the people the opportunity to extend any friendliness to him
and his children, interpreting their slowness to accept him as
active dislike. He was an American and the other white people
in our Islands were New Zealanders. But he could not appreciate that these foreigners were reticent with a stranger, especially one with such talent as he. Because he was an American familiar with what American readers expect to find in a
book about the South Sea Islands, Frisbie deliberately laid a
heavy hand on the romance — solid down-to-earth New Zealanders, probably unaware that the romance of their Islands
truly existed, rebelled against his approach to his subject. Frisbie retaliated by taking every opportunity to criticize and belittle New Zealand in print, forgetting that it was New
Zealand which was offering him, a foreigner, sanctuary when
other countries had rejected him. So Frisbie snarled and New
Zealanders snarled back; he retired into a shell of loneliness
and introspection that had become so legendary in the Pacific
that newcomers to the Islands no longer made the attempt to
offer him friendship and consolation for the fears that tortured him. The only close friends now left were Andy Thompson, the faithful Lionel Trenn, and ourselves.

Like the majority of white men who seek escape from the
difficulties of civilization in the South Seas, Frisbie first came
to Tahiti. A short period of active service during the 1914–
1918 war had left his nerves so shattered that he felt he

could no longer stand the hustle and competition of his own country. He had had a little experience in newspaper work in Chicago and had made up his mind that, in the peace of the Islands, he would find a subject matter most fitted to the style of writing that he hoped to make peculiarly his own.

He was fortunate in meeting James Norman Hall who went out of his way to help young writers. Hall had recently installed in his home another young man whose ambition it was to become an author, Lionel Trenn: the two apprentices formed a friendship that was to last until Frisbie's death, even though Frisbie succeeded in his work while Lionel collected rejection slips and filled his wastebasket with unfinished manuscripts. Frisbie while in Tahiti wrote nine full novels, only one, *My Tahiti,* ever being published. Despite this he refused to believe that he would always be a failure but accepted employment with a Cook Island trading company to run a small store on the isolated atoll of Puka Puka. There in solitude Frisbie decided that if he could not write fiction then perhaps he would find success as an essayist.

He had married a Tahitian but after she bore him one son he divorced and remarried. He told me very little of his first wife; I gather that she was unfaithful and that his first years in his atoll home were unhappy. His second wife Nga, of whom he writes so sincerely in his book *Island of Desire,* proved the ideal companion for him, their four children were a delight and his happiness is clearly and beautifully expressed in his first success, *The Book of Puka Puka.*

Frisbie wrote this chapter by chapter, submitting each completed cameo to the editors of the *Atlantic Monthly,* the publishing firm that Hall had always told Frisbie he should make his goal. Now, with Hall far away and out of touch in Tahiti, Frisbie was fortunate that he found in Edward Weeks, editor of the *Atlantic*, another who recognized his talent and provided the encouragement and praise that was so essential if he was to do his best. *The Book of Puka Puka* was a success that Frisbie was unable to enjoy, for shortly after its publication Nga succumbed to tuberculosis, her grave in Puka Puka an intolerable reminder of past happiness to the husband left alone with four small children.

Frisbie's second success, *Mr. Moonlight's Island*, typified the loneliness he was feeling. It was a stroke of bad luck that this book should reach the public at the outbreak of war. Soldiers and their families could not be expected to immerse themselves in the abstractions expressed by a bereaved hermit on a desert island; but Frisbie formed the conviction that his poor sales were the result of "not enough of what the public wants, romance." By the small sales of the rest of Frisbie's books, the public showed that it did not want romance mixed with philosophy, repetitious philosophy at that, and the author went from publisher to publisher always seeking for the one who could make his latest book as popular as the first had been, but gaining in fame only from the essays published from time to time in the *Atlantic Monthly*.

Because Tom and I refused to treat him as an oddity, Frisbie accepted gratefully our offers of friendship, and if a day passed when he did not wander into our house we knew that he must be ill. At first when other people arrived he would rush away without explanation, but gradually he overcame his contempt for our New Zealand friends and enjoyed their company as much as we.

To Frisbie, the acceptance of an article by the *Atlantic Monthly* was mecca reached. I had never even heard of the magazine but Frisbie determined that, following the example of Hall in helping new writers, he would raise my mediocre scrawling to the level of what he termed "imperishable prose." I was surprised at his interest, for, by his own admission, his golden rule was that to offer help to a young writer was to court trouble: if he praised them he was damned for insincerity, if he criticized he made another enemy. Although he was at this time working on his novel *Dawn Sails North,* a volume chock-full of romance, he found time to call in to see what progress I was making. After a month or two I came up with an article that, perhaps because it concerned Frisbie's favorite island, Suvarrow, he deemed fit to be sent to the *Atlantic,* enclosing it with a letter to Mr. Weeks explaining his particular interest.

The same mail that brought me a barren rejection slip (my first and, to date, my last from the *Atlantic Monthly*) returned to Frisbie his own manuscript of *Dawn Sails North.* He would have to cut out and rewrite two hundred full pages. What a dejected couple we were that day.

It was Christmas time, the gayest time in the South Seas, but somewhere in my Yuletide celebrations I must have met with an outsize centipede for I spent the New Year nursing a bad case of blood poisoning and trying to reassure Frisbie who by this time was depressed to the point of contemplating suicide. He had been so content but a short time before, for the first time taking a place in our small world in Rarotonga; now, after the publisher's rebuff, he was again drawn into himself, rushing towards physical and mental collapse. He considered that he was as good a judge as any of the merit of a writer. Like Hall, he too wanted to have a protégée, but, unlike Hall, he took his pupil's failure as a personal slur on his judgment and as a further proof that he was unappreciated.

As Tom was frantically trying to clear his surgical list before leaving the Island on vacation, it was left to my uncertain hands to reassure our friend, to encourage his eldest daughter Johnny to look after him even more carefully than she had always done in the past. Privately I heartily agreed with the judgment of the *Atlantic Monthly* in their opinion of my effort, but I would not have dared tell Frisbie of this.

On Leave

MY three-year term of service in Rarotonga was nearing an end; I should be due for three months' leave — and then what? Would the authorities renew my appointment, and if so under what terms? In the beginning it seemed to me that we should need at least ten years to clean up and revitalize the Islands, but lately, in teamwork with Pat Irwin, we had been making faster progress than that. Apart from my medical work I had been able to assist the natives in a most critical situation: I had become proficient in their dialects and had amassed a large amount of anthropological data, both in English and in Rarotongan, which I felt might some day be valuable.

Still in the back of my mind was my hoped-for deep-sea cruise. I had had valuable lessons in practical seamanship from Captain Andy in my travels on the *Tiare Taporo;* I had been able to keep up my practice of navigation and to gain experience in the handling of a small ship at sea. Yet a boat such as I wanted was going to cost a great deal of money and that was something I simply did not have.

After talking the matter over with Lydia, I decided that rather than spend my precious three months at some New Zealand resort, we would point for Australia and there — if it were possible to have my leave extended — I would study for the postgraduate diplomas in tropical medicine and tropical hygiene at the Sydney School of Tropical Medicine. Sydney was noted for its tough academic standard in postgraduate work, but I felt that if I could apply myself sufficiently to obtain those two diplomas they would be a big help when the time was right to apply for the position of Chief Medical Officer for the Cook Islands.

It would be expensive for the four of us to travel to Australia and we would have to find some means to earn money while we were there. I had no indication, either oral or written, of what the feelings of my Government towards me might be, or even whether they would want me to continue in the Islands. But it was time I knew. I wrote to the Department of Island Territories and stated my case, asking that my three months' leave be extended to cover the course at the School of Tropical Medicine and that I be reassigned to the Cook Islands for a further three-year term after I had gained the diplomas. I explained my financial situation and expressed the hope that New Zealand might offer me assistance. Some of the Government officials in Rarotonga, who knew that I had done this, were cynical. According to them the authorities were just waiting for the termination of my contract in order to be rid of me once and for all.

But the skeptics were silent when back came word from New Zealand that they approved of my plan for postgraduate work, would extend my leave as long as was necessary, would pay my fare to and from Sydney, and in addition would grant me a generous proportion of my salary during the time I was absent from Rarotonga. Their only stipulation was that I promise to return to the Pacific Medical Service for another three-year term.

I shall never forget the evening that news arrived. It traveled fast and by five o'clock that afternoon, at a celebration to herald the advent of yet another of our friend Ron Powell's numerous daughters, everyone in Rarotonga, both natives and Europeans, knew of my good fortune. To the Islanders the news was a relief, they had been apprehensive that my support of their revolt against the Administration had ruined my career; the Government's acceptance of me signified the acceptance of all the Cook Islanders. For myself, I knew that my position was at last officially secured and that I now had tangible evidence that I had not been considered wrong in supporting my people's efforts.

As is likely to happen when one's personal troubles seem to have smoothed out, I now experienced a feeling of euphoria — the Polynesians have a neater word for it, *ngakau-parau* — and with it, as I now know, goes an amount of overconfidence. To explain what happened, I have got to turn back some months before we made our decision to go to Australia.

At the end of my first year in the Islands I was restored to the operating room and from that time forward my record of successful treatments mounted to the point where patients came to me from the furthest islands, and some even from neighboring territories. The operations went well; I was averaging about five a day; and I suppose it was inevitable that I should go up in my own esteem. The Islanders knew when my term expired, and they began to flock in to see me in my last year, those on whom I had operated sometimes bringing with them their ailing friends for last-minute treatment. There were days when as many as twenty or thirty queued up outside the hospital waiting for me to arrive. "When is my turn coming, Tomu Taote?" they would call out to me, and it was hard for them to understand that with the hospital already full it might be another week before we would have an empty bed. Even those who had nothing wrong with them began to insist that I operate on them in case something might flare up after I had gone away. I used to explain that a surgical operation was dangerous business, at which they would only laugh at me. "I'm going to come back here day after day until you agree to look inside me," said one man who had nothing whatever the matter with him but wanted the extra assurance of having his appendix removed.

Right in the midst of this activity, a young man named Apera came in on homemade crutches from an outer village in Rarotonga. Eight months earlier he had fallen from a tree and dislocated his hip. Although his family had urged him to come straightway to the hospital, he, experiencing no doubt that reluctance to submit to surgery which is common to all of us, kept postponing the evil day until the last minute before I left. Now, so long after the accident had occurred, he begged me to help him. He was a husky youth and apart from his injury was in perfect health. I knew that major surgery was necessary to repair the hip and that it would be complicated by the tissue growth in the joint as well as structural alteration in the bone formed round the joint. However, in view of his general condition I did not hesitate to go ahead, and, using local anesthesia and keeping a careful watch on his progress throughout the long operation, I managed what I regarded as a very neat repair. Apera was returned to his bed in the ward none the worse and very grateful for the work the hospital had done for him. Examining him after the operation I found his condition encouraging, no sign of exhaustion, and no threat of collapse, and I returned to my house satisfied that I had done a successful piece of ticklish surgery.

Like other surgeons, I have always relied on instinct when I have felt any doubt over a case and now, quite suddenly, that instinct told me to be doubly careful. I hurried back to the boy and examined him again. He was bright, alert, and still none the worse. His pulse was normal, so were his respirations, yet something in the back of my mind still told me that the lad needed transfusion. Even so, for some perverse reason, I persisted in relying on the textbook symptoms of collapse and relegated my inner promptings to the background. I examined Apera regularly every hour, for these promptings were becoming unendurable, and I was obsessed with anxiety. Again and again I sat by the patient's bed, questioning him and puzzled by his reassurances when in the back of my mind I was so certain that, despite his obviously excellent postoperative condition, something was going amiss. Several times I started to order the nurses to set up the transfusion apparatus, then, thinking back to my training, each time told myself that they were not necessary. Apera came out of the operating theater at 11 A.M., and at 11 P.M. that evening I paid my umpteenth visit to his bedside, examining and watching, yet still not calling for the treatment which my instinct told me he needed. Now, actually while I held his wrist for the pulse, I felt it beneath my fingers as it soared, fell, then stopped. The patient had died, from shock. I had been wrong, that unheeded voice right. My elation and my success had driven me to turn a deaf ear to an inner prompting that might have saved a boy's life. Now that life was gone. In treating Apera I had depended too much on textbook reasoning and too little on what the textbooks cannot describe — the humble approach, the instinct to treat each case individually.

In talking with Apera's family, I remember their reaction, and although it might have been expected to lighten the load on my conscience it did not.

"Dr. Tom, it is not your fault. We blame the boy himself, for it is many months now since we first urged him to come to you. He was afraid, or he treated the matter lightly. It is hard that he has paid with his life, but no matter what you tell us, none of us will ever hold you responsible for the boy's delay in making up his mind."

Their trustfulness added to my humiliation. It had not been easy to build up the natives' confidence in surgery. I could only hope that during my absence their confidence would not be lowered.

❧

I have to stop and count how many times Tom and I have changed our address. Fifteen times in thirteen years, I think it is, and the routine still follows the same pattern. I do all the packing and Tom springs into action two weeks after we are settled into the new address, at which time he is sure to find that I have discarded some valuable garment that needed only a new top, bottom, middle. Nomads as we are, we do not acquire furniture, thank heaven, but I am no less acquisitive than the average woman, and my pile of knickknacks, when assembled in one heap to be inserted into various boxes, always makes me feel slightly ill. The packing up for Australia ran true to form.

I was looking forward to the change, for the narrow confines of Rarotonga had, for some time, been pressing in on me. However, I was dismayed at the thought of leaving our friend Frisbie. Knowing that we would have to earn additional money while in Sydney, I was very doubtful whether my articles and stories would be salable without the valuable editing Frisbie had, in the past, so generously given me. Lately there had been talk of our writing a book together: working in collaboration with him would have taught me a good deal and I was eager to begin after our return. But I could see that

Frisbie's health, never very good, was taking a turn for the worse. He came to the house even more often than before, but he seemed worried about his physical and mental state and seeking for reassurance.

The household was now in that state of utter confusion that always accompanies changing our address. Tere, the cook, had inadvertently become pregnant, a lapse on her part (in view of her past experience in such matters) I regarded as downright careless of her, an opinion in which old Maria most thoroughly concurred.

"Tere," I remonstrated, "how could you be so silly! What about all that fancy Maori medicine you talk about? Didn't you try some of that?"

"Mummy, medicine no good. To make the best medicine for not having babies, you must have the red berries that grow in the taro swamp. All the rain we been have wash the berries away. The old lady down in Avatiu give me another medicine, but it no good. Make me too sick to swallow, so now I have baby inside."

"Well, Tere, you've got just nine months to get that baby outside, weaned and living with your granny, so be sure that everything is in order by the time I come home."

"Silly girl," Maria said with a sniff. "Always having the boy friends. In the evening, always walk on the road, then run in the bushes. Ought to know better, look at her now."

As Tere sang somewhat off-key, Maria was unsympathetic with anyone who so misused her spare time as not to join her singing group. In any case Maria thought little of Tere's cooking ability. If guests were expected I noticed that Tere was sent out of the kitchen while Maria took over. This was Maria's opportunity for the final touch to the reorganization of my domestic affairs.

So Tere waddled around puffing and blowing at the exertions of housework while Maria followed her, everlastingly expressing her disapproval of girls gone wrong. I discovered that the lad responsible for Tere's fall from virtue had left the Island to work for the phosphate company in French-owned Makatea Island. I approached the company's agents to see if I could force the boy to support his child, but found that there was nothing to be done. Free love in Rarotonga is free by law. Tere wasn't worrying, so I stopped worrying too, and began to look ahead.

The Government, in addition to the many other assistances offered us, had even rented a house for us in Australia. In 1949 the housing situation in Sydney was as desperate as in other parts of the world. I knew that people were living in tents and caravans through lack of a permanent roof so that the rental of nine guineas a week for a furnished house, though far more than we could afford, would have to be met by some literary effort on my part. Frisbie, his book *Dawn Sails North* now finished to the satisfaction of his publishers, decided that we should write a book together, of course with his brains and my hands. He had chosen as the subject the fantastic tale of murder, treasure, and romance that is part of the story of Suvarrow Atoll.

Frisbie had already written for the *Atlantic Monthly* a series of three articles with Suvarrow as his subject, and had devoted half of his book *Island of Desire* to the short period when he stayed on the atoll after his wife's death. The conclusion to that period had been the frightful hurricane which had almost destroyed the tiny coral *motu*. Suvarrow Atoll had brought bad luck to others than Frisbie. As far as we could ascertain, in the attempts over the years to retrieve the treasure hidden there by pirates early in the seventeenth century, there had already been five men murdered on the atoll, another had committed suicide. John Pratt had seen his yacht, *Vagus,* disappear into the storm in the 1942 hurricane. Tom's own grandfather had lost a fortune trying to convert Suvarrow into a copra station. But at least one man had found Suvarrow to his advantage. An American, as Americans will, actually dug up a substantial sum in doubloons. Rumor had it that there was still treasure to be had on Suvarrow, but in these modern times the riches on the atoll seemed now to lie mainly in the lagoons in the form of pearls and shells matured from the baby shells planted by Grandpa Harries's copra workers. Ambitious traders were again looking towards Suvarrow with an eye to easy profit.

Over a period of years Frisbie had amassed a pile of references to the history of the Island: these, together with his entire library, had disappeared in the Suvarrow hurricane. Now that I was en route to Australia, we planned that while in Sydney I should visit the Mitchell Library (that source of every fact about the Pacific Islands) and gather the facts again; then, on my return, Robert Dean Frisbie (in large letters) and Lyd Davis (in very small ones) would somehow write the book of the century.

Then, a week or two before we were due to leave Rarotonga, Tom telephoned me from the hospital early in the morning.

"Lyd," he said, "bad news. Frisbie has just died. You'd better come over and see if there is anything you can do."

The blank statement left me stupefied. I knew that Frisbie had been ill for many years, and Tom had often told me that he would die suddenly, but it seemed so tragic that this should happen just at that time when he was finding a new enthusiasm for life. He had few friends among the New Zea-

landers on the Island, and now there were three little girls left
with no one to care for them. Fortunately the boy had been
sent to New Zealand some months before his father's death.
In his books Frisbie had expressed his opinion of my countrymen in no uncertain terms, yet it is a tribute to their kindness
that these people whom Frisbie had always regarded as beneath
his contempt came forward immediately and offered to give
homes to the children and take care of the formalities of death
which no member of the family was old enough even to understand.

Frisbie's grave lies in a far corner of the churchyard of the
London Missionary Society in Rarotonga. I think he himself
would have chosen some other retiring place; his family were
devout Catholics. His coffin was followed, not by Puka Pukans, but by white civil servants, traders, and residents of
Rarotonga, come now to show the respect that had been re-
pulsed by the living man. A hiss of disapproval ran through
the mourners when the missionary, no doubt acting in good
faith, piously announced, "We must pray that this man will
lead a better life now than he has on earth."

That remark will be forgotten as will Frisbie's life on earth
be forgotten, but one thing will remain, his true fairy story
of the South Seas, *The Book of Puka Puka,* surely one of the
classics in the literature of "the islands."

Frisbie's financial affairs were left in a turmoil, but faithful
Lionel Trenn doggedly straightened out the myriad accounts
and correspondence, for, like Tom and me, Lionel had always
found much to admire in our friend.

So often where a white man fathers half-caste children they
are regarded as of less importance than if they had been of
full European blood. Frisbie's love for his "cowboys," as he
always called them, was genuine. Working with his eldest

daughter, Johnny, who had for so long been the mother of the family, together they produced that lovely children's tale *Miss Ulysses from Puka Puka*. The skeptics scorned the fact that Johnny's name appeared on the cover, but knowing the child so well, how she thought, and those things that impressed her most, Frisbie had edited her childish expression with a remarkable skill. He always gave Johnny full credit for her book and was prouder of it than of any of his own. His one ambition was that some day Johnny would write books of her own better than her father had ever done.

Frisbie wanted his name to live after him, and I think it has. There is scarcely a book on the South Seas printed today that does not tell of the long-jawed recluse of Puka Puka. With the exception of James Norman Hall's tribute in the *Atlantic Monthly*, none of the descriptions of Frisbie's character come from a genuine knowledge of the man. I myself knew him only in the last two years of his life, and a finer friend and teacher there could never have been. Perhaps one day Lionel Trenn will recall those days when he and Ropati used to chew their pencils in Hall's guest house, and give us the full story of one of the saddest and most eloquent men to escape to the South Seas.

CHAPTER XVII

Samoa and Fiji

IT seems to be a family tradition that every time the children and I set off on an expedition with Tom we carry with us high hopes and little cash; our trip to Australia was up to standard. The Government agreed to fly us to New Zealand where we would catch a liner for the trans-Tasman crossing; so we began the game of island hopping that would cover the roundabout journey.

After a full day's flight from Rarotonga, we stopped at Upolo, the largest island of the Western Samoan group, west of the Cooks.

In contrast to the ascetic-featured Cook Islander or Tahitian, Samoans are stockily built, rather coarse-featured and quite dark-skinned. Having been under the domination, successively, of the Tongans, the Germans, the British, and the New Zealanders, the Samoan has built up a resultant resistance which has earned him the title of the "Irishman of the Pacific." Elsewhere in Polynesia the natives have reached out innocently, at times almost greedily, for the good things that civilization seems to offer them; when an unpleasant situation occurs, they are content to allow time to smooth matters out. Not so the Samoans.

Samoans will not wear white man's trousers, preferring to wrap their hips in ankle-length *lava-lava*. For some reason when they drape this straight piece of material, they roll it inwards instead of outwards as other Islanders do. And it slips. Every few steps the burly Samoan men out-Rand Sally as they unfold their robes for another safety twist. John voiced something that had puzzled me when he stopped a ferocious-looking native and asked, "Do you wear pants under your skirt?" We were not to know because the man laughed so much he never did answer the question. Later inquiry revealed that some do, some don't.

The majority of the Samoans wear a maroon-colored *lava-lava*, the badge of the Mau movement which was organized in protest against the Administration with the slogan "Samoa for the Samoans." New Zealand silenced the rebellion with gunfire, and resentment still smolders. This is what so easily might have happened in Rarotonga. Today when Samoa is enjoying unique prosperity through copra and cocoa trade, the people have at last been given a voice in their own affairs, a voice which is quickly becoming dominant. New Zealand still holds an advisory position. Samoa has been a difficult territory to administer, and within the next few years the planned independence of the Samoa group should prove an interesting development to watch.

A European-type house in Samoa is a rarity, for the natives prefer their picturesque *fale*, probably the best type of native house in the Pacific. It is raised up on a circular cairn of coral stones, open on all sides: instead of walls it has pandanus root mats which can be rolled up and strapped against the roof during the day and then let down at night or in rainy weather. The roofs are made of plaited pandanus rising to a central peak. As the houses are quite open, tidiness is displayed: neatly made beds, orderly rows of household utensils and piles of tightly rolled mats show the housekeeping of the owners. The cooking premises, as is general in Polynesia, are set apart from the dwellings and there, in the same native oven used in Rarotonga, the women cook up the traditional recipes.

As I have never lived in Samoa I have only a visitor's impression of its way of life: the stubborn retention of the old tradition and the aggressive resistance to innovation has not apparently harmed the Islanders. In one respect, as Tom would point out, this has been harmful: the people are unwilling to co-operate with white doctors. It has been very difficult to institute any public health program in the group, with the result that various diseases have taken a needlessly large toll of the population. But perhaps, as is already planned and hoped, the Samoans will one day have sufficient young doctors of their own people to facilitate the improvement of the health.

Apia, the main settlement of the island of Upolu, is a name well known to civilization as it was here that Robert Louis Stevenson made his last home. Stevenson brought to sweltering Samoa (average shade temperature 86 degrees) the architectural nightmares of Victorian Scotland, and the thick gray stone walls, tall towers, and, of all things, the fireplaces of the home he built stand as a monument to the Britisher's determination to go on being British even in Paradise. After building that tropical monstrosity, "Vai Lima," Stevenson left instructions to the perspiring Samoans that on his death his coffin should be carried right up to the mountain top to "Here let me lie." His bones now admire the view from the highest peak in Samoa.

In Apia, it is fashionable to make a pilgrimage to Stevenson's tomb atop the peak. I did not. The prospect of toiling up the steep overgrown path, sweating in the heat to look at a stone slab upon which thousands of tourists have taken it upon themselves to add their names to that of the great Louis, did not appeal to me.

Fortunately for later residents of Apia, Stevenson's design for a home in the tropics was not imitated after his death. Today only the poor Governor steams to liquid in "Vai Lima," mopping his brow, and listening to the ghost of Louis as it taps in the chimney. Housing affects health: it is significant that successive occupants of "Vai Lima" do not remain robust for long — neither did Stevenson.

There are two striking features of Apia's waterfront. At the time that Germany controlled Western Samoa, the First World War was imminent. The British battleships quietly moved in ready to take over in case war should be declared. The ships of both nations were politely lined up in the sheltered waters of the harbor when a most unusual hurricane struck the Island. The British made out to sea and safety while the German ships piled up on the reef where they still are, so many rusty derelicts. Nature had taken a very decided hand in the settlement of an international affair, but it is doubtful if the natives were grateful. German colonial administrative methods proved suitable to the Samoans. Stern discipline with no touch of cruelty was just what Samoa needed, while the agricultural methods taught by German experts were well suited to local conditions. The lessons of so many years gone by are still a big factor in the present prosperity in Samoa. The Germans freely intermarried with the Islanders and their descendants now hold responsible positions with the Samoan Government. The Asian labor imported to handle heavy work has been banished by New Zealand, a policy that we could not but admire in view of what we saw at our next stop, Fiji.

The other landmark of the Apia waterfront puzzles the

visitor — a long line of small wooden buildings standing over the waters of the bay and connected with dry land by means of rickety boardwalks built up on stilts. In his round-the-

Pacific tour on behalf of the Rockefeller Foundation, Dr. Lambert preached everywhere the doctrine of hygienic latrines. He considered that the Samoans living near the lagoon would be best advised not to dig deep holes with expensive "cup and saucer" installations, but instead to foster sanitation by erecting their "small houses" over the water . . . and beyond the low-tide mark.

The Samoans went ahead as advised, but, growing tired of building lengthy causeways, they soon did not bother to observe where the tide mark was. The houses became more and more elaborate: one-holers, two-holers, even six- and seven-holers sprouted up at the water's edge. Some had windows with real glass in them, some had bamboo wall blinds so that the occupant could poke his head out and admire the scenery while at his devotion. Some were painted blue, red, green, even striped, while the variety of roofing design was endless. Some built the "small house" first, then started on the boardwalks, grew tired of that, and said to their families, "I'm tired. I'm going to sit down in the shade now. You'll have to learn to jump that last yard or so."

Islanders are not noted for keeping their possessions in good repair, and it is some years now since Dr. Lambert first recommended these sanitary landmarks. Now most of the doors have fallen off, and the windows are broken, the roofs blown away, and often the whole four walls lean crazily against the wind and weather. Yet the Samoans continue to put their houses to good use, sitting al fresco and chatting with the neighbors as they pass, or waving to the tourists as they drive by. Like people the world over, they sometimes take a comic book along with them and sit down for a quiet read.

I still think that the drive from Faleola airfield into Apia is the most beautiful in the world. But now it is spoiled. An Englishman shared our taxi one morning when we were hurrying to catch a plane. He was an old island hand and he gave me a tip, the acceptance of which I regret.

"My dear," he chortled, settling his long-distance eyeglasses into focus. "Ay'm quaite obsessed, for years Ay've been taking this drive and though Ay know the shore view

is beautiful, these last few years Ay'm always so busy counting the ones with doors, the ones without, and the ones with
no shelter at all, that Ay really haven't looked at those lovely
villages at all. Today Ay think Ay'll concentrate on the ones
with more holes than three. Oops, there's a five-holer, almost
missed it."

And I started to count the ones without doors. The next
trip I counted the ones that still had doors. Blast that man!

There are eighty inhabited islands in the Fiji group, two
hundred and fifty in all, and we flew down to Nassouri, the
airport town of Viti Levu, the main island of the group, to
have our first view of how the British colonial service is administering their territory in the Pacific. Fiji is not within the
Polynesian triangle, but is inhabited by the more Negroid
Melanesians. The territory is vastly more extensive than any
of the Polynesian islands: from the air we could see endless
acres of sugar cane, pineapples, and copra plantations as well
as veritable seas of virgin jungle. In great stretches of swamp,
tender green rice was growing, something we had never seen
in our own Islands.

The Fijian people are almost all six-footers, even the women
too, and their height is increased by the incredibly dense mop
of black fuzz that is their hair, standing six or eight inches
from their foreheads. They stalk along, straight as arrows,
indifferent to the Indians who swarm their Island or to the
white men who rule it, their very bearing proclaiming their
belief in their racial superiority. But at work in the fields I
noticed only Indians or Chinese. In the labor gangs at work
on public projects, of which there are many, again only Indians. In the myriad shops, markets and curio stores in Suva,
the main town, only Indians. In the cobblers' workrooms, in
the offices, and in the hotels, Indians again. The number of

Indians in Fiji slightly exceeds the number of Fijians and on subsequent longer visits to the territory I was able to get a clearer, if still only a tourist's, picture of the conditions that have arisen from the importation of Asian labor.

Although, like the Samoans, the Fijians too had once been subdued and garrisoned by the Tongans, they resisted the in-

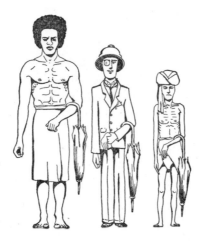

vasion of white men with vigor. They were fierce and often cruel but they put up a good fight to keep their land for themselves. When they realized they were beaten, they shrugged their shoulders and said in effect, "Go ahead and take the land but don't expect us to work for you."

To the British colonizers, Fiji represented a fine potential source of wealth, but without the help of the natives supplying labor to plant and tend plantations it would be impossible to exploit the resources. Accordingly the inexhaustible bank of Indian labor was drawn on: the sugar, rubber, copra and rice plantations went into rich production and the new-found gold mines, leased from Fijian chiefs, were worked with the aid of the Indian immigrants. The Fijians have little use for money with which to buy the comforts so loved by foreigners: if they wish to amass a small sum for any particular purpose, the chiefs send a group of villagers to seek employment from the white men. These work hard but hold their positions only long enough to earn the amount required, then courteously but firmly resign their jobs and return to their homes. This was their policy in the early days of the colony; it is the same today.

The Fijians seem undisturbed by the number of the intruders in their land. Imported disease, plus their stubborn refusal to co-operate with white doctors rather than their chiefs and native medicine men, have decimated the native population. When measles suddenly came to Fiji some years ago, lack of immunity to the strange disease brought the death total to an appalling figure. The threatened outbalance in the numbers of the two races worries only the British, who, despite the lack of co-operation by their indigenous subjects in Fiji, do love and respect the race. The Fijian gives the impression of more shoulder shrugging. "They wanted the country, let them work the problem out themselves if it's worrying them. If these little Indians ever get together long enough to start any fights with us, they won't last long. Let's go back to the *burre* and drink a little *yaquona*."

And so off they go to gather round the carved wooden bowl that holds their *kava*, clap their hands in ceremony and sing of the cannibal kings of the old days: how they buried a live man beneath the corner posts of the chief's new house, his spirit to stand guard against evil; how they banished and killed off the useless; how they fought their neighbors and kept the cooking fires busy boiling the remains of the vanquished. What good stories those must be. They let the world go by. Not for them the worries of commerce and the exhaustion of labor to produce more than you actually need for your own family. As long as there is just enough taro, *kumera,* banana, plantain and breadfruit, there will always be enough fish in the sea to go with it. Not too much, just a little over for the gift to the chief and that will be sufficient. A new shirt? Two day's work on that new pipe line will take care of that.

On the other hand, the Indians are demanding slightly more than they have a right to receive in this country that is not their own. They plot and plan, increasing their families, working day and night to increase their wealth, the richest ones traveling overseas for study so that they may return to executive positions in Indian affairs. While the Fijian strolls the streets in the evenings plucking his guitar, the lights burn late in the Indian workrooms. They dream of some day making Fiji theirs. During the Second World War their sentiments towards their governors was made only too plain: the Fijians welcomed the opportunity for battle against the enemies of the Allies, and their record in the Pacific theater is legend now; but the Indian company from Fiji had only one solitary volunteer. However, like their relatives at home, the Indians in Fiji are of so many different religious castes that at present it is unlikely that they will unite firmly enough to start real trouble.

Despite all this internal confusion, the Fijian group seemed to me the most progressive in the Pacific. There is little doubt that in the past the mother country used the territory mainly for profit; today that policy has changed and everywhere are signs of tremendous expenditure for the good of the Fijians. Educational facilities for Fijian youth are extensive and advanced; agricultural methods are improving by continued research done on the spot; constant coming and going of planes to all parts of the world has raised the economy of the territory immeasurably; an obliging hurricane centering on the main street of Suva, in 1951, completely demolished the eyesores of most of the old buildings so that now a new and modern city is rising.

The filthy fly-covered market that was one of the sights of Suva has shifted into modern premises. I mourn its going but am impressed with the spotless cleanliness of the new premises, kept so only by constant supervision. Gangs of mosquito inspectors, and protégés of Mr. Amos with whom Tom started our program in the Cook group, patrol the island. Their instructions, so rigorously observed in our home territory, fall here only too often on deaf ears.

The Fijians obey their chiefs, the Indians obey their religion, the Chinese go their own sweet way while the Englishmen, Australians, and New Zealanders click their tongues.

And yet, with all the underlying discontent among the races, Suva is a gay place. The bright sari of the tiny Indian women, grubby white dhoti of the men, the faded blues of the Chinese, the scarlet and black of the Fijian police, the grace, gaudiness and bearing of the Fijians themselves as they stride by in their ground-length *sulu* (another version of the Samoan *lava-lava* — though apparently more securely twisted) all go to make Suva the brightest spot in the Pacific. After dark the natives stroll the roads, strumming their guitars and singing their own songs, in contrast to the whine of the Indian chants that come from the open doors of the mosques. Along the sidewalks the sweetmeat man pushes his barrow laden with sticky flyblown cakes, the ice-cream man trundles along ringing his little bell, the Hindu peanutseller does a noisy and roaring trade, and all the while in many languages everyone screams and shouts, jostling for a place at a counter, a seat on a bus.

As Tom had Cook Island students to see at the Medical School in Suva and was intensely interested in the huge tuberculosis sanatorium at Tamabua, he was always preoccupied, leaving me and the children to amuse ourselves. I like to see things by myself rather than be led by the opinion of others. Riding on buses presents the cheapest way of covering the most ground in the shortest time.

Buses in Fiji fall into two social categories, those on which peanuts may be eaten and those on which peanuts must certainly not be eaten. The British residents of Fiji, though not at all averse to traveling on native buses, usually prefer the non-peanut variety. I like peanuts, on or off buses, and the one I always chose gloried in the name of the "Atomic Power Charabanc." It takes longer for the peanut bus to get under way, for the peanut vendor is a busy man and he never accepts anyone's cash without argument. The buses are low-roofed; no matter how deeply you bend your knee, in finding a seat you are bound to crack your head at some point, all of this adding to the enjoyment of the other passengers. On one side sit the Indians, on the other sit the Fijians, and they ignore each other. The children and I would install ourselves on the back seat the better to view the excitement, for on any bus-ride in a strange land, there is bound to be excitement.

In Fiji you do not pay your fare as you enter a bus, instead you settle up when the ride is over. This takes ages as the driver, always an Indian, will never believe that you are telling him the truth as regards your point of embarkation. He is always particularly suspicious of his Fijian passengers but in view of their physical dimensions I noticed that drivers pressed the arguments about the size of fare only with their own countrymen. There are no prearranged stopping places; if you want to flag a bus, you wave, yell, shake your fist and, if necessary, lie down in front of the wheels. There are many accidents and no wonder: loose gravel scarred at the side of the road, broken fences and wreckage of less fortunate vehicles do not worry the drivers, they skid along at a steady fifty miles an hour, the loose pieces of their chariots shaking the very teeth out of your head. The driver deigns to watch where he is going only rarely, the best part of the time his head is screwed over his shoulder while he chats to a friend in a rear seat.

Many of the passengers seem to be shifting house. They are loaded up with cases, boxes, bundles, children and livestock. It takes time for everything not actually human to be piled onto the roof and some member of the family must ride with his head hanging out the window to see that nothing falls overboard; if it should, the driver does not mind grinding to a stop, backing up and collecting the debris. Need I say that Fijian buses rarely keep to timetable.

All the time everyone chews peanuts, the discarded shells lie ankle-deep on the floors but we crack more nuts and munch on, the Davis contingent no less energetically than the rest. I persuaded Tom to come for a bus ride in Fiji only once. We had an exceptionally entertaining ride, I thought, but Tom still prefers to go broke paying taxi fares rather than endure the local color of buses.

Because Fiji drivers always picked up friends who lived up side roads, I saw a great deal of the country in Viti Levu. Housing, both Fijian and Indian, struck me as appalling. The Indians took pride in their horrible shanties built out of packing cases, flattened-out biscuit tins and anything else they could gather. The constant rain of the Fijian climate (at least around Suva) turned the gardens into swamps and, though the Indians are evidently making a greater effort to cultivate domestic crops than are the Fijians, no where are the gardens models of neat planting. In the fields beside their houses Brahman cattle are yoked to primitive Indian plows, young children and sometimes women shout and encourage the cumbersome animals in their work. This is the East trans-planted to the Pacific.

The Fijian houses are picturesque but, as is too often the case in the Islands, obviously unhealthy. The homes are usually circular, sometimes square, all very small; and their walls, instead of being made of the clean aerial roots of the pandanus plant such as we see used in the other Pacific groups, are built of unplaited strips of banana leaf. They look like untidy bee-hives, their grass or coconut thatching just as straggling as the walls. There are no windows in these houses, just one small door out of which pours thick black smoke from the cooking fires. The native houses were not too bad before disease hit the people, but now I could well believe what I had heard of the high tuberculosis rate among these people. And yet on one occasion when I wandered away during one of the many breakdowns of my bus, I discovered living conditions in an Indian family that were little better.

An Indian woman asked if I would like to rest in her house. My gorge rose as I noticed a young boy about sixteen years old, thin and flushed with obvious signs of tuberculosis. He was sitting at the doorway of the house holding a small earthenware bowl. The poor lad was hemorrhaging copiously from his lungs, but his family ignored him. The boy, rather than hold his head over the step of the doorway or use the bowl he held in his hand, was bleeding onto the floor of the house over which two infants were crawling on their hands and knees. I did not envy a medical officer his task in teaching these folk the elements of hygiene. The family would not allow me to help the lad. They thought of him only as a life that would inevitably end very soon, not understanding the risk to which he was exposing the other children.

This pathetic incident taught me more clearly than any other the receptiveness of the Polynesians, who had proved themselves so amenable to their health instruction and so alert in the realization of their past mistakes.

The people of Fiji are not uninterested in their own welfare. In their high chiefs they are fortunate in having leaders who in their integrity, their university education and their close understanding of their own people and of the British administrators, dispense a justice that is admirable. These chiefs, trained in their chosen professions, have married Fijians and are educating their sons to the standard they themselves have reached. As Fijian leaders increase in number and influence perhaps then will come the solution to the problems which beset the Islands at present.

Tom, on returning from various Pacific conferences, had often told me of the ability of these leaders: the one I came to know who will serve as the beau ideal is Edward Cacabou. Edward is a grandson of the last of the paramount chiefs of the Fiji Islands. Strangely he is only one-quarter of Fijian blood, the rest is Tongan for the Tongan conquerors were careful to see that they intermarried with only the best of the vanquished. And so Edward, though Fijian in build, is Tongan in face; through his education at Oxford University and the Temple where he took his degrees in law, he is British in comprehension, and, to the downfall of many, Polynesian in his sense of humor. Edward's practical jokes, recounted in polished accents, are legendary.

Like his brother George Cacabou, Edward has until recently been magistrate for one of the large districts of his home territory; in that district, the meanest native holds him in respect, for he has never perpetrated an unjust decision. His integrity, not to mention his sense of humor, makes him among the Europeans the most sought-for companion in Fiji; and even with the little Indians, Edward commands as great a respect as he does with his own people. With all this, Edward never forgets that he is a high chief and he tolerates no presumption on the part of a Fijian commoner. Tradition means much to him.

As a man and as an administrator Edward is typical of other Fijians who have been educated to help their people. In men like him I hope will be found the solution to Fiji's problems.

CHAPTER XVIII

In Charge

WE were away from the Islands for eight months, and for six of these I worked full time at the School of Public Health and Tropical Medicine at Sydney University. It was enormously stimulating to find other medical men as keenly interested as I was in the problems which I had thought unique in the Cook group, and it crystallized my thinking to work side by side with them in the laboratory and lecture rooms. I came to Sydney satisfied that despite the opposition I had done a fair bit during my three years in the Islands, but I soon began to shed this illusion; the more I talked with older men who had gone through somewhat similar experiences, the more I realized that there were other measures I might have used had I known of them and which I certainly would make use of in the future. When we sailed back to Rarotonga I took with me two new degrees, but more than these academic symbols was the knowledge of how to cope with epidemics and of new approaches to such old enemies as filariasis, leprosy, and tuberculosis.

While we were in Australia, Mother's letters had told me that she had not been well and had flown up to New Zealand to consult specialists, but I was not prepared to find her as ill as she was. Her upright carriage and her commanding presence were altered: she had shrunk into a little old lady, quavery and uncertain, completely bedridden and seriously ill with a kidney disease that I realized was incurable. Pat Irwin had looked after her in my absence, and when his term of office came to an end he entrusted her to Doctor Blackwood who had been sent to fill the post until my return. Doctor Blackwood and Mother became good friends, and I know he did his utmost for her. Then he too had departed and now the responsibility was mine.

My sister Mary flew in from Auckland to be with Mother; we had not seen each other for years, and when I met her at the airport I was struck by the fact that she had become a beautiful woman. Whatever she may feel, Mary remains outwardly undisturbed even when things are not going well, and her presence was very soothing to Mother; although her visits to Rarotonga had been few, she had never lost touch with the Islands which she had loved as a girl. Mother's bed would be brought out to the veranda and there they would talk of the past, of Mary's husband, Ian Harvey, and of their home in Auckland, and of their two daughters, Mary Lou and Sandra, who were in boarding school. At meals Mary would tempt Mother's appetite with island delicacies, the sea eggs and purple sea snails which she loved.

At the time of his illness I had been amazed at little Tim's will to survive: now I saw it again in my mother. For weeks she clung to life. With each new treatment I prescribed to ease her pain, she would nod her head and murmur, "Whatever you say, son." But when she saw that there was nothing further medicine could do for her, I remember her telling me, "Tom, I know that you have done all that you can, now it is for me to help myself. I am not going to die yet because there is something I must do for you."

What that something was, I was never to know. I felt that she wished to give me some message or explanation, for although she had talked to Lyd of her earlier life, this was a subject she would never discuss with me. But the barrier continued between us even in these last days of her life. It was Timothy, always her favorite grandchild, who was her particular joy; his demonstrations of love, so spontaneous and unaffected, made Mother feel that she was still the energetic and healthy woman she had been on those days when he had been the one in need of care and love.

The two weeks I had first thought would be left to Mother stretched into four months before the end came, and all that last night in my old home up on the hill there came and went a constant stream of Islanders from the villages to pay a final tribute. It was summer, and white-clad they walked up the steps of the house carrying long sheafs of Christmas lilies and creamy frangipani. They stayed on through the night, sitting cross-legged on the long veranda and chanting the songs for the dead which are such a beautiful part of the island tradition. Those searing voices, rising and falling against the distant beat of the surf and the closer rustle of the palm fronds, had sounded eerie when I heard them in the homes of others. Now they brought only comfort and a feeling of pride that my mother had been so much appreciated during her life. The individual note of consolation, the high falsetto sounding as if it came from a far distance, gave to the singing a unison, haunting and elusive, defying analysis. The words of their songs told of the story of Life, the life that is earth's gift to each man; its joys, its problems, and the inevitability of the body's death: beyond this, the words went on, lies the immortality of the soul, heaven's gift to man.

One of my first official duties after my return to Rarotonga had been to present myself at the office of the Resident Commissioner, he who had been the kindly friend of my childhood and my mentor in my years of service. His attitude towards me was now much more considerate than it had been before my leave. While I was in Australia, Lyd and I had received several letters from him, and their friendliness had touched us. Residents of the South Seas are not noteworthy for the volume of their correspondence, but the Commissioner had gone out of his way to keep us posted on local events.

"We're glad to have you back, Tom," he said, "I'm so very sorry about your mother's illness. We're none of us getting any younger. I've been feeling pretty depressed myself these days, I guess I'm off my tucker, but I'll get down to New Zealand for a month or so and that will help. You'll be Acting Chief Medical Officer; so far there's been no official confirmation of your promotion, nor any notice of another doctor being appointed. We'll wait and see, and meantime I know you'll carry on as you did before. We are all proud you have those new degrees, and I promise you we're glad to have you here again."

It was ironic that on the day of Mother's death I was informed by radiogram that I had been appointed Chief Medical Officer. This promotion had not come easily. On my return I had an outspoken session with the Public Service Commissioner who was on visit from New Zealand. He explained that there was some misgivings about appointing me to the chief authority, and I countered by pointing out my unwillingness to serve any longer in a subordinate capacity in the Medical Department. "If," I said, "another officer is to be appointed over me, I should prefer to accept the offer of the British Colonial Medical Service who say they would be glad to have me."

He thought this over and finally assured me that my case

would be reconsidered. When the official confirmation came through three months later, I felt as if a weight of uncertainty had been lifted from my mind. At last I could put my own program into practice.

The Islanders were openly pleased by my promotion: to them it had long been inevitable. The European community may have had some doubts, but they too gave me their congratulations. The events of the past three years had shown them that my ideas were not as far-fetched as they had first thought. Medically, I knew they trusted me, for virtually all the Europeans had requested my personal attention during the time I was assistant.

My hands were at last free and my problem was to set up a Medical Department adapted to the territory. I had learned that an imported European staff was expensive and too often on a temporary basis. I believed I could run the entire service for 18,000 people with only one European matron and one district nurse to attend to the care of preschool-age children. During my first six months alone in Rarotonga I had not found the work too much for one man if the assistant medical practitioners were properly used, so an assistant medical officer seemed to me an unnecessary luxury; however, my Government still considered the work too much and assured me that an assistant would be provided. I would have no difficulty in finding something for him to do, and my matron assured me that if the New Zealand nursing service insisted on sending her qualified sisters to help in the practical work of the hospital she would make every effort to keep them amused.

I had learned to appreciate the value of a good matron. Miss Hawkes, who had been in charge when I first arrived, may have been old-fashioned in her methods in the beginning, but she showed herself eager to adopt the new ways, co-operative with the medical staff, and in sympathy with the patients in her charge. Unfortunately, after repeated open quarrels with my Senior Medical Officer, she had been rudely dismissed. Other matrons had come and gone, but now, in Miss Reynolds, I had a prize, for her capability had earned the affection and respect of the Islanders. Under her direction we instituted a training curriculum for the twenty-five student nurses which approached the standard maintained in New Zealand. Where before we had always been short we were now flooded with good applicants. Male nurses too were trained in the main hospital, and we gave every incentive to those candidates coming from the outer islands of the Cook group whose small population precluded the employment of a full-time doctor. Their training was mainly in preventive medicine, including elementary dental care, child health and sanitation. The assistant medical practitioners, who were several ranks above the male nurses, instead of being sent to an outer island and forgotten for several years were to return to Rarotonga every eighteen months for refresher courses.

We were just beginning to recondition the hospital when the Resident Commissioner became seriously ill, necessitating my visiting him several times each day. Then and during his long convalescence we had many intimate conversations.

"Tom," he would say, "I didn't always agree with your policies and I still don't agree with some of them, just as you often can't understand my way of doing things. But always bear in mind that no matter how we differ I realize that you are doing what you think is right — and that I am no different. You know I wasn't always Commissioner here, that I gradually worked my way up from a very junior position. Back in those days I watched the men on top and made my own judgment of what they were doing. When my turn came, I carried on what I thought was the best of my predecessors' methods, just as others who come after you will carry on what they think was your best. For I can't see that you will stay on in Rarotonga many years longer, Tom. It took me over twenty years to get to the top, you're there already and bound to advance in your profession, as I know you will." I assured him that I had no thought of quitting now when there were so many things that needed doing here at home.

There still seemed to me a rather wide gap between my department and the various communities. To close this gap we asked each village to elect a Committee for Health; each committee was to nominate one of its members to serve on a Hospital Board, which would be in direct contact with the Medical Department. To this Board we added representatives from the already existing organizations, such as the Child Welfare Department, the Island Council (an advisory body to the Commissioner), and the heads of the various Government departments. In so doing I was breaking no new ground, but merely reverting to the ancient tradition when the people had a voice in all things. Here again I encountered the opposition of the Administration, whose argument ran as follows:

"This has been tried in the past and has never worked. The Islanders pay nothing for their medical service and have no right to have any say in how that service should be administered. The only policy is to tell them 'This is what you need, we happen to know, and this is what you are going to have given to you.'"

This philosophy with its disparagement of native understanding did not surprise me. For many years the people had been deprived of responsibility in their own affairs and in the process their reticence and timidity had been interpreted as ignorance and stupidity. I cannot say that the first meetings of my Health Committees were a signal success. Even though the people trusted me, it was only too plain that they were quite unused to speaking up in their own interest. So I adopted the method of quietly spreading propaganda among the people of the villages. The church deacons were of particular assistance here. If I was able to win their approval of an idea, I felt certain that it would be quickly circulated in the meetinghouse. Sure enough, it was not long before my Hospital Board started making suggestions to me. Once the Board realized that I really was willing to adopt their ideas, they lost no time in originating others in addition to those I had planted.

We set two primary goals for the Committees and their Board. The first was to enlist their help in injecting modern medical methods into the pattern of the local culture. We had to arouse the enthusiasm of the community for their new responsibility and the results were often amusing. We carried out regular inspection of yards and gardens, using a band of trained boys known as "Mosquito Inspectors." These lads arrived, polite but unheralded, and outdid Sherlock Holmes in their efforts to uncover mosquito breeding places. Where before rumors had warned the careless of the imminent inspection, now householders, realizing more clearly the dangers of allowing such breeding places to accumulate, were not in the least sorry when their neighbors were publicly disgraced for being untidy in their rubbish disposal, nor were they above quietly informing "the Inspectors" of the best places to search!

We took another step towards the improvement of public health when we began to carry out a strict inspection of food sales. Very quickly the baker who had a fly buzzing round his dough found himself without customers, and the scramble of the European store managers to find the cheese cover when a Board member hove in sight was to me as pretty a picture as I could ask for.

Our second goal was to involve the people in the operation of the official Department by encouraging them to contribute their own money to the building program. We suggested that each village erect a health center including a small dispensary where the district nurse could work, babies could be weighed, and ambulatory patients seen by the visiting practitioners. The villages gathered funds with enthusiasm and soon they received help from an unexpected source. The Education Department in the Cook Islands was extending its activities in a new program of adult education and the departmental heads were enthusiastic over my community centers. The idea of the people building and maintaining the health centers fitted in perfectly with the Education Department's plans. We teamed up and enlarged what would have been purely a medical center to one which would encompass the activities of the other program too. The health centers now would be part of a larger community center; sports were included, and it was proposed that an experienced New Zealand educator would visit and instruct the community in any subject in which they were interested. Gradually the village was coming into its own. Similar community participation was extended to the outer islands of the group too, where the male nurses and assistant medical practitioners did such excellent work on returning to their own territories. I was amazed at the sums of money these people, living on islands that were very far from prosperous, collected in their efforts to improve their medical facilities. The buildings they erected with their own hands may have been less substantial than those planned by the Government architects, but at least they were up and in use, not merely lines on blueprints.

It was gratifying to see how the people responded. The women of Rarotonga decided to hold a baby show and demonstrate publicly the care they were lavishing on their infants. To raise funds for prizes, they first held a bazaar, even the poorest native contributing something, either food or handwork. Lydia told me that although the bazaar was not scheduled to open until 11 A.M. the doors were burst open by sheer crowd pressure by 9 A.M., and at 10:30 the "SOLD OUT" notice went up. The baby show itself was the most lavish ever held in Rarotonga. If some of the prizes went to the wrong babies, it was because Lyd was adding up the marks awarded by the judges, and she says that a mob of over eight hundred babies, each with its mother, combined with a 90 degree temperature, produced a confusion which may have affected her addition.

In committee meetings I spoke of the seriousness of tuberculosis and how devastating was its effect on the people of the whole Cook group, accounting as it did for almost forty per cent of the yearly deaths; how, although we had a sanatorium and various other curative measures, the people themselves would work along with us to combat the disease. I explained how the disease was communicated and how this problem demanded the personal co-operation of every Islander if we were to lessen the death toll.

Evidently the committee members had gone back to their villages and passed on what I had said, because the immediate response was that whole families demanded X-rays, the sanatorium overflowed and little isolation huts began to crop up where patients could be properly cared for by their families without undue risk of contagion. In this way we were able to deal with the overflow of patients whom it would have been more ideal to treat in the sanatorium. Recovery percentages were good and advanced cases began to dwindle.

Committee members were invited, gowned and masked, into the operating theater to see for themselves what surgery meant: soon the fear of operations began to disappear and in time they came to be regarded as only a little more complicated than the swallowing of a couple of pills (which at the outset had once been very fearsome).

Elephantiasis, the all too frequent complication of filaria, had attacked many of the men in a very sensitive place, enlarging portions of their anatomy to the extent where gents' suiting took on the cut of sugar sacks. Policeman Kimi was the first volunteer for radical surgery for his complaint, and I well remember seeing him in the main village, shortly after his discharge from the hospital, surrounded by a circle of unsightly fellow sufferers, as he turned this way and that for them to admire the neat fit of his new pants. "You too can again look like me," he seemed to say.

Instead of an official inspection tour by the Resident Commissioner, Chief Medical Officer and chiefs of the Island, the village representatives now held their own inspections in the center, enforcing the lessons they learned in sanitation and hygiene. When the villages were to their satisfaction, they came to me of their own accord and demanded a purely medical *tutaka*. And how different that *tutaka* was from that one I had made shortly after coming to Rarotonga. There was no longer anything for the householder to hide. Mosquito breeding areas were cleared, rat breeding places eliminated, gardens neat, houses clean and tidy. The children were pushed forward for inspection, healthy and clean-skinned. We neglected not a single house on the Island during that inspection and each district made ready a feast hoping that some house in their village would win the prizes that the board was to award for the neatest house and the neatest village. The village that carried off the silver cup for being the best on the Island was inspected by everyone in Rarotonga. That village would have a hard time holding onto their cup the next year.

Because of my familiarity with the dialects, I could facilitate our community program more easily than a medical officer who had no grasp of the language. I felt that his handicap could be best overcome by utilizing the importance of the Suva-trained practitioners and our locally trained nursing staff and that I must continue to raise their professional standards and create for them real positions of authority, positions which were at that time noticeably lacking. Once these posts were established and competently filled it would be difficult for another qualified European doctor to ignore them. Here would lie the permanency of our work.

The conversion of what had been an indifferent hospital into an alert training school received the approval of Dr. Cruickshank in Fiji; he made available to us facilities in his own large hospitals and laboratories so that Cook Island staff who had completed their local training could carry on with more advanced work and return fit for more responsible positions. Cook Islanders in the Medical School in Fiji in Dr. Lambert's day had been considered the best of any of the island students and it was deeply satisfying to receive the excellent reports of this new generation. I was not short of teachers in my own hospital and I observed that the lecture audiences were not confined to staff only, for a solemn group of older natives would gather to listen outside the "lecture theater" (the veranda of the nurses' home). They went back to their villages and repeated what they heard: if some of this was garbled it did not matter as long as interest and subsequent questioning kept the ball rolling.

So we come to my special pride: the assistant medical practitioners. The Government supported me wholeheartedly in my proposal to allow them three-month terms in Fiji for post-

graduate training in a specialized field. Manea Tamarua was the first to take his extra training. The literal translation of the name Manea is "beautiful," and by Polynesian standards Manea is "beautiful, beautiful." He is large, and fat, and happy, his only grudge against fate is that he has a bald head — very rare among Polynesians — but even that he turns into a joke. Manea chose tuberculosis as his specialty. I must admit that I had a moment of panic when visiting the huge tuberculosis sanatorium at Tamavua in Fiji: the medical superintendent at the hospital showed every sign of kidnaping Manea for good, so valuable had he proved. Manea, for his part, had busily taken charge, still giggling over his baldness, still cracking jokes with his swarm of patients, and apparently vastly amused at my uncertainty over his returning to Rarotonga. He did overstay his time a little, but on being assured that on his return he was to have full charge of his own sana-

torium he lost no time in coming back, beaming more widely than ever.

Manea's wife, a Rarotonga-trained nurse, replaced the European qualified sister in the sanatorium, and from that time on neither Miss Reynolds nor I had any further staffing worries with our all-Rarotongan tuberculosis hospital. Our patients there were just as happy and cheerful as their doctor and his wife.

John Numa followed Manea to Fiji. John had been one of the black sheep among the assistant medical practitioners when I first met him, but now his character had so changed that it was difficult to recall the days when he had been another of the "bad boys." John's purity of Polynesian ancestry shows in his appearance. Apart from his classical features, John's gentleness in handling his patients never failed to arouse my admiration. I have always tried to sustain what is known as a "bedside manner" myself; with John that manner was just natural. European mothers of young children in

particular would usher John to the door, after his examination of their child was complete, with perfect confidence that he had just worked a miracle. And in truth John was very efficient. He had not been in Fiji long before he was given full control of the Central Leper Hospital at Makogai. With over seven hundred patients in his care, there was no question his ability had been recognized.

These were the same men who had been regarded as useless but three years earlier. Ngaei Tou, generally known as the handsomest hula dancer in the Pacific, while marking time for his turn at postgraduate surgical experience, began to specialize in obstetrics, and to my amazement and delight

European maternity cases were soon seeking his care. The fact that the most conservative New Zealand ladies evinced such faith in one of the native practitioners seemed to me the answer to a dream.

Excepting for the occasional difficult case, I did little practical medicine myself in my last term in Rarotonga: it was hardly necessary. The assistant medical practitioners vied with each other as to who could perform the neatest surgery or could arrive at the correct diagnosis. "Beautiful" and the "Hula champ" may still be carrying on their feud over who does the neatest repair on a hernia case. They were hard at it when I left Rarotonga. During influenza epidemics, of which we had several during 1951, these young men personally attended four and five hundred cases in village homes, gladly devoting their off-duty hours to see that each case was given personal attention. I like to feel that my insistence on their having regular hours off duty at this time was one of the reasons why none of them ever succumbed himself.

Tekao Tinirau, perhaps my favorite among the hospital men, had been stolen from me. The Administration had come to regard Tekao with as great a respect as I and now he was replacing a European official as Resident Agent on the island of Puka Puka.

His salary in his new capacity had almost tripled, a fact that I was able to utilize in obtaining substantial increases for my other assistant practitioners. Now all salary increases were awarded on a basis of capability rather than length of service. The assistants had something to work for, and work they did, for Tekao's success was undeniable and an example at which they too could aim.

As Resident Agent of Puka Puka, Tekao did not relinquish any of his medical work, he merely added to this the duties of magistrate, postmaster, treasurer and general department of information — a department that, on a Pacific atoll, covers a million and one problems and adjustments. Tekao was instrumental in arranging that the Puka Pukans, who had been in such a state of depression when we had visited them in 1946, save enough money to purchase the island of Nassau which they had so badly wanted for copra production: at last it is in their hands and on it flourishes a settlement of chosen people from the main atoll. Today I am told that Tekao has left Puka Puka: he has moved on to take charge of two larger atolls, Manahiki and Rakahanga, the largest exporters of copra, shell and pearls in the whole group. He holds a heavier responsibility than the other Resident Agents in the Cook group who are Europeans. How far will he go in the end? I know that his greatest interest is in his medicine, yet he is gradually being led away from that into the field of administration, a field that beckons other of my senior assistants as well.

But I am getting ahead of my story. At last I could honestly say that the medical service I had hoped and planned for was approaching its goal. Our chief drawback was the shortage of trained personnel. Some of the islands large enough to warrant the employment of a full-time assistant medical practitioner, trained nurse and sanitary inspector were not only still without them but were also without the facilities for housing such a staff. I knew that plans for such facilities were in the hands of the Government architects, thanks to the support given me by the New Zealand Government and by Dr. Cruickshank in his capacity of Director of Pacific Health Service. I also knew that it would be another four years before the twenty-five Cook Islanders in training in Fiji would be ready for active service.

The sincerity of New Zealand's interest in the improvement
of the health service to the Cook Islands was unquestionable
and they were making every effort to build up a sound educational program for the Islanders. In other islands of the Pacific the news of the work in the Cooks was well known. In
Tahiti the taxi drivers insisted on going out of their route in
order to point out to me unsanitary messes they considered
should be corrected. When I landed on the small island of
Bora Bora, the people were insistent that I examine every
child on the Island, despite the fact that this is French territory and I was therefore openly reluctant to do any medical
work. The Cook Islands, if not yet a model, had become a
place to envy, for with the appointment of a young Assistant
Medical Officer we had been able to institute thorough attention to every schoolchild on our island, giving them regular
prophylactic treatments for many of the complaints that had
previously caused trouble and loss of life among the younger
age group. Preventive medicine at last!

Encouraged by the keen interest New Zealand was now
taking in its island possessions, I now tried to excite a parallel
interest in the economic development of the group. True, one
or two of the islands were more than well off, but the majority were still poverty-stricken, these being the islands that
produced mainly perishable goods. There seemed to be a fear
in the mother country that if island export should be increased, the New Zealand growers would be embarrassed.
Since during the great part of the year New Zealanders could
not buy an orange or banana anywhere in their country, I
found it difficult to be reconciled with this "protectionist"
attitude.

Once a year, for four years in a row, I spoke up at the annual meetings of the Cook Island Legislative Council, em-

phasizing the increasing need for economic welfare. Each year
I met with the same response: "Confine yourself to matters
medical. Agriculture, marketing and economics can be
handled by our 'experts.'" Of course we had men who knew
far more about economics than did I but I could not resist
pointing out that good health, sound economy and a rising
standard of living are inseparable. No one could deny that
poverty in some of the outer islands was impeding my health
programs but there was far too little realization that these two
issues are linked together. What troubled me was that the
Islanders might interpret this lassitude on the part of the authorities toward increased prosperity as rising out of a fear
that, if prosperity should come to the Cooks, it would inevitably be accompanied by a change of administration, or worse
still the fear that New Zealand would lose the little Islands
altogether. To my way of thinking paternalism is the surest
way of severing the link between the dependency and its
protector.

During the four sessions of the Council which I attended,
the discussion would invariably center on finance and expenditure, and there the European officials and the native representatives could never agree. No one can deny the advantages
that go with the expenditure of large sums of money to cut
roadways through sheer coral, to blast great gaps in an encircling reef, to buy expensive imported trucks to transport
fruit from plantation to packing shed or to build houses for
technical experts imported from New Zealand. But what was
understressed were the resources of the Island, developed and
undeveloped. The fruit and other export crops of the Cook
group are already there, it wants only ships to get them to
markets. The people again and again expressed their willing-
ness to carry the fruit on their shoulders and tramp through

the bush and rough coral to get it to the ships if only the ships would come; but their zeal did not find an answering response. Year after year the expenditure by New Zealand for the Cook group increased. My own department benefited but even so I felt it would be better if we could detour part of our allowances towards the betterment of the economy of the natives.

Jane Tararo, an *ariki* from the island of Mauke, expressed the general opinion of the Islanders towards New Zealand's policy as interpreted by the Council when she said:

"Everything we ask for here we ask because we as Cook Islanders deem it important. These things we are not given. Everything that seems to us expensive and untimely, we are given whether we want it or not."

During my last term in Rarotonga I was chosen to represent the New Zealand Department of Island Territories at several conferences outside my own territory, and on these occasions, as had been possible when in Australia, I was more easily enabled to view our local conditions as compared with those of distant territories. In conversation and discussion with government representatives from other countries, I found that in the Cook Islands I had been viewing in miniature the very same forces which have resulted in the loss of the colonies of the empires. To the 18,000 Cook Islanders, these forces are quite as tangible and as important as to the millions in Malaya or India. I have told you how nearly Communism entered our paradise and might very easily have stayed.

Perhaps mine may be a lone voice when I plead that now is the time when intelligence must be used in dealing with the uncertainties of underdeveloped races; that the resources of sociology and anthropology should be applied in a practical manner and not, as is only too obviously the present attitude, as a collection of museum curiosities; that the potential economy of a people be given an amount of attention equal to the paternalistic gifts of education and good health. This is no experimental pilot project: health and education are as necessary to underdeveloped races as they are to America, the United Kingdom, or industrial Europe.

The only result of paternalistic giving can be ultimate resentment on the part of the recipient, and the sole means of lessening such resentment must be repayment for the paternal gift. No matter how nominal the charge for service may be, that small charge will always remain a strong thread in the retention of pride and personal self-respect.

CHAPTER XIX

Trouble in the Laundry

NOW that Tom was established as Chief Medical Officer, John off to the little school for European children, Tim in shining health, and Maria organizing my house almost out of existence, I could have expected a life of ease. But Rarotonga prides itself on never having a dull moment, and New Zealanders outdo Englishmen in their abuse of the midday sun.

We saw very little of the children. John, when not busy at his morning school classes, was always to be found down on the wharf, doing exactly what Tom had done at the same age: closely examining the structure and rigging of the visiting yachts, pestering their skippers with endless seafaring questions, and vanishing out of sight in "borrowed" tenders. With the European children he played cowboys and Indians, with his Rarotongan friends he learned to trap wild fowl, ride bareback, and use an underwater shanghai to spear fish. Tim too visited his own home only at meal- and bed-times, but his pursuits were slightly more cautious than his older brother's. Tim swam, but never out of his depth; he did not dive off rocks until he was quite sure the depth of the water was just right, and he always returned from his "hunting" expeditions in the mountains before nightfall. The children were happy, and they were healthy too. Island children always seem to resemble something that has crawled from under a log and mine were no exception, but I knew that once in a more temperate climate they would more than hold their own.

The natives had given up their tennis clubs because of the unavailability of sports gear and lack of money with which to buy it. Our garden had a tennis court, and I wrote to New Zealand for rackets, balls and nets so that the village could again take up this sport in which they had excelled in the past. Old-timers warned me that I would soon be picking up the balls and cutting the grass for my tennis team and how right

they were. The local lads played from 8 A.M. until dark. At first only half a dozen were interested but soon the garden overflowed with players; they brought their wives, children, aunts, uncles, and grandmothers, who sat all over the flower-beds and watched the menfolk perform. To come into the garden they passed by the gate and stepped straight through the fence, until the surroundings looked as if the rats had been at it. Young vegetable seedlings collapsed beneath large brown feet and my cherished lily bulbs gave up the struggle. I pinned a notice on the gate: "TWO SETS AT A TIME ONLY," but forty or fifty players in an afternoon was the average and there was barely a trace of grass left on the court.

On Sunday, which should have been my day of rest, the veranda resembled a canteen as Maria and I jostled round handing cups of tea and more and more sandwiches to the

European tennis enthusiasts. Most of them would stay for lunch, linger for afternoon tea, and as the sun went down pull out extra chairs and sip chota pegs while they discussed life. Maria muttered in the kitchen premises, and I offered hopeless prayers for a little peace and quiet.

I let them enjoy themselves for as long as I could stand it, then took the net down, hid the rackets and watered the barren court. Immediately tennis courts sprang up in other people's gardens. Trucks circled the island on Saturday afternoons bearing teams and supporters off to challenge other villages, while I adjourned to the club and played pat-a-ball with the ladies. I missed the rousing games I had had with the native boys but thought that at last I could have my garden to myself.

Then boxing came into vogue. Tom had a hand in this and volunteered to coach our village team and referee the matches. Instead of tennis players, we now had muscle men all over the garden, banging away at punching bags slung to our loveliest trees. These brought along their little brothers who started private scraps in odd corners of their own, falling all over the flowerbeds and breaking the trees with homemade dummies, junior size.

Outrigger canoe racing should keep people away from my garden — and for a little while it did. The local yachting enthusiasts formed a club where, twice a week, tight-lipped men piloted tiny sailing canoes round a six-mile course marked out on our largest lagoon. Ron Powell had been crewing for Tom but when Ron built his own boat the only other candidate Tom could find who was small enough not to impede the speed was me. It is the duty of the crewman to see rocks in the lagoon. I cannot see through water, and after several weeks of rousing record-breaking races the inevitable hap-

pened. We bumped into just one rock too many and over we
went, the force of impact on the coral head snapping the
mast, stays and everything else snappable. Tom was not angry.

"That's a pity; now we'll have to build another canoe."

He built the canoe to his own design. With Ron Powell and
Puia, he laid the keel on the front veranda. No sooner would

he start work on the boat than he would be called out on a
case; the work progressed by inches and for four whole years
that wretched shell took up half the veranda. At night people fell into it, by day we walked round it. All the furniture
was jammed onto the far end of the veranda to make space
for the shipyard while the children used the hull as a parking
space for their toys. Over the side of the veranda, the lily
bulbs choked and gasped as they battled to fight their way
through inches of wood shavings. In the old canoe (with a
little help from me, of course) Tom had set the all-time record for outrigger sailing, but it was a great disappointment to

him that the new boat was never finished. The finest canoe ever designed or built now streaks round the lagoon with an outboard motor stuck on the end, the property of a fishing enthusiast who hates sailing as much as I do.

Rarotonga is rightfully proud of its Girl Guide Association;

yet if Queen Elizabeth, the Patron of the overseas Guide movement, could see the way we keep Guiding alive in Rarotonga, I wonder what her reaction would be. At first I captained a group of adolescents in our most isolated village. They spoke Rarotongan and I spoke English, and if you have ever tried to define the word "honor" by gestures only, you will appreciate my difficulties. Some of my Guides were married women with children, some of them were unmarried with children and most of them were using their spare moments to reach a similar status. However, I was soon convinced that Guiding, adjusted to local conditions, fulfills an important role in the education of the young girls in the Pacific. They were all eager to learn the European ways, cooking, sewing, looking after children, nursing the sick, even learning the Morse code, flag signals and, in the extreme, the deaf and dumb language. The more obscure or strange a subject, the quicker did they reach proficiency. They showed little interest in the subjects we introduced because they were Polynesian: hat weaving, native cooking, nature study and swimming were things they could learn at home, whereas the weekly Guide meeting was a golden opportunity to learn to become a little more like the European captains.

As secretary to the local Guide Association, I was able to come closer to the other European women on the Island, and to enlist their help in various charities we had found necessary; and ultimately, to find a way of helping some of the people of the Pacific who will need that help wherever I may be.

On one of his attendances at conferences, Tom had joined in an official tour of the Central Leper Hospital at Makogai. His main concern was with the welfare of the Cook Islanders who were patients there, and although these people were progressing well medically he was most upset to find that they were mentally downcast because their own people seemed to have forgotten them.

At Tom's suggestion, I had gathered a band of kindly women who were helping me to collect clothes and materials for the crippled children requiring hospitalization in New Zealand and for the patients in the tuberculosis sanatorium. My requests to New Zealand firms and women's clubs there had been answered overwhelmingly; we lost no time in diverting our excess materials to the Cook Islanders at Makogai. A group of responsible natives raised large sums of money to ensure that their own people should no longer feel forgotten. The Cook Islanders at Makogai were happy, but what of the other patients?

Many years ago, through the efforts of one lone man, Percy Twomey, New Zealanders had established a Trust Board for the Lepers of the Pacific, regardless of race, creed or color, and the money and gifts collected by this Board had increased to the point where there is not a single leper hospital in all the Pacific territories, whether French, British, or New Zealand's own, that does not benefit from the efforts of a country which has itself no patients suffering from the disease. Unfortunately a man whose name, at first glance, could easily be confused with the Board Secretary's, had on his own account started a door-to-door collection on behalf of the lepers and pocketed most of the proceeds. The Board, although aware that this was happening, did not wish to prosecute as they felt, and rightly, that such publicity would be most harmful to them. Whether they wanted it or not the publicity was inevitable when members of the public protested through the editorial columns of the newspapers, and it seemed that donations would fall off just at a time when, due to improved medical treatment for leprosy, comforts and financial aid were most necessary.

Armed with a New Zealand newspaper's credential, I persuaded Dr. Cruickshank, in Fiji, to allow me to visit the hospital at Makogai and, after seeing for myself what the New Zealand public had been able to achieve there, to write some newspaper articles to encourage the people to continue their help to the lepers.

Dr. Cruickshank, like every other doctor of my acquaintance, regards journalistic activities with deep suspicion, but feeling that my motives might after all be unselfish he arranged for the cutter from Makogai to come over to Suva and take Tom and me over to the hospital for a tour of inspection. My reception by Dr. Austin, superintendent of the leper hospital, was surprisingly warm; he has been in charge of the settlement at Makogai for twenty-one years and as no journalists ever visit his Island he has not yet learned to dislike them.

From a fictitious account I had read of Makogai I expected to see barbed-wire entanglements separating male from female, unclean from clean, with policemen on guard to see that the rules were observed.

The only policeman in sight was sitting on a fence engaged in an argument with one of the patients; the only barbed wire was in use to keep the cattle from straying into the patients' gardens. No one could have guessed that this lovely Island was different from any other. Certainly the housing was varied; Samoans were living in *fale*, Fijians in *burre*, Cook Islanders in pandanus houses, and Indians and Chinese in neat wooden bungalows. Certainly there were large well-kept dormitories and modern kitchens, but the majority of the patients preferred to live in the type of house that they had known in their home islands.

"Look at my silly people," said Dr. Austin. "We've built these beautiful neat dormitories for them, and here they are; they've set up house under the floors. Don't blame them; you know, it's much cooler down there and as long as they're happy they can stay there.

"Our dormitories are beginning to look like trains nowadays. With over seven hundred patients instead of the usual four hundred, we have to keep tacking bits onto the end of the buildings. If people like your Dr. Tom don't stop sending me patients, we'll fall off the Island soon."

The Makogai housing problem was a serious one. The apparent success (the experts still refuse to make a statement that they have a cure) of the new sulfatrone treatment of leprosy has filled the leper islands of the Pacific to capacity. Because this treatment has shown a miraculous effect on the skin lesions that have long been the most distressing feature of leprosy, the beds in the hospital wards are almost empty, the patients being accommodated in the community villages. With so great a majority of patients living an almost normal life, it is now more than ever essential that they be given some occupation during the long period of waiting until the doctors pronounce the disease cured for them.

Here is where the work of organizations like the Leper Trust Board has proved such a boon. Makogai Hospital is administered by the authorities in Fiji; drugs, hospital equipment and salaries are paid for by the British; the staggering parade of luxuries and small comforts so much a part of the hospital are all the gift of the people of New Zealand.

Makogai has two workrooms, one for women, one for men; the women's is equipped with modern sewing machines and every other device of occupational therapy that an Island woman could wish for; the men have a carpentering workshop, with all the most modern tools. The children have playrooms, toys and sports equipment; the Boy Scouts of Makogai, all young sufferers from leprosy, have the most impressive collection of musical instruments and Scout gear I have seen. There is in the center of the Island a huge open-air theater and recreation hall, while in each section, male and female, there are lounges, furnished and equipped to a standard that the patients have dreamed of in their more primitive island homes. The X-ray building, together with all its equipment, is the gift of New Zealand while the two schoolrooms, one for the boys and one for the girls, are models of tropical design, furnished and decorated to a standard far above the usual island school.

"All these people you see working so busily, arguing, learning and planning for their future, have a chance to return to their old world and resume a normal place in life," Dr. Austin told me. "Our nuns and the Fijian nurses who help them no longer have to spend their days dressing the ulcers that were so repulsive; today they peer down microscopes counting blood cells. I sometimes wonder where to put my new patients, but thanks to New Zealand I can keep them amused and teach them something useful while they mark time before going home free of the infection."

I saw no signs of the misery and despair which I had been taught to associate with leprosy, only hope. It is true that there must remain on the Island many patients who, because of deformity, would be happier to spend the rest of their lives in the hospital rather than live again with their own people, but for the great majority the training and education received while patients in the hospital will bring an improved status on their return to normal life.

The estimated number of lepers in Africa, India and China is appalling. Yet in the Pacific leprosy may well disappear. Penrhyn Island, which provided most of the Cook Island cases, had not a single case during the last leper survey there. Manahiki and Rakahanga, Palmerston Island too, all in the Cook group, had no fresh cases to report. Those persons who by laboratory test were proved to be suffering from the disease left the Cook Islands willingly and with hope in their hearts, without fear of the isolation they must submit to during their stay on Makogai. If people of other countries will give lepers the proper medication and rehabilitation and reassurance, leprosy might well recede into Biblical legend.

On my return from Makogai, I transformed the guest rooms in our house into a small warehouse; willing friends came to help sort and pack the small gifts we had been able to collect; and right in the midst of this, my fate caught up with me.

With the small legacy that had come to him from his grandfather's estate, Tom bought "the boat." She was as nearly the Tom Davis dream boat as could be imagined. Tom had watched her being built in Auckland sixteen long years before but never dreamed then that she would be put up for sale at just the moment he would be able to make her his own. The *Soubrette* was quickly renamed the *Miru* in memory of the first daughter of the Polynesians.

The *Miru* was everything I hoped she wouldn't be. A ketch, she was built for ocean cruising, and it seemed from the bulk of her that the bigger the ocean the better she would like it. Instead of planking, her hull was built of triple skins of precious New Zealand kauri, sheathed in copper. Her mainmast was the joke of New Zealand yachtsmen, so solid and defiant does the oregon spar stand. Her rigging seemed made for the North Sea gales, yet despite her broad beam and stumpy 45-foot length, in the water the *Miru* still managed to look a lady.

"We'll sail to England on her and I'll do some postgraduate work when we get there," said Tom gleefully. "Of course, before we go, I'll get a deckhouse put on, pull the galley out and install it aft, yank out those two bunks and shift them to the deckhouse, get a new set of sails and renew the rigging, have her repainted and a few other odds and ends."

"After you've done all this and paid for it, what are you going to use for money? We'll have to eat on the way, remember," I reminded him.

"Money? Oh, that. Well, I'm off down to see Ron Powell to work out these specifications; we'll worry about money later on." And Tom, now "Skipper," would disappear.

Study of the map, although it showed England a long, long way off, at least proved that we would be sailing in favorable winds and through the tropics. The succession of strange lands lying between Rarotonga and England quite outweighed my reluctance to take part in any epic voyage Tom might conceive. However my optimism was short-lived, for no sooner had we settled on a route for a westward passage than the opportunity came for Tom to do some postgraduate work in America — in Boston, to be exact. Another look at the map, and my heart sank. The American academic year began in September, that meant that we would have to cross the Pacific in midwinter. From my reading of the history of our ocean, I knew only too well that this voyage had never been done before in a small craft and had been attempted, unsuccessfully, only once. But, from those who knew what they were talking about, I received no sympathy.

"Jeez," said Captain Andy, looking at the map. "Across the Pacific south of the line and in midwinter! West to east. Jeez, if I could only come wid yous. Whut's your route to be, Taam?"

"We'll sail from New Zealand and go straight over the Roaring Forties to Peru. Maybe stop in at Rapa up in the Australs, and perhaps Easter Island, but I'd prefer to do that stretch all in one bite if we can make it."

Six thousand odd miles all in one bite! I sighed.

"Peru! Jeez, you can make it, Tom. Cut up into the Hum-

boldt Current round about Easter Island and you'll fetch up
at Callao. Finest port in de world and what a calaboose dey
got dere!"

"If we keep south of the horse latitudes," continued Tom,
"and north of the ice, I estimate an eight-week sail right
across. With the *Miru's* build, her storage space and water capacity, we should do it. After Peru we'll use the engine and
run up the South American coast, through Panama, the Caribbean, and on to Boston. Do you think it's possible?"

Ron Powell wailed. "A midwinter crossing of the Roaring
Forties and me with five daughters! They say it isn't possible
to go west to east in the winter. It's possible for you, Tom, but
what about me?"

What ideal shipmates those two would have been!

Certainly I did not relish that crossing to South America,
yet to get to a new piece of dry land I was quite prepared to
suffer the water in between. To Tom, this was a dream come
true, and for me and the children to have stayed behind or
followed by more conventional means the dream would have
only half its worth. Although all my life I have lived in sight
of the sea, and during the years in Rarotonga virtually on top
of it, I have never come to like it. The gentle waters of the
lagoons I loved, but the angry ocean outside the reef I could
never like. At night I would listen to the endless pounding of
spray on coral, beating, thudding, then hissing greedily onto
the beach, obsessing me with the idea that some minute the
coral would give up the unequal battle with the surf and the
waters would rush over the Island.

At sea, during other cruises, the water even in its calmest
moments seems to be lying in wait for that one mistake which
will make us victim to its greed. In this is the very challenge
that Tom loves so much; for him there is no greater satisfac-

tion than to pit himself against this most voracious of the elements. I have watched his face as he sits at the tiller during the storm, his eyes shifting over the sails, the riggings, glancing at the wake, reveling in the green seas as they pour over the decks and spray onto his face. At those times I am afraid even to look at the ocean. I keep telling myself, "Nothing lasts forever, tomorrow this will be another memory."

I did not think that the passage from New Zealand to America would be dangerous. We had a good ship, and if it had been otherwise I knew that, even if he was prepared to risk the journey himself, Tom would not endanger his whole family. He knows how much John and Tim love the sea and ships, and I suppose he hoped that I would at least suffer in silence. After all I do not get seasick, only miserable.

My chief concern for the long voyage, which we would start early in 1952 when our leave from Rarotonga was due, would be the ordering of food. We planned to carry stores for ten weeks, both fresh and canned; and our last weeks in Rarotonga became one vast confusion of letters to the yacht builders who were refitting the boat, letters to the New Zealand Government (who disapproved our visiting America), checks to the various firms who were working on the boat, letters to New Zealand manufacturers in one last appeal for the lepers, hastily written manuscripts to be sent to America in the hopes that I might earn some dollars after our arrival: food lists, clothing lists, lists of ships gear, checks, checks and still more checks. If this went on, we would set out for America in the same financial state in which we had arrived in Rarotonga, seven years before.

Packing our belongings reduced me to hysteria. Tom is one of those people to whom even a small piece of string or a rusty bolt might come in handy. As fast as I discarded his collection of mechanical antiques, he carefully rescued them, solemnly informing me that this corroded piece of wire might soon be the final link between life and death.

In one room lay twenty-eight packing cases for storage in New Zealand; in another lay twenty-three packing cases for storage on the *Miru*. Between the two piles shunted my old enemy the Public Works Sports Association, determined to have the winning goal in our seven-year-old game. I lay awake each night wondering how many cases from the *Miru* pile had mysteriously crept into the store pile. It transpired that only one had transferred itself; this case contained our radio receiving set, but by the time the Sports Association had paid the bill for the case to be flown to us in New Zealand I felt that I had won the final goal.

Exactly one month before we were due to leave the Cook Islands, the farewells began. In the welter of stores, packing cases, correspondence and outgoing checks, I had little time for regrets at the parting or fears at the voyage. For me those years in Rarotonga had been good even with all the worries and doubts. I had seen Tom's plans mature, his faith in his people prove well founded; John and Tim were none the worse for their years in the tropics and the friendships I had formed in Rarotonga were so firm that I did not think a temporary absence would end them; almost by accident, I seemed to have slipped into a profession that, as it had done during our months in Australia, might provide an income for us while we were in America. My parting from the faithful Maria I will never consider as other but short-lived for she is as much one of our family as are the children. A part of Rarotonga, the tiny plantation now so soon to be coming into production, is really ours; perhaps one day we will make our home there, reviewing the past, which at this moment is so un-

certain again, as a memory worth the suffering for the remembering. Tom was leaving something he had taken years to
build, and that is never easy.

⌒⌇⌒

I did not regard my leaving Rarotonga as a desertion of
duty. In the seven years I had worked in the Cook Islands I
felt I had laid a foundation that would be for the permanent
good and this overcame my personal sentiment. The Islanders
commended my decision, but in the speeches made to me at
the feasts in our honor I was distressed to detect again a note
of uncertainty and lack of self-confidence.

"You have allowed us to play a part in your work, but if
you leave us will our voices again be silenced?"

"That is in your hands," I told them. "If you continue to
work with my successors as unselfishly and energetically as
you have done with me then you won't need to worry; your
achievements will speak for themselves. Keep it this way
and your value will grow, not only to the Medical Service,
but to all the other services that your Government offers
you."

During these final talks, I was gratified to discover how
much understanding the Islanders had of our work. Our lessons in public health education had really taken hold.

The attitude of the Europeans towards my leaving was little different from that of the Islanders. As the Islanders had
done, the Europeans pleaded, "What has been the use of your
working to build up a Medical Service? You must know as
well as we that you will be scarcely out of sight of the Island when that service will start to fall apart again."

Again I could answer in all honesty, "No matter if the present service does disintegrate, I know that down at the bot-

tom will still remain a foundation stronger than the one I found to build upon seven years ago. You all know what is possible for modern medicine to give you even in the partial isolation of the Cook Islands; I have no doubt that, in the knowledge of what you can expect, you yourselves will see that this is what you get."

So now it was good-by. I had gone to Rarotonga because I knew that there was a job to be done. When other positions had sometimes tempted me, I had stayed there because I recognized in this small Pacific Territory a first-class training ground for a young doctor in practical and administrative medicine. I had worked in a developing community with a partly educated indigenous people and had gained a full experience handling an officialdom that I found was no different from that in other small dependent areas.

I had reached the objectives I had set myself much earlier than I had ever hoped for. There was now only a very small effort necessary on my part to maintain present momentum. Probably no further progress could be made for at least another five years when fresh personnel, now in training at the Medical School in Fiji, would be ready to return to Rarotonga.

I felt that the time had come for me to look further afield and to add to my knowledge of medical administration; America would offer me that opportunity.

My final meetings with the various committees and organizations we had set up to help with the Medical Service were always terminated by tears on the part of my well-wishers. My hospital staff, numbering well over one hundred, entertained me formally and on a grand scale, but on the day following this event there occurred an incident which I shall never forget.

I was sitting in my office at the hospital, clearing up my files of correspondence, when my secretary, a young European clerk, knocked at my door.

"Excuse me for bothering you just now, Doctor, but would you mind coming down to the laundry, there's trouble down there."

Now the laundry is the one part of my hospital setup in which, as regards its location, I take no pride. Somehow it became the one thing which received the least attention, and although over the years I had made periodic efforts towards its improvement I regret to say that all our hospital washing was still being done in a very Heath Robinson establishment down at the bottom of the hospital grounds. All day long a group of ancient old ladies, their children, grandchildren, pet dogs and close friends took turns in scrubbing, rinsing and — after draping the hospital unmentionables on various clotheslines, rocks and coconut trees — ironing under a corrugated iron roof. And so there was often "trouble" in the laundry, the settlement of which I discreetly left to the matron.

"Tell Matron to settle it, I'm busy," I told the young man.

He left my office hesitantly but in two minutes he was back.

"I'm sorry, Doctor; but things are getting pretty serious down there. Matron would like you to come and help her straighten things out."

There seemed no help for it, I was to have one more "run-in" with the laundry staff.

But what a surprise I had that morning. No sooner had I put my head inside the door of our washing premises than I found myself showered in *ei*. On a spotless white cloth, laid over a borrowed table, stood an array of bottled goods. An enormous teakettle held a generous supply of home-brew. The old washerwomen stood, their faces wreathed in smiles, while they waited for the oldest of all to act as their spokeswoman.

"Our son," began old Mama Manu, "you are our guest. We know that last night all of us who have worked for you showed the people of Rarotonga how much we have learned to love you. But this is not enough. Our love is not only for you as a doctor but as a man as well and today we are joining together to show that love in the way we know you like best. Puia, bring the guitar, and fill the glasses."

Touched though I was, I could not refrain from glancing at the pile of unwashed linen.

"Now don't you worry about the work," said Mrs. Manu. "We've had this party planned a long time now, and the work will be finished as usual. First relay to the tubs, and let the party start."

The unofficial hospital farewell began at 9:30 in the morning. To the accompaniment of scrubbing, rinsing and bustling out to the drying lawn, with the alternating comings and goings not only of the hospital personnel but of half the villagers as well, under the delighted eyes of the patients who climbed out of their beds and watched the proceedings from the ward verandas, I succumbed for the first time to the sentiment of these wonderful island people.

I joined my voice with theirs as we sang the mournful chants of old-time Polynesia. When my *ei*, quite drenched in tears, had to be replaced with a fresh one, our mistress of ceremonies called for a riotous drinking song, and interspersing our melody with belly grunts I showed them that I had not lost the art of dancing a hula. The teakettle was refilled again and again. And when we felt hungry, the villagers brought bundles of cooked food to keep the party going. Matron dashed back and forth to the hospital to ensure that work was progressing as usual, or, if not quite as usual, that it was at least being done. Friend Puia, always the sober one of the party, organized the work-relays. I knew that the great ball of the preceding night had cost each staff member almost a whole month's salary, yet here they were, giving still more.

Always since working in this South Sea Island, I had refused to allow a lowering of standards on the grounds that "This is the Islands" might be a good excuse to do things differently from the methods taught in more advanced countries. But now, for once, looking round me, I had to admit that only in the South Seas could a party like this happen. I tell myself, too, that only because a part of me is Polynesian can I truly appreciate the greatness of heart that has made strangers say, "This is the Islands, this is paradise."

CHAPTER XX
Below Deck

OUR departure from Wellington harbor was not the hilarious leave-taking that seemed to be the lot of other small craft off on a long cruise. Although our friends gathered at the wharf to wish us good luck, their kind thoughts seemed to be tinged with the color of doom, and none of them could conceal that they thought we were all committing suicide.

Tom had now acquired two crewmen. There was no shortage of applicants — almost everyone we met longed for a sea voyage to America. Tom finally selected a young man named Neil Arrow, whom he had met at the sail-mender's. Neil had had a lot of sailing experience and seemed a fine choice. The selection of the second crewman we left up to him, more familiar than we with New Zealand yachtsmen, and he soon settled upon Bill Donovan, a young man just twenty-one.

We would sail at 1 P.M., and the landlubbers milling all over the decks, slippery with the pouring rain, were not making things easier for the crew. Tom was worried over the weather forecast. Something was brewing outside the coastline, but as our sailing date had already been delayed four weeks we must go now or give up altogether. John could not have been less concerned at the commotion around him; he sat and read comics; Tim was curled up on my bunk, asleep. I accepted various small gifts from the endless stream of farewellers, and felt very brave and rather sorry for myself.

I retired to the main cabin and continued to knit Tom a

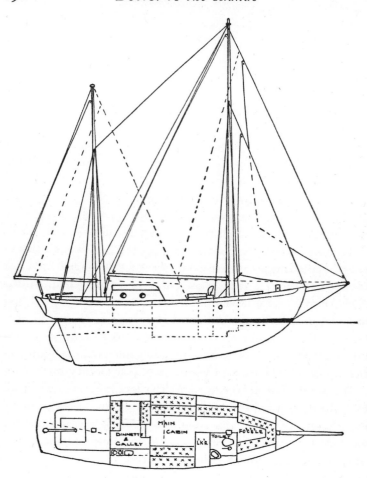

storm hat. The emotions of Madame Defarge as she busily clicked her needles were as nothing compared to mine at that moment. If only I had the courage to grab the children, run ashore and say, "I'm not going, I'm scared." Pure cowardice in the face of the resulting scandal kept me at my knitting.

"If you want to take photographs, come up," shouted Tom from the deck. "We're casting off."

"Come on, John," I said, grabbing my camera and struggling into my mackintosh. "Don't you want to say good-by to New Zealand?"

"Poof, I don't care about New Zealand," said John settling down to another comic. "When will we get to America?"

Only God could answer that one so I left John to the realms of Tarzan and Terry and the Pirates, and prepared to take pictures. Bill had kissed his weeping mother for the last time, and was now aboard wielding the boat hook to keep our bow from under the wharf. Neil was hoisting the staysail, and rather than ask Bill to assist him he was launching our vessel in blood; the staysail block had evidently connected with his nose, and he had smeared the resulting gore all over the rest of his face with a piece of cotton waste. Tom was performing a rather clever acrobatic: he stood at the tiller, shouted good-by with one side of his mouth, yelled to Neil with the other, and gave orders to Bill through the middle, all the while hanging over the side of the vessel to grab his movie camera which was being handed to him from the wharf.

We were away. Up on the masthead, a carved tiki that Ron Powell had given us for luck was screwed to face the bows, our homemade house flag also fluttered a tiki, St. Christopher's medallion was screwed to the deckhouse bulkhead, and everyone's fingers were firmly crossed. As Wellington disappeared into the distance, I went below and made a nice cup of tea.

To me there is nothing lovelier on the sea's face than a harbor. The sight of rocks, buoys and other ships may worry the skipper, but for the cook how precious is the lack of motion in sheltered waters. My cooking facilities consisted of the barest necessities: two kerosene primuses swung on heavy gimbals, one pressure cooker, three saucepans, one frying pan, and a kettle. With such reliable tools I knew that nothing could go wrong. Let others have their alcohol stoves and their bottled gas, we would always have hot food. Making that first meal was easy, for even outside the harbor, despite the ominous skies and falling glass, the motion of the *Miru* was comparatively gentle. But this respite was short-lived. Within a few hours both Timothy and I had succumbed to seasickness, Timothy enduring the sneers of the more hearty John, and I privately vowing that I would show no action in the culinary department until my interior had settled.

On deck, young Bill too was feeling the motion. Tom was undisturbed, as usual, but Neil, having read somewhere that a glass of salt water would settle the most delicate of stomachs, had made the mistake of swallowing a pint of sea. Whoever started that legend was only too clearly a liar. However, the boys had to keep working, taking watches, two hours on and four off, attending to the sail and attempting to clear up the gear still to be stowed. Rough weather was so speedy in coming that the men took the line of least resistance and jammed all the loose gear under the galley table. What their opinion of my defection as cook may have been I will never know, and at the time I felt too miserable to wonder.

After two days of complete neglect of my duties, during which the men cooked for themselves, I issued forth. Timothy was rid of his seasickness, and none the worse for the experience; John was getting in everyone's way on deck. Bill and Neil were still suffering from seasickness, but this had not impaired their appetites; for the last two days they had all been eating canned food, so I prepared to make up for my shortcomings. There was no stanchion beside the galley bench, and as there was nowhere to wedge myself while cooking a meal the best I could do was to pounce on my pots and pans each time the *Miru* rolled to starboard, the galley side. Despite this, that first day I produced an excellent chow mein and restored my status in the eyes of the menfolk.

We were carrying only two hundred gallons of fresh water; we did not want to ration this out to a set number of pints per day, preferring to refrain from washing and to drink as much as we wanted. The children, for whom there is no greater sport than sozzling with soap and water, were also put on their honor to leave the fresh water alone. The prospect of going without washing their faces delighted them and there was plenty of sea for sozzling purposes. I had planned on using no fresh water at all in the cooking, and washed our dishes in a saucepan of hot sea, liberally sprinkled with soap detergents. The dishes were reasonably clean, but as there was no place to set a dish down without its flying under the galley table, clean utensils were apt to contain a small lake of sea and soap upon their next presentation, for they could never be dried or rinsed.

Like most small boats, the *Miru* had no provision for a locker in which the men coming off watch could hang their oilskins or stow their sea boots. Consequently these large, cold and dripping wet pieces of equipment were draped all over the galley. The chart table, at which we ate our meals, was also in the deckhouse, so with navigation gear, oilskins, radio parts, and all other pieces of equipment that had to be left in readiness for any emergency, there was really little room in which to do my cooking.

I discovered very early that under the seat at which Tom worked out his navigation I had stowed my most often used foodstuffs. If I said, "Excuse me, could I get at the flour," I invariably chose just that moment to interrupt a delicate computation, which would have to be done all over again. If, to make room for a plate, I shifted something, it was apt to become irretrievably lost. Small cans of oil, or other liquids which must not be upset, found a resting place on top of the gimbals; if I put them aside to cook a meal they tipped over. It was all too clear that a small yacht out on the ocean is no place for a woman's business. How I longed for my sunny veranda in Rarotonga and the efficiency of Maria. A few days out from New Zealand Bill left one of the hatch boards lying on top of the deckhouse and a sea swept it away. Now for the rest of the voyage I would have huge seas filtering onto my stoves and down the back of my neck for the gimbals were set just below the main companionway.

One week out from New Zealand John suddenly became rather green and within a few hours he was covered with spots. He had picked up measles and at a most inopportune time, for the glass fell and we were in the midst of a hurricane. I shifted Tim over onto the bottom of the mate's bunk and installed John in my place, cramping myself up at the bottom, with my knees up to my chin and water pouring onto my head from that darn leaking skylight. I was too worried about John's discomfort and lack of the rest he needed to notice much about that storm. Tom saw more of it than I did.

The hurricane at least had one good result. I was so bruised from being thrown around the deckhouse when working at the galley that Tom had at last rigged me some support. This was a length of rope with a spring clip at each end attached to the porthole bolts above the bench, but it kept me in one place even if it did dig a ridge across my seat. Meals improved, and there was slightly less food on the galley floor. The storm had not been followed by a calm for the seas were still raging.

Fortunately we all had our sea legs by this time, but the strain of always clawing one's way from place to place, coupled with the everlasting suspicion that the man on watch might have been washed overboard, was beginning to tell.

I had been obliged to shift both the children out of the forecastle which was soaking and still pouring in water with each wave coming over the bows. Tim was now permanently installed at the bottom of my bunk; when the skylight leaked he squeezed up beside me while John, speedily convalescing from his spots, was occupying a makeshift bunk just aft the forecastle. The arrangement worked reasonably well as the children could now play on John's bunk and keep out of the main cabin, allowing the men, exhausted from the strain of the storm, to get a little rest. The presence of Tim taking up a good half of my already limited sleeping quarters caused discomfort, but as there was no alternative accommodation for little Tim I kept quiet and wondered if the pains in my joints were really just cramps or whether I was succumbing to sailor's rheumatism.

The deckhouse and main cabin were now in a state of the most appalling untidiness. Even Bill, who had started out so neatly, had to remove everything from his locker to find what he was looking for. The cabin floor was three or four inches deep in water, and anything that slipped off a bunk or the table was immediately soaked. We wore sea boots all the time except in our bunks; Tom's textbooks, carefully brought along to be used at the all-too-distant School of Public Health, had fallen from the shelves and were ruined; everything breakable in the crockery locker had to be thrown overboard. From now on we would use the few plastic dishes. From the constant deluge of seas breaking over the decks, the two primuses in the galley poured soot all over the boat. Our new paint work was black, and so was I. We were all suffering from "the itch," and in need of lots of soap and fresh water.

Bill and Neil always combed their hair before going on watch. They couldn't explain why; perhaps subconsciously they were hoping that we would pass a luxury liner, but luxury liners don't come down in the Roaring Forties.

Timothy was the most fortunate. Being only five years old and consequently not far from the ground, he found it easy to clamber round no matter how marked the motion of the vessel. Both he and John were more than paying for their passage in fetching and carrying for us clumsier adults. Because of the continuous rolling of the vessel, there was no hope of John starting his correspondence lessons. He lived in constant fear that we might strike calm weather; he need not have worried, for three days after the first hurricane darned if we didn't strike another, this time much worse.

Tom ordered all sails down, lashed the tiller in an effort to head the boat up into the wind, and we settled into our bunks determined not to watch the glass but to pray silently that this storm would not last the four-and-a-half days of its predecessor. Where earlier the winds and seas had caused us discomfort, this time I think that we four adults were actually afraid. The *Miru* was on her own. Could she possibly survive the pounding she was receiving? The wind, now raging at what must have been ninety miles an hour, screamed and whistled through the rigging, and breaking waves caught the *Miru* beam on. The effect on those below the windward bunks was like a punch in the chest. Expectantly, we sensed each wave a second before it broke. "Hang on!" someone would call, and Tom in the bottom bunk clawed at his bunkboard while I grasped the beams above me, tensing myself for the blow.

From John's bunk, in the comparative security of the lee-ward side, I heard, "I'll have Mr. Snip the tailor's son, then I'll have Mrs. Chop the butcher's wife." Busy playing a card game of Happy Families, the children were blissfully un-aware that the rest of us were waiting each moment for our vessel to fall to pieces.

Hurricane or calm, we still had to eat; it wasn't so bad in the galley once I had climbed into the security of my precious rope. I managed to cook up some steak, peas and rice, and produce my usual brew of coffee. I admit to feeling rather no-ble concerning the preparation of this meal, for a hurricane is always considered the perfect excuse for the ship's cook to take a day off. After the meal I climbed back into my bunk and prepared to hang on for the rest of the afternoon. Tom teetered up into the engine room to see how things were far-ing there.

No sooner had he left the main cabin than I found myself sitting on Bill's chest without the slightest recollection of how I got there. All my breath had been knocked out, my back hurt like the devil, and my shins were quite skinless. Dazedly looking round, I saw that the deckhouse table had been torn from its bolts and had crashed over against Bill's bunk. I had been thrown bodily out of my top bunk, struck the table and torn it loose, and finished up with Bill.

The two crewmen, whom gravity had stuck fast to their leeward bunks, stared at me in bewilderment and a little fear. I was not seriously hurt, having added only a few bruises to my already alarming collection, but when I struggled to re-gain my own quarters, another buster caught us and over I went again, this time straight on to our kerosene heater, the only means we had for drying clothes.

John put his head round his corner. "Mummy, whatever

are you doing? Why don't you go and lie down instead of falling all over the place?"

Not deigning to answer, I made a third sortie and scrambled back where I had started. During all my commotion, Tom had been having some private adventures up in the deckhouse. When the buster hit us he had been thrown across a can of oil, upsetting its contents all over the already swimming floor, then tossed onto the deckhouse table which his weight had broken off its hinges, so that he was pitched down between the unbalanced table and the side of the vessel, his head amongst the gear crammed on the leeward side, and his heels in the air. Stuck in this position he had not been able to come to my assistance, but when he had at last regained the upright and lurched down to the main cabin again, his reaction to my perambulations took me aback.

"For God's sake," bellowed Captain Bligh, "who did that to the table, and look at my heater!"

Crouching in my top bunk and hanging onto the beams for dear life, I felt rather as if I had taken a little hatchet and systematically smashed things up. Reeling and crashing, Tom managed to dig up a piece of heavy rope and lash the wildly careering table to the side of Bill's bunk. Bilge had now collected to the point where with each roll of the vessel it slopped against the sides of our bunks. Tom returned to the engine room and attempted to start the electric pump; when he came back he was speechless. Our pump had given up the struggle just when it was most needed. If this was the state of things below, what must it be like abovedecks? It was unsafe to go and look, but we prayed to God that the hurricane would blow itself out quickly.

From John's bunk still came those piping voices: "Now give me Billy Bun the baker's son, I know you've got him because I gave him to you myself. You're cheating. Mummy, Tim's a cheat." How I wished I too were only ten years old and without a care in the world.

After Tom and I had reinstalled ourselves, we took Neil's bunk board and wedged it on top of mine, which had proved

so inadequate. Each breaking sea threw Tom onto the floor. It wasn't far to fall and he was not being hurt, but every descent threw him into six inches of bilge water. He wiped himself off and climbed back philosophically. "Now we'll have to put into land, the nearest is Rapa Island, thirteen hundred miles away. We'll have to dry out after this and get the pump fixed and that table bolted down again. God knows what the rigging will be like now. I doubt if we'll have an inch of unspliced rope left. As soon as this dies a bit we'll know the worst. I never dreamed any yacht would stand up to this pounding. Let's hope she can last the night. Woops, into the bilge again!"

This time the Pacific seemed to have decided that the little

Miru had passed all tests, for next morning the wind had fallen and the barometer was rising. The hull of our vessel was quite undamaged after the beating of the last twenty-four hours, but the decks were swept clean. All gear stowed in the cockpit had gone, all our inflammable fuel which we had kept on deck for safety had disappeared, the standard compass, so carefully checked for correction before we had sailed, had been lifted bodily out of its box atop the deckhouse and had vanished. All that remained on deck was the dinghy (under which we had stowed a sack of potatoes), the deck mop and the boat hook. The *Miru* had never before or since looked so tidy topsides. The pieces of sheepskin which we had used for chafing-gear on the stays were now snowy white, for the *Miru* had been under water right up to the masthead. The rope rigging was in a mess, and by the time repairs were made Tom counted fifty-two splices.

We still had 6400 miles to go before we reached Peru — and we had to have more rope. New Zealand was but three hundred miles to the west, but because of the completely adverse winds it would take us almost as long to cover that short distance as it would to keep on going to Rapa Island. We all had decided that the sea had thrown its whole book at us and we had come through with our vessel none the worse, and ourselves, apart from exhaustion and damp, none the worse. But Rapa must be reached soon for the men had not a single dry garment between them. Sleeping in wet clothes had soaked their mattresses, their skins were chafed raw, and we adults had all assumed suspiciously gray complexions. On the other hand, the children were blooming. Although they had not been able to go out on deck ever since we had left New Zealand, they had never complained, inventing games that could be played sitting together in John's bunk. The prospect of a call at another Polynesian island was to them merely a source of annoyance. Why didn't we hurry up and reach Cowboy Land? Who wanted to look at any more Polynesians?

For some reason, although few Europeans have ever visited Rapa Island, this tiny speck of land has gained itself quite a reputation throughout the Pacific. "That is the place where there are seven women to every man. Tom will get killed in the rush if you go there," was the advice I had received. Rapa's claim to fame proved to be purely geographic.

From the sea, Rapa is fantastic. Bora Bora and Rarotonga are justly famous for their sky lines, but beside Rapa they are tamely insignificant. Dozens of weird peaked castles rise straight from the sea, cliffs hundreds of feet high drop sheer to the pounding surf while sudden rolling hills break the anger of the looming rock. There is no protecting coral reef here to guard the land whose stormy birth and struggle to survive against the ocean is borne out by the strength of its soil. The only barriers are low reefs of soft coral; unlike that which surrounds the more tropically situated islands, it is brittle and easily broken, and no great danger to ships.

Across the mouth of the harbor entrance our charts showed us a reef, but we knew we were back amongst Polynesians when we puzzled over the meaning of dozens of markers standing up over the coral. The Rapans seemed to have a private system of warning boats, and it was not until a longboat loaded with natives, all male, came out to us, that Tom would take the risk of seeking an anchorage. Rapa had been expecting us, but not all in one piece. Rarotonga had radioed only that morning to tell Rapa that the *Miru* had been caught in the worst gales of seventy years off the New Zealand coast. It was thought that the skipper might have tried to head up to the Austral Islands, within which lies Rapa, but since the

Miru had not been heard of for three weeks it must be pre-
sumed lost. Would the Rapans kindly keep an eye out for
pieces of wreck, half of which would be the property of the
French Government, who owned the Island, the other half
the natives would be welcome to?

The Rapans were little different from any other Polynesians. They were slightly darker-skinned, but wore the same
tattered clothes and straw hats perched on top of their heads
as do the Rarotongans. Their language proved to be similar to
Tahitian, so although I could barely make myself understood
in my newly acquired Rarotongan, Tom had no trouble con-
versing with them. He learned that the proportion of fe-
males to males was just over 50 per cent, so away went another legend. We had also heard that Rapa is not well supplied
with food; for visitors that may be so, but the natives
cultivate sufficient for themselves, and from the sale of
beef which runs wild on the Island they also make enough
money to buy the few European luxuries that every Islander
likes.

I was surprised at the un-Polynesian attitude of the Rapan
natives who came to sell us food. Immediately they realized
that we had shirts to exchange, the price went up. Two shirts
for six eggs, all of which proved bad, made me certain Rapa
was suffering from inflation. They asked a bar of soap for two
small crayfish, ten fishhooks for a basket of wild oranges.
Even the two Frenchmen stationed on the Island seemed to
think that Christmas had come. As we had said we were on
our way to America, the official in charge of the mail and radio station would not accept sterling in payment for our
stamps and radio messages, and our precious dollars had to go.
We couldn't barter with the Rapans, for if we were unwilling
to pay their price they would take the goods away. Our only

alternative was to live on our ship's stores, eked out by a little fish that we had been able to buy at reasonable prices.

The Islanders had formed a co-operative society for the export of their beef. They divided the profits and divided their local produce too. On Friday, the day they distributed their rations among the villagers, they were kind enough to send a generous share out to the *Miru,* while the two Frenchmen and the local native doctor turned on what was to be our last island party for a long time. Dancing the hula among the empty wine bottles on the long table, I could not help wondering how long it would be before we would be doing this again. When Tom and Bill upset the canoe on the way home and fell into the freezing lagoon, we knew that we were following the old tradition of yachts visiting a South Sea island.

The food situation was not as troublesome as the rigging. We had heard that the schooner *Tagua* might be expected in a fortnight from Tahiti to pick up beef; there was no rope or stores to be bought at the one tiny store on Rapa and the *Tagua* was our only chance if our broken rigging was to be replaced. We decided to wait two weeks. This would give us ample time to make internal repairs, though it would also add far too many extra meals to the number for which I had stored our provisions. With our rifle the crewmen were able to add some beef to our Deepfreeze, but we needed more staples for the long six weeks it would take us to reach Peru.

After fourteen days of waiting, the *Tagua* sailed into the lagoon. She too had been through the gales, and was little better off than we. However she did carry good supplies of rope and a little spare food, but here again the skipper insisted that he be paid in dollars. Knowing that New Zealand sterling was easily negotiable in Tahiti, I was so infuriated over the unfair-

ness of this that I stubbornly refused to buy anything more
than a few tins of butter, one can of biscuits and a little
sugar. Tom bought a full supply of spare rope without arguing the exchange. Even if we might go a little hungry, we
would at least have the security of knowing we could replace
our rigging if we struck another hurricane.

As the Rapans were well occupied chasing cattle on the
morning we set forth, Tom piloted the *Miru* out by himself.
The day was calm, he had coaxed the engine into activity, and
the clearness of the waters of the lagoon made the negotiation
of the channel fairly simple. Then the engine subsided. Shortly
before this Bill had mistaken the fuel can for one of water.
Now came the result, but as the breeze was coming off shore
we were able to get sail up and reach the safety of the open
water before anything worse happened.

The meteorological observer at Rapa had assured us that we
could expect fairly reasonable weather for the next few days,
and though the weather was steady the huge seas, so much a
feature of this part of the ocean, were still with us, tossing
and rolling us day and night, but spinning the log over into
steady runs of between 150 and 160 miles each day. We were
cutting down south again into the Roaring Forties, and the
decks were again awash.

A day or two after leaving Rapa, Bill flagrantly disobeyed
an order from the skipper. We had been given two chickens
as a farewell gift, and Tom had asked Bill to kill and pluck
them.

"I'll kill them," said Bill, swallowing hard against another
bout of seasickness, "but I'll be keel-hauled before I'll pull
their feathers out."

Bill was determined, so Tom relegated the job to John, who
attacked the first bird with enthusiasm, stripped half of it,

then, growing bored, had to be bullied into attending to the other half. Resigning himself, Tom sat in the cockpit, steering with his foot, and prepared to pluck the second bird. With only one wing to go, we heard a heart-rending scream from the deck. We rushed up the companionway prepared to see the skipper's body lunging over astern.

"My chicken, my chicken," roared Tom. "That goddam wave took my chicken, and only the parson's nose to do."

Bill, who loves food better than anything else in the world, privately vowed that never again would he balk at any job connected with eating.

Below decks we were more shipshape than we had ever been. Most of our spare gear, which had always occupied the floor under the galley table, was now in use replacing that which we had lost in the two hurricanes. The cursed skylight was battened down tight with canvas and now we expected to be dry in the cabin. The winter sunshine at Rapa had dried and aired all our mattresses and we were well washed again.

I had cut meals to two a day, with only cups of tea or coffee at noontime, and we could continue in this way for another month before it might be necessary to institute rationing. We knew each other well enough now to evaluate each other's stories, to know that the worst was behind us, and that no matter how rough the weather might be, the long stretch of ocean ahead of us would be more than anything a test of endurance.

Tired of sitting on watch with soaking trousers, the two crewmen had followed Tom's example of wrapping their hips in native *pareu,* the gay blue and white flowered loincloth to be bought only in the Pacific Islands. The boys were not as skillful as Tom in rolling the cloth securely. Bill in particular repeatedly threatened to come entirely apart, but at least now they did not sleep in wet clothes, and the skin rashes would not recur.

On the 13th of July we found ourselves plumb in the middle of the Pacific Ocean. To me this day was significant, for each run we made from now on, no matter how short it might be, would bring us nearer to South America and farther from New Zealand. Our prospect of living comfortably after the completion of the voyage had also improved, for the *Tagua* had brought me a letter from the *Saturday Evening Post*. Thanks to Hal Coolidge the *Post* seemed to believe that we would really complete the voyage and they wanted me to write an account of the trip. It was quite impossible to start on the articles while we were at sea; my typewriter had been deluged by the leaking skylight, and even if it had been working I could not have kept it steady enough to use in these huge seas. Each day I continued to write a little in my diary, but the very sameness of the succeeding entries remind me now how barren were those days between Rapa and Peru.

We struck two calms and two storms in the 4750 miles. The calms gave the men the opportunity to attend to damaged rigging while during the storms we hove to, sat in our bunks, and read books. Once we passed a pod of whale, once we saw some jellyfish, but apart from the ever-present sea pigeons and albatross the seas were deserted and our main interest lay below decks in the galley regions. I had to strain my ingenuity in making our two meals worth waiting for. I gradually extended my culinary talents to making tarts, scones, buns, puddings, anything to vary the menus yet not use up too much of the precious stores. And I had learned the ship's timetable and how to keep my cooking out of the men's way.

One night while we were hove to during a storm, Tom and Bill decided out of sheer boredom that they would attack the galley and show what "we men can do with the cooking at sea." After more than an hour's concentrated effort, Tom emerged triumphant bearing a plate full of wet round grayish balls. "Doughboys," he said, but we could think of other names. We ate them for the sake of the precious flour they contained, but Tom and Bill kept away from the galley after that. Neil occasionally gave a demonstration of his cooking ability; the results were very good if one was prepared to wait for them and did not mind the array of burned pots stacked in back of the lockers.

On the first of August we feasted. I had carefully hoarded up three chickens, peas, potatoes, ice cream and canned fruit for this day, for this was John's tenth birthday. Not only had John reached double figures, but we had entered onto the third and last 2000-mile chart of the Pacific. While John unwrapped his bundles of salt-water presents, we looked longingly at the great stretch of land on the right-hand side of the chart. Our previous two charts had been clean sheets of paper, regularly ruled off into neat squares with a couple of fly spots representing the only good solid earth. My spirits rose as I looked at our present course, for no matter how slowly we might be moving, every day would bring us a little farther from the left-hand margin, a little closer to that good solid earth.

While John gloated over two sweaters, a pair of bathing trunks, a slightly mildewed fruitcake, a pocketknife, half a packet of plasticine, and a five-dollar bill, we lit the one coarse tallow birthday candle, and as John blew each of us wished that the miles might pass a little more quickly.

After our birthday feast I collected all the food left aboard, for now we would have to institute strict rationing. My collection of edibles was not appetizing. The last tin of biscuits had lost an argument with a can of kerosene, the dry cereals had burst their wrappings and become mildewed, the gallon can of soya oil, the last of my cooking fat, had sprung a leak. Rancid butter would have to be used instead. Of sugar we had none, but there was a little jam and honey left. That would be used in our tea and we would try to avoid the seeds in the bottom of the cups. My inventory did have one happy result, for I unearthed a precious case of homemade preserves, the ones Mother had brought to Lyttelton for us. We had stowed them in a far corner of the hold and forgotten about them; now with a measured ration of the remaining flour we could have an occasional jam tart for dinner.

Tom estimated that it would be possible to reach Peru by the 21st of August, and therefore the food must be divided into twenty-one rations. Scones for breakfast, nothing for lunch, one third of a can of beef, one sixth of a can of vegetables, one third of a cup of rice, two tablespoons of custard with a little jam strewn on top, would be the day's food. We had plenty of dried milk, and I dug out a head of very high cheese. I had forgotten that I had bought two of these, one of which I had thrown overboard, and all these weeks had been wondering where the strange smell was coming from. The cheese was now pale green with black flecks in it, but it was still cheese, and, when eaten in chunks with one's head outside the companionway, provided a fine substitute for our missing luncheons.

Even though we were short of food and the boat was sailing herself without assistance from the crew, the days were not boring to me. I had launched out on a complicated piece of knitting, and while I slipped one, dropped one, I reveled in the knowledge that each minute land was coming closer. The children were in better health than they had been for years. They rarely quarreled, and the only breaks in the peace of our days occurred when John and I had our daily argument over his correspondence lessons; he much preferred watching the waves to completing the day's assignment, but I was determined he should keep up with his schoolwork. One day I admit that he infuriated me so much I actually bit him, then suffered agonies of conscience. Heavens, I wasn't as hungry as all that! The sums were gradually done, the answers correct, odd seafaring poems laboriously learned and recited, and John's haphazard education continued.

Timmy had started out on kindergarten work, but he showed an alarming determination to read and write backwards. I could not be guilty of biting both my offspring, so handed the littlest one some plasticine, some pieces of wood, and a pocketknife, and left him to work out his own salvation. He became fascinated with model boats, but when I found that all my handkerchiefs had been neatly cut into triangles for the construction of "waggle sails" and my precious fishing lines had been hacked into small lengths to provide the miniature rigging, I realized that though Timmy had been quiet and contented during these long days he had been quite as mischievous as any other small boy.

On the 20th of August the food was almost finished but it was impossible for Tom to estimate an accurate position. For five days there had been no sign of sun or star, the horizon was obscured by thick haze, and the water a flat calm. That day we knew that South America was truly behind the clouds, for alongside floated a dead pelican. We don't have pelicans on the western side of the Pacific. South America, where are you? Tom connected up his radio transmitter and tried to contact Lima, but the only stations we could pick up were in Chile. The sun came out, but, darn me, if it wasn't in eclipse.

A sight taken that morning put us somewhere up the Amazon. That night we kept double watches, and for the first time in eleven weeks since leaving New Zealand I was given a job at the tiller. It was bitterly cold, and repeated dunkings in the oil tank with the end of the deck mop showed our fuel almost finished. Tom is never at a loss; he poured a couple of cans of the kerosene I had been using to keep the primuses alight and on we went. Though we peered into the darkness, we saw no sign of a light. A faint flare in the sky promised land not too far off, but South America is a large continent, and we did not know how far north or south of our port we might be.

The next morning we finished the last remaining crumb of food — one can of bully beef and some fried buns concocted out of the remains of the dried milk, custard powder and cocoa. They were horrible; even Bill, our hardiest eater, couldn't tackle them.

When a fishing boat loomed out of the mist, we quite forgot that it had been forty-five days since we had seen another human being. The swarthy men aboard spoke what we gathered must be Spanish. We tried English, vile French, viler Italian, perfect Polynesian, and legal Latin. The combination of all tongues confirmed that Callao was just fifteen miles up the coast, and the sky reflection Tom had taken for Lima the night before was indeed Lima. Abel Tasman struck Espiritu Santo twenty miles south after eight days' dead reckonings; Tom Davis had beaten him by five miles.

At the Helm

OUR voyage in the *Miru* as far as we can ascertain was the first west-to-east crossing of the South Pacific to be completed successfully in a small boat in midwinter. The route has once before been attempted; that was in 1922 by Connor O'Brien, but one of his crewmen developed a poisoned finger two hundred miles off the New Zealand coast and he returned to port. I really had no choice in my route for my only alternative was to have set off in the other direction, a journey that would have taken at least a full year to complete. As matters stood, I was supposed to be in Boston by the end of September if possible. Actually it was not possible due to the dilatory workmanship of the shipyard in Wellington which was supposed to have completed the fitting out activities while I was finishing my work in the Cook Islands. In the end we were delayed a whole month in Wellington making ready for sea. I would be the last to say that when we eventually sailed the *Miru* was ready for the trip ahead of her, but I had always promised myself that when my turn came I would "set the date and go."

I figured that I would need two crew members for the safe conduct of the ship and here I think *Miru* set another record: she landed in Boston, five months after setting out on one of the hardest passages ever made in a small vessel, with the same ship's company that she had in the beginning; more important, we were still all on speaking terms. The choosing of a suitable crew for small vessels always has been difficult: men who are willing to undertake a dangerous and uncomfortable voyage are not usually the most stable of individuals, and stability is an essential where lives will ultimately be at stake. The experienced sailors who have stability are usually weighed down with responsibilities of family, home and business so that the crew-seeking skipper has, as a rule, only adventurers from whom to choose.

Eventually I chose two young men who seemed, even if not experienced at ocean-cruising, certainly to promise pleasant company and strong backs. Neither Neil Arrow nor Bill Donovan (mate and able seaman to the *Miru*) gave me the impression that they would ever break down in an emergency. In this I proved right: though Neil and Bill knocked themselves and the *Miru* about, they did what they were told for five months on end and even if sometimes they had difficulty concealing resentment of my orders they performed those orders without question, ultimately learning to love and respect our vessel as much as did I.

Neither of the crew understood engines, radio, or navigation. Lyd had learned to be an excellent dry-land navigator, her computations are impeccable, but she would be the first to admit that one of her sights taken on a rolling boat might put us in a position halfway up the Congo River. I had hopes of teaching the crew simple navigation: Bill gave up in despair very early, Neil continued to nibble his pencil and exasperate himself in his efforts to plot an accurate position. I, never a genius at mathematics, had taught myself navigation years ago and on this voyage I used star sights and worked my position with the aid of Hughes air navigation tables. I chose to use star sights because a simultaneous three-star fix

gives latitude and longitude with a minimum of effort. I
plotted our position daily, for I consider this good practice no
matter how many thousand miles a ship may be from land.
It was good for the morale of the ship's company as they eagerly examined the great bare charts each day to see how
much farther we had progressed.

My knowledge of engines had improved since the days of
my old motorbike, Hurry Up. In the *Miru* we depended upon
a seventeen-year-old Ailsa Craig Diesel motor, a British model,
which exerted her full 27 English-rated horsepower down in
the bowels of the ship. There were times when I had to work
to keep her going. An excess of zeal on Neil's part when filling the oil tank forced me to remove the entire engine head,
do a valve-grind job, and reassemble it when in the midst of
the second hurricane, but even that is possible when the devil
drives.

My tentative plan was to sail straight from Wellington to
Peru in the Roaring Forties between Latitudes 35 to 50, an
uncomfortable part of the world for a 6750-mile crossing in
midwinter. During our first three weeks in the Pacific, as
Lydia has said, we struck two hurricanes. At the outset I followed the varied advice I had gleaned from reading the numerous "epic voyages," and in the process I lost all my spare
lines and both my sea anchors as well as a couple of heavy
sails improvised to make-do sea anchors. I also learned a lesson that none of the books had mentioned. I will not pre-
sume to lay down a law that this is the correct method of riding out a hurricane, but when the experience of others and
my own invention had failed, then I discovered that *Miru*,
left to herself under bare poles, settled into the safest position to face the winds and the raging seas. She eased into just
that angle where she would take the least movement in any

part of her: my 24-ounce canvas, a weight fitted for the old giant barques, would not stand; my ropes chafed through. *Miru* made sure that I had expounded every effort to help her, then turned round and showed me how it was done.

In the second hurricane I hauled down all sail and left her

to look after herself from the beginning. Without wishing to generalize, I should say that this was merely the demonstration of a very simple law: one may lean on a wall but one may not walk through it. *Miru* leaned on the wall of the storm at the best angle for her particular design: she did not want to be pushed through, and it is my opinion now that, provided a small vessel is well and strongly built, this method is the safest when the wind force has reached a velocity that could be dangerous.

I do not say that during the hurricanes we were comfortable below, that is impossible on any vessel. Although in the rest of the voyage we ran into no more hurricanes, the regular forty-mile-an-hour wind that is part of the scenery in the winter Roaring Forties and the cyclones and high velocity gales we struck during the remainder of the journey I handled with an eye to the lesson I had learned during the two hurricanes. Gale force winds allowed the use of a riding mizzensail and no longer did we hang onto the sides of our bunks and worry as to how best we might help the ship: instead we read detective books and rested secure in the knowledge that the *Miru* knew her business and would bring us through safely.

The loss of my spare rope and the innumerable splices now in my running rigging demanded that after the hurricanes we put into the nearest land for repairs and a well-needed rest. We made for Rapa Island in the French Austral group, still another 1600 miles to the northeast. This involved some very ticklish seamanship in using the elements to advantage. The seas were always immense and the winds always at least gale force and from the northwest, west, or southwest. In these huge seas I had to let the *Miru* run before, but I noticed that when the wind changed from one western point to the next, for about twelve hours during and after the change, the seas died a little, sufficiently for me to alter course due north before again running before the new sea. It was a zigzag course that kept everyone on the alert for the coming wind change: even in our bunks during sleeping hours we three men were alert to any altered motion of the vessel and would rush on deck to take full advantage of our short opportunities for a northing.

I was considerably worried about the accuracy of my navigation, for during the hurricanes I had lost overboard my navigating compass so that I had to use the steering compass, placed directly above the engine and completely uncorrected for deviation. I had to do these corrections as I went along taking azimuth and amplitude sights on every new change of course. The steering compass was in perfect correction by the time we sighted South America.

At Rapa we rested, washed, battened down in those places that had proved not watertight, painted our topsides again, and, after waiting two weeks for a passing schooner (the *Tagua*) to call at the island and replenish my supply of rope, moved out on the long 4500-mile stretch of the Pacific.

My main concern during the six weeks' voyage from Rapa to Peru was with the morale of those aboard. The two children were behaving normally, irritating at times, but no more than is usual in small boys, and always finding new ways to amuse themselves which the rest of us envied. So long as we were approaching a large piece of dry land Lyd remained cheerful. The galley was her chief concern and she was kept more than busy thinking up new ways to produce our one big and appetizing meal of the day. Thanks to our Deep-freeze we had pork chops, roast chicken, roast beef — except during those first bad weeks when we were living on rationed stores, more often cold than not. The number of calories consumed daily would pass muster with any dietician, the frequency and variety of meals would amaze a fresh-water yachtsman. The two crewmen remained cheerful; Bill was finding the Pacific Ocean rather larger than he had bargained for, and Neil, inspired no doubt by the fact that Lyd had been offered a very profitable contract by the *Saturday Evening Post* to write an account of our voyage, was launching out into a brand-new career of journalism.

I was careful always to watch for any signs of fatigue, for it is fatigue that is responsible for the accidents and inefficiency and sometimes even the loss of life on a small boat. A man is tired, he is not alert, he slips or trips on some object he would ordinarily avoid, and overboard he goes. I did not have life lines right around the *Miru,* but I made sure that my two crewmen were always alert enough not to have to rely on such safety devices. With never more than four hours' sleep at one time (the watches were two hours on, four hours off), I tried to give us all a break, a rest and a boost to morale by occasionally heaving to and breaking out a bottle of Lyd's gin. Then we would hold a private party no less gay than if we had been on dry land with all the comforts of home and in the morning we would sail on again, heads aching perhaps, but our spirits considerably higher and the time we had lost in carousing more than caught up by the renewed vigor.

About five hundred miles off the coast of South America the horizon was quite obscured by haze, and, knowing that the junction of the Pacific and Humboldt currents had produced this phenomenon and that I could not expect a clear sky until almost against the land, I realized that the remainder of my navigation into Callao would have to be done by dead reckoning alone. Our only chart of South America covered the area between the Gulf of Mexico and Cape Horn, scarcely an accurate indication of the precise location of the pinpoint on the Peruvian coast marked Callao. For five days I set the course by using my wind changes (if the diminishing zephyrs could be called wind) and the reading of the ship's log. That log had come a long way, but its accuracy was proclaimed by the fact that we came into the Peruvian coast just fifteen miles to the south of Callao; and after six weeks of ocean, monotony, and rationed meals, no land was ever hailed more gladly than the barren deserts and rocky peaks that rose out of the mist, just as my people back on the other side of the ocean had predicted they would.

That crossing of our earth's most vast and angry ocean had offered me every problem that a small-boat skipper might ever expect to confront him. In the initial stage of our journey, when the elements had been so vicious, I had occasion to wonder whether I had been overconfident in thinking that I could ever hope to achieve the midwinter passage, and mistaken in subjecting my wife and small sons to discomforts that I felt sure were unparalleled. Yet here we were, all of us in glowing health and spirits, and with a satisfaction in our hearts that we will seldom approach again.

I was following an ancient path in that long haul across the Pacific, but one which had been given fresh prominence by Mr. Thor Heyerdahl's best seller, *Kon Tiki*. By a quirk of fate, when I was studying for my certificate as an amateur radio operator, back on Rarotonga, I was one of the three amateurs who located the Kon Tiki raft just after she was wrecked on Raroia in the Tuamotu Islands.

We Cook Islanders regarded the Kon Tiki expedition with more than usual confidence. We felt certain that the raft would reach Polynesia if it would only stay afloat. But Mr. Heyerdahl's theory of the origin of our people we thought of as a rather amusing misconception. Our song and legend and our history have told how Polynesians visited Peru in the days gone before: how the leader of the expedition, Maui Maruma-mao, had led his fleet of double sailing canoes in a smaller outrigger canoe in which, with his own family and his own *taunga,* he had set the course, controlled the supplies, and watched over the less speedy boats in times of ill weather; how he had laid his course from Raiatea in the Society Islands, down through the Tuamotuan group, and across to Easter Island, then on to the "land of ridges," the Andean chain on the coast of Peru. The old folk often sang the story of how Maui stayed on in Peru searching for a land like the lush islands he had left, but, finding none in the barren section by the sea where the Incans lived, had settled himself and the members of his expedition in the coastal caves, lingering in this

foreign country long enough to be impressed by the culture of the strangers and to absorb from it those elements which would best fit into the prevailing Polynesian systems, social, religious and educational.

Our songs told too of how Maui died while in Peru, and how, before his death, he instructed his son Kiu to carry on the study of the Incan culture and return to Polynesia to teach his people the lessons learned; how Kiu gathered his expedition once more and sailed back to Easter Island, staying there to formulate the improved tradition, carving on the tablets that have caused so much mystery and speculation among scientists the symbols of society that would henceforth be displayed in the tattoo patterns marking the various social strata of the Polynesian people.

We modern Polynesians do not regard this expedition of our ancestors as such a great miracle of seamanship, for our people of that time, sixty generations ago, were wise in the ways of the sea, sky and the elements. The members of the expedition to Peru were no mere adventurers out for sensation, but a carefully selected group, expert in fishing and navigation.

Perhaps the Incans did drift across to Polynesia, but they left nothing behind them or on their way that could be regarded as distinct proof of their coming. The presence of the *kumera* in both countries is explained by Kiu having brought it on his return journey. Our legend and song tells of no story of an Incan visit. The Incans were never the great navigators that the people of the South Seas were and are. The poetry of Polynesia proves that the ancestors of the modern generation were familiar with the strange land so far away, for when I myself sighted that land, through the description given me before I left Rarotonga I was familiar with several of the landmarks outside the port of Callao.

When I was living in the Pacific I was never unduly concerned over the error of the Kon Tiki theory of migration, but after I reached America I was appalled to find how widespread and accepted the theory had become . . . that is, by laymen. I am thankful to say that scientists, anthropologists, and other students of Polynesia are agreed on what really happened.

Between Peru and Boston there lay another 4000 miles as the gulls fly, but with land so near, fuel depots and food supplies at hand, not to mention well-equipped marine supply stores, we all of us regarded the rest of the journey as a hay-ride. The Atlantic could do its worst, we almost challenged it to outdo its rival.

I used the engine all the rest of the way — of course with sail — and my problems now mainly revolved around my efforts to keep "Old Ailsa" started — or, once started, in continual revolution. The transit through the Panama Canal, I had been warned by other yachtsmen, could be very damaging to small sailing vessels. However, we made our transit alongside one of the small coastal banana boats, and with plenty of lines kept taut to our escort when rising, and to the top of the locks when being lowered toward the new ocean, the *Miru* said good-by to her home waters with all her usual grace and dignity. I will not deny that making the transit was a great strain, but by obeying the orders of our canal pilot, and keeping a close watch on what my two crewmen were up to, I was able to control the speed of the engine, handle the tiller, and still enjoy the novelty and engineering wonder of the Canal.

The Caribbean offered us the easiest sailing to date, although there was always the threat of hurricanes here during the last weeks in September. But luck was with us, and the only one who carried an umbrella was Lyd; with the memory of our early bad luck still very vivid in mind, she spent the entire two weeks that it took us to cross to the North American coast studying the sky and various booklets she had collected on the hair-raising subject of "Hurricanes: What Signs to Look For."

Our first American port was Key West, in southern Florida, and there it was brought to our notice that it has never been customary for New Zealanders to enter the United States without first procuring visas from the consul in their own country. Our homeland being rather far behind us, our arrival date in Boston already looming later than it should, and our motives for coming to America being above question, we were at last allowed a dispensation from Washington to continue our journey. Unfortunately we had chosen the season of the equinoctial gales for our journey up the east coast of the States, and even carrying the maximum sail that the brisk winds and heavy seas permitted, and with the engine doing her utmost to push us along, we were making little more than fifty miles each day. Bored at the lack of progress, I changed course towards the coast again and made up my mind to travel the rest of the way, at least as far as Virginia, in the Inland Waterway, a route of scenic beauty according to the various yachting publications, but, as I soon found to my sorrow, rather unsuitable for the passage of sailing vessels drawing as much as eight feet, as the *Miru* did.

The engine needed repairs, and while I attended to this at a wharf near the entrance to the waterway I kept up my contacts with the American radio amateurs to whom I had first been able to speak shortly after leaving Key West. These friends we never saw were kind in the extreme, forming a network down the length of the coast, keeping regular schedules with me, and offering every possible assistance to hasten our journey. But "haste" is not the word to apply to those three weeks we spent in traveling the 900 miles between Florida and Virginia, a distance we would have covered in ten or eleven days had we been able to sail outside the coast. We sailed by day and night and the channel is elusive after dark: on thirteen occasions the *Miru* grounded on the mud banks, and we were forced to wait for the incoming tide before we could hope to move. Lack of courtesy on the part of the speedy powerboats disgusted us, but for only one or two of our mudlarking adventures can we blame their wash: our other mishaps were due to my doggedness that we travel at night, and to the howling nor'easterly that repeatedly drove us off course in the narrow waterways.

The wash from the powerboats made our cook very cross: Lyd considered she had had more than her share of mopping up spilled food when we were out on the ocean. To one powerboat, however, I take off my hat. Seeing us stuck hard and fast on a bank early one morning, this gentleman raced up and down alongside us at full speed, creating a large enough wash to enable us to wobble off the bank. Unfortunately I was so amazed at the skipper's politeness that I did not take the name of his craft: so I make my salute here.

By the time we had reached Norfolk in Virginia, where we would again sail out on the Atlantic, the date had crept up to October 28, a full month past my expected arrival in Boston. If a nor'easter had been blowing at the time, we would have had to wait or continue inland, but this time Fate smiled, and the wind veered to nor'west, gale force, as is routine for the *Miru,* but at least going our way strongly enough to accomplish this "last mile" with a three-day flourish — and a broken gooseneck on the mainsail. On November 2, just five months after setting out from Wellington, we sailed into Boston harbor. I had enjoyed every minute of every mile. From the Harvard School of Public Health, from yachting enthusiasts, from Boston friends who, too, came from "down under," we were given a reception which showed that there were others who could appreciate the fact that New Zealand is a long hard way from Boston. Americans gasped at the size of little *Miru,* though to us yachts don't come bigger or better.

I will never regret choosing *Miru.* Even after the rigors of our long cruise, it would be hard to believe that she had not recently arrived from a week-end trip from Cape Cod. When we hauled her onto the slips, I could hardly credit it when I saw that her hull and keel had survived two full-scale hurricanes as well as every variety of the lesser hazards of deep-sea sailing. Her masts and rigging stood as firm as ever, the copper sheathing on the sides of her hull was barely scratched and even the scraping she received on the mud of the inland waterway had loosened only an inch or two of the keel-sheath. One or two stanchions were loose, the result of carelessness by people clambering aboard, and poor old Ailsa was badly in need of overhaul though I am assured by the Diesel experts that she was good for as many thousand miles again.

Only great necessity would entice me to repeat that west-to-east Pacific crossing in winter time. I have shown that it is possible, but I doubt that it will ever be repeated. It is difficult today to have a vessel built and rigged to sufficient strength to counter anything the Roaring Forties has to offer, and it is even more difficult to obtain a crew willing to face nearly 7000 miles of open ocean and remain human beings at the end of it. We hoped that our two crewmen would remain our friends long after the voyage was completed, even though living as closely together as we had been it was inevitable that we should come to know the bad as well as the good in each other.

The skipper on such a voyage has to stand up against the elements, and be ready for any responsibility that may fall on his shoulders. The old sailing skippers had plenty of troubles: take all of these and add to them the job of keeping a complicated Diesel engine in working order, a Deepfreeze and its generating plant running constantly, all the electric installations in perfect nick, and a radio constantly ready to receive or transmit, and there you have a bare outline of what the modern ocean-going yachtsman must expect.

I was fortunate in that I had the company of my wife and the diversion of my children, but I suspect that Lyd did not enjoy the long voyage as much as I did.

Postscript

IN the days when we drove round the streets of Dunedin on old Hurry Up with Tiger panting at the rear wheel, we were "well-known characters." During the first three years in the Cook Islands, we were "suspicious characters." During the last three years in the Islands, we were just "Island characters." Then in the States (and for a short time) we seemed to be "celebrities," and all because of a long, monotonous voyage.

Here in America, people like us to talk to them. We both have plenty to talk about: the problems of the people of the Pacific Islands, the administration of a health service for a semideveloped territory, the various isolated islands we have visited and the rehabilitation of patients who are being treated for leprosy; least in importance, we could talk about the dangers and experiences in crossing 12,000 miles of open ocean in a 45-foot sailing vessel. Yet always it is this last that intrigues people the most and ourselves the least. We are reluctant heroes, stealing every opportunity to sneak in an observation on Polynesia among the welter of nautical recollection so eagerly assimilated by those who cruise, by anxious mothers of small boys, and myriads of other kindly people who must take their adventure vicariously.

It is on those too rare occasions when we are able to tell of the difficulties, the gaieties and the aims of our life in the Pacific that we notice a distinct atmosphere of puzzlement and disillusionment in our audience. The legend of the glamour of the South Sea Islands is no less unreal today than it was when it began growing one hundred and fifty years ago. Because the first stories of the Islands were couched in language as flowery as that of the fairy stories of our childhood, the people of the more conventional countries of this world stubbornly refuse to believe that those Islands are inhabited by people whose problems from day to day and for the future are as real and urgent as our own.

We have moved far away from our home Island but there is no fear in our hearts that we will ever forget Rarotonga, its people, its beauty or the lessons we learned there. Knowing how difficult it is for those hard-working people to find time to write letters, we savor to the full each word we do receive on the infrequent steamers that travel between the Cook Islands and the United States. We chuckle over local gossip (known at home as the "coconut wireless"), as each letter gives a different and growing version of the same story. The dividing ocean robs none of the gossip of its interest, while each little incident that concerns the Medical Service convinces us anew that there is still something that will remain of the establishment we left behind.

From England, an occasional note from the Commissioner now in retirement shows that he is as eager for news from the Islands as we are.

The last of the candidates for postgraduate medical training has left for Fiji, and those returned seem to be fulfilling their promise. Dear fat Manea, still so "Beautiful," seems ready to leave the hilly confines of his tuberculosis sanatorium and rush down the hill to the rescue of anyone, native or European, who needs his services. Ngaei, the hula champ, and handsome John Numa are equally in demand for their specialized services. Matron Reynolds still rules the hospital, and we think her love and understanding of the Islanders is to be counted upon. From a newspaper clipping we read an account of the success of the establishment of community centers for village health services and adult education, an experiment unique to Rarotonga that has proved an example for other similar territories. Hurray, it seems to be working as we thought it would.

From our old factotum Puia, we received a letter postmarked "New Zealand." Puia has found it impossible to make an adequate living from cultivating his fruit for export, he has turned away from his home to look for employment in the city. He tells us that the emigration of Islanders to New Zealand continues at the high rate we knew of in recent years. The old story continues, the distinguished *ariki* says everything is fine, yet the island "man in the street" is still having a hard time to live at the standard he has set for himself. But Puia includes another item that piques our curiosity. He tells us, in the vaguest of terms, that the Government is again willing to subsidize and revive the Cook Islands Producers Co-operative Association. That is good news, for evidently the people are still keeping faith with their Government.

Technical assistance programs, which have played such an important part in the postwar development of small territories, are being furthered to the utmost by New Zealand in her small island territories. At last a giant cold storage plant is being erected, and the fruit no longer need rot on the wharves for lack of a ship to take it away. Experts in this and that continue to visit the Island, but the coconut wireless tells us that these days they confine themselves less and less to paper work and try to come into closer contact with the people than has been the practice in the past. And from the Central Leper Hospital at Makogai and the Leper Trust Board in New Zealand we hear of an increasingly expanding program for aid to the leper patients.

Individually, our old friends progress. Tekao is now indisputable lord of his two rich atolls; never once has he denied the faith we placed in him, and there will be few to remember the day when he was regarded with anything other than the highest respect. Ron Powell now displays above his curio shop the large sign, "RON POWELL AND SONS." Twin sons have at long last saved his reputation, but we predict that in ten years' time those five beautiful Powell daughters will be a new legend in the Pacific. We hear that Ron regards our diary of the *Miru* voyage as one of the most illuminating pieces of literature in existence, so Ron is evidently still in love with the sea. Captain Andy Thompson continues to cross the waters between the Cook Islands and Tahiti, but we are sure to his desolation his present command runs not by billowing canvas, but by smelly Diesel motors. Andy's little court of old-timers, held so regularly on the veranda of his house at Aorangi, must be dwindling now, and for him the waterfront bars of Papeete must be peopled with the ghosts of Frisbie, Nordhoff and, his dearest friend of all, Jimmy Hall. Andy told them tales, they made the tales legend all over the world. Lionel Trenn is the only one left who knew all of that group. We can only hope that before it is too late Lionel will stop registering births and deaths, and, remembering the lessons James Norman Hall taught him so many years ago, put down the rest of those stories before they are forgotten.

But of all our old associates, the busiest one of all has been . . . who else but Maria? First she bustled off to New Zealand and found employment on a large sheep station, there to reign as chief cook. But the climate was a little cool and the social life a little dull for Maria's taste. Soon she packed her-self onto a train and burst upon a waterfront town in one of the main cities. And where else would Maria be most at home but the local hotel? The social life of a hotel cook was evi-dently all that could be desired, but the climate still was not to her taste, so off again further north . . . to another hotel. As housekeeper and undisputed ruler of the kitchen of one of New Zealand's largest hotels, we have no doubt that although the rest of the staff are leading a busy life, that hotel has greatly improved with the addition of our Maria. She is our best correspondent, never forgets a birthday or anniversary, keeps us posted on the doings of all the Islanders who have moved to New Zealand, and always ends her letters with a prayer that we can be together again soon.

And we will, Maria. We don't know where or when but the lessons we learned in the Islands have made the obliga-tion of helping the people of the Pacific the most steadfast thing in our lives. It is wrong for anyone to think that be-cause we made a dangerous trip to reach another country, that trip was made without purpose. The purpose is always to add something to ourselves which can ultimately be used for the benefit of those Islands that we shall always call home.

We had come to regard the *Miru* almost as a living member of our family, as something that would always be with us and that must be considered in any plans for the future that we might make. But then on November 6, 1953, just twelve months after our triumphant arrival in Boston, the *Miru* faced her last hurricane. Dragging her moorings along the harbor of famous Marblehead she piled on the jagged rocks, helpless and beyond our aid. She had stood the storms of the Pacific so bravely and had taken care of us so loyally that it was hard to admit to ourselves that the weather had beaten us all at last, forcing us to leave *Miru* to meet her end alone. There against the rocks she lay smashed to pieces, a victim to the greedy hands of souvenir hunters, and the prying eyes of the curious. We didn't care to watch that.

Tom and John were stunned at our loss, but Timmy, the family philosopher, just sighed and said, "It's a pity *Miru* is wrecked, but she gave us all a lot of worry."

Perhaps by the time our American citizen, Robert Harries Davis, born in Salem, Massachusetts, November 12, 1953, is old enough to climb the ratlines, there may be a second *Miru*, this time with an all-Davis crew.

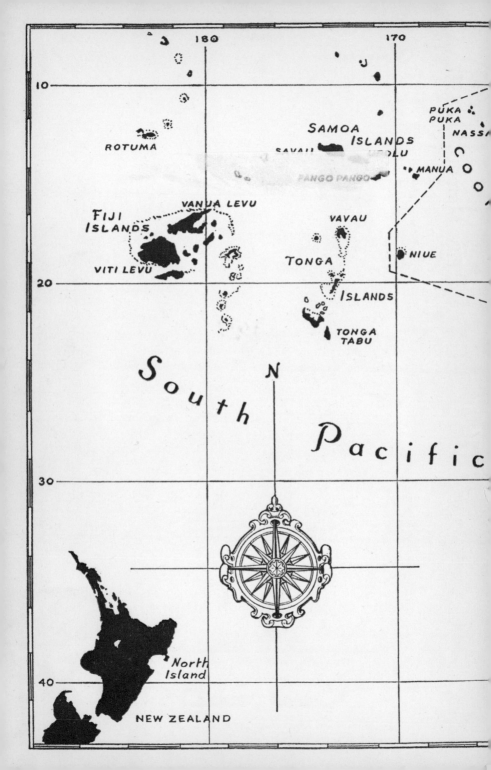